JOE HESCHMEYER

THE EARLY CHURCH WAS THE CATHOLIC CHURCH

D1194352

Catholic
Answers
Press

Published by Catholic Answers, Inc.
2020 Gillespie Way
El Cajon, California 92020
1-888-291-8000 orders
619-387-0042 fax
catholic.com

Printed in the United States of America

Cover by ebooklaunch.com
Interior by Russell Graphic Design

978-1-68357-246-6
978-1-68357-247-3 Kindle
978-1-68357-182-7 ePub

To Stella Maris Heschmeyer, my beloved daughter, who brightens the lives of her parents and all who meet her.

"Imitate a little child, whom one sees holding tight with one hand to its father, while with the other it gathers strawberries or blackberries from the wayside hedge. Even so, while you gather and use this world's goods with one hand, always let the other be fast in your Heavenly Father's hand, and look round from time to time to make sure that he is satisfied with what you are doing, at home or abroad."

—St. Francis de Sales

CONTENTS

Why Care What the Early Christians Believed?

ANY CRITIQUE of Catholic teaching falls into one of two categories: either Catholics are getting blamed for believing what Jesus taught, or they're getting blamed for straying from what Jesus taught. If you're looking for ways to answer the first kind of argument (that Catholics shouldn't be so faithful to Jesus), there are a lot of good books for you, but this one isn't it. My goal is to reach those who believe that Jesus' original teachings were good—but that the Church lost her way over time.

There are different ways of formulating this. Some Protestants will argue that the Catholic Church strayed from the truth of the gospel. Others will argue that the "true Church" declined and was replaced by the Catholic Church. But the basic thesis is the same: the early Christians got the gospel right, but over time, error won the day. Charles Reign Scoville (1869–1937), a popular Protestant preacher at the turn of the twentieth century, paints the picture this way:

> For 300 years there was one Lord, one faith, one baptism. For 300 years there was one shepherd and one fold, one way and one door to that fold. For 300 years the disciples

wore one name—the name of Christ.[1] [But] after the first 300 years, [the Church] drifted along 1,100 years through the dark ages and consequently drifted from the straight and narrow way, until we have the Roman Catholic Church.[2]

Likewise, the church historian (and Presbyterian minister) J.A. Wylie begins volume one of *The History of Protestantism* by tracing how "the spread of Christianity during the first three centuries was rapid and extensive" owing in part to "the fidelity and zeal of the preachers of the gospel, and the heroic deaths of the martyrs."[3] But after the legalization of Christianity in the early fourth century, Wylie claims that "the faith which had maintained its purity and vigour in the humble sanctuaries and lowly position of the first age, and amid the fires of its pagan persecutors, became corrupt and waxed feeble amid the gorgeous temples and the worldly dignities which imperial favour had lavished upon it."[4]

You can find countless variations of the claim that early Christians believed Protestant things: Mormons who claim that the early Christians believed Mormon things,[5] Muslims who claim they believed Muslim things,[6] non-religious people claiming that they didn't originally consider Jesus divine,[7] and various other religious groups making similar claims about how their teachings were what the earliest Christians *really* believed.[8] Almost all of these arguments follow a similar form: the first followers of Jesus got the message right, but eventually, things go wrong, and that's how we end up with Catholicism.

But notice that all these critiques of Catholicism turn on specific historical claims (or assumptions) about what the early Christians were like. And that makes sense. If you say Jesus' teachings were good, but the Catholic Church got them wrong, you've got to say either that (1) nobody (until you?) understood his teachings or (2) these teachings were originally understood but were eventually *mis*understood. The problem with the first of these two ideas is that Scripture shows that the earliest followers of Jesus *did* understand the gospel, at least eventually. Jesus promises the apostles at the Last Supper that "I will pray the Father, and he will give you another Counselor, to be with you for ever," whom he calls "the Spirit of truth" (John 14:16–17). This "Counselor, the Holy Spirit, whom the Father will send in my name, he will teach you all things, and bring to your remembrance all that I have said to you" (v. 26), and "when the Spirit of truth comes, he will guide you into all the truth; for he will not speak on his own authority, but whatever he hears he will speak, and he will declare to you the things that are to come" (16:13). St. John can thus speak of "the truth which abides in us and will be with us for ever" (2 John 1:2) and describe how he has no greater joy than "to hear that my children follow the truth" (3 John 1:4), suggesting that it wasn't just the apostles who understood Christ's teaching, but also their spiritual children. St. Paul writes to the Colossians:

> And you, who once were estranged and hostile in mind, doing evil deeds, he has now reconciled in his body of flesh by his death, in order to present you holy and blameless and irreproachable before him, provided that you continue in the Faith, stable and steadfast, not shifting from the hope of the gospel which you heard, which has been preached to every creature under heaven, and of which I, Paul, became a minister (1:21–23).

In short, the earliest Christians got the gospel right. That doesn't mean that everyone without exception got everything right, but it does mean that the truth of the Faith was well known, and widely held, and that the task of the next generation of Christians was to remain firm in this faith and to "contend for the Faith which was once for all delivered to the saints" (Jude 1:3), not to go searching to find where the true Faith had gone.

And contend they did. Although the early Christians weren't perfect, what we see of them is inspiring. An early (perhaps second-century)[9] Christian author describes the state of Christianity in his day by saying that although "Christians are indistinguishable from other men either by nationality, language or customs," like their neighbors with regard to "dress, food and manner of life in general," there is nevertheless "something extraordinary about their lives" in that they are radically centered upon Jesus Christ:

> They live in their own countries as though they were only passing through. They play their full role as citizens, but labor under all the disabilities of aliens. Any country can be their homeland, but for them their homeland, wherever it may be, is a foreign country. Like others, they marry and have children, but they do not expose them.[i] They share their meals, but not their wives. They live in the flesh, but they are not governed by the desires of the flesh. They pass their days upon earth, but they are citizens of heaven. Obedient to the laws, they yet live on a level that transcends the law. Christians love all men, but all men persecute them. Condemned because they are not understood, they are put to death, but raised to life again. . . . As the soul benefits from the deprivation of

---

i   That is, the Christians differed from their pagan neighbors because their neighbors killed unwanted infants by leaving them on hillsides to die.

food and drink, so Christians flourish under persecution. Such is the Christian's lofty and divinely appointed function, from which he is not permitted to excuse himself.[10]

The famous Baptist preacher Charles Spurgeon (1834–1892) connects this radical message (and lifestyle) of early Christianity with the fact that these Christians suffered persecution:

> The fact is . . . most of us are vastly inferior to the early Christians, who, as I take it, were persecuted because they were thoroughly Christians, and we are not persecuted because we hardly are Christians at all. They were so earnest in the propagation of the Redeemer's kingdom, that they became the nuisance of the age in which they lived. They would not let errors alone. They had not conceived the opinion that they were to hold the truth, and leave other people to hold error without trying to intrude their opinions upon them, but they preached Christ Jesus right and left, and delivered their testimony against every sin.[11]

But as the Reformed theologian Michael Kruger writes, this "weak, fledgling, persecuted Church" of the second century "not only survived, but eventually spread across the empire and the entire world," because of its members' faithfulness to being distinctively Christian in their "worship, doctrine, behavior, and writings."[12]

In this book, we'll take a brief look at five topics.

First, we'll debunk an important objection that undergirds everything that will follow: What if the Catholic Church just corrupted the original, pure doctrines and practices of the Apostolic Age? What if a creeping heresy compromised everything we now know about the early Church?

Then we can move on to each of the four areas that Kruger mentions.

2. **Doctrine:** What did the early Christians believe that baptism did, and how did they think believers were *born again*? As we'll see in chapter two, they universally held that being *born again* is something that happens in baptism, and that baptism has the power to wash away your sins and save you.

3. **Worship:** What was Christian worship like in the first 200 years? In chapter three, we'll look at what they said about the Eucharist being the body and blood of Jesus Christ and of the liturgy (which we now call the Mass) being a *sacrifice*.

4. **Behavior:** As Kruger writes, "it wasn't just what Christians *believed* that made them unusual; it was how they *behaved*."[13] He has in mind Christian sexual ethics, which were (and once more are) at odds with secular culture. But I'm interested in exploring another aspect of Christian living: How were their churches structured? It's common to hear it said that the original churches were disorganized, or else were two-tiered (with elders and deacons). Chapter four will show that this isn't true, and that the three-tiered structure, with a bishop in each local church, dates back to the apostles.

5. **Writings:** Kruger rightly acknowledges "the distinctive role Scripture played in [second-century Christians'] religious life."[14] As we'll see in chapter five, it's through these Catholic believers of the second century that we know about the four Gospels.

In looking at each of these four areas, I've generally confined myself to looking at Christianity from about the year 200 and before. It's not a hard and fast rule, and I bend it whenever it seems justified, but I have a few reasons for sticking with just these earliest of the early Christians. First, Christianity explodes in size after this point, making it difficult (and confusing) to accurately trace the currents of thought throughout the Church. Second, some of you may hear *A.D. 280* and think, "That's plenty of time for the rot to set in." Using 200 as more or less the cutoff date means we're looking at Christianity *before* it faced many of the most famous of the early heresies. This is Christianity before Manichaeism, Donatism, or Pelagianism existed, and it's long before Emperor Constantine legalized Christianity in the fourth century.

The final reason to look at Christianity in the first and second centuries is that Christians from that time had something that we don't: living memory. As the biblical scholar Markus Bockmuehl explains, "the end of the second century was the last time that personal memory of the disciples of the apostles could still be truthfully invoked in order to confirm or challenge a particular interpretation of the apostolic gospel."[15] At the close of the second century, you still have people who learned from the students of the apostles and who had personal knowledge of what the apostles meant by their writings and what they said in their preaching. In Bockmuehl's words, we find that "a relatively short and identifiable chain of living *personal recollection* reaches back to the apostles themselves."[16] In fact, as we'll see in the next chapter, we even know quite a bit about some of these second-century followers of the apostles.

1

Creeping Heresy?

BEFORE WE LOOK at the chain of personal recollection running from the apostles through second-century Christianity, let's begin with an objection. As we saw in the introduction, Protestants, Mormons, Muslims, and secularists may not agree on much, but they do frequently agree that the Catholic Church corrupted the "original teachings" of Jesus . . . even if they can't agree on what those alleged "original teachings" *were*. Anyone making such a claim should be able to show three things: first, what Jesus originally taught; second, when and how the false Catholic teaching was introduced; and third, how that false teaching supplanted the true one.

Broadly speaking, there are two ways of approaching this challenge. One way is by articulating a specific historical claim. Take, for instance, Dan Brown's popular novel *The Da Vinci Code* (which sold more than eighty million copies). Although a work of fiction, *The Da Vinci Code* was widely assumed to be set against the backdrop of real history. The marketers of the book were only too happy to promote this view, printing "read the book and be enlightened" (taken from the *Washington Post*'s review)[17] on the back of the paperback.[18] In the novel, Sir Leigh Teabing claims that Jesus was originally viewed simply as "a mortal prophet . . . a great and powerful man, but a man nonetheless," until the First Council of Nicaea, at Constantine's urging, voted to declare Jesus *Son of God* instead. Teabing concludes that Constantine thus "turned Jesus into a deity who existed beyond the scope of the human world, an entity whose power was unchallengeable."[19]

The advantage to the specific approach is that there's a clear theory presented. In this case, Brown is making clear his belief that prior to the reign of the emperor Constantine (306–337), Christians didn't believe that Jesus was divine. But the flip side is that it's easy to demonstrate the falsity of such an explicit claim. Besides the biblical evidence (e.g., St. Thomas calling Jesus "My Lord and my God!" in John 20:28, or John describing Jesus as both "the Word" and "God" in John 1:1), there's an abundance of evidence that Christians before Constantine considered Jesus divine and worshipped him.

The other approach is vague historical hand-waving. Instead of specifically claiming that a particular heretic introduced a heresy, just say that heresy *crept in* (as if ideas created themselves!). And instead of saying this happened in a particular year, or even a particular century, just say it happened *over time*. A clear example of this can be found in the writings of the Founding Fathers of the United States, in an 1820 letter from then-former president Thomas Jefferson to his predecessor, John Adams. Jefferson held to the belief that God, the human soul, and angels are all made of matter. Explaining his theory to Adams, he said that "to talk of immaterial existences, is to talk of nothings. To say that the human soul, angels, God, are immaterial is to say, they are nothings, or that there is no God, no angels, no soul. . . . At what age of the Christian Church this heresy of immaterialism, or masked atheism, crept in, I do not exactly know. But a heresy it certainly is. Jesus taught nothing of it."[20]

The advantage to the vague approach (from the perspective of the person arguing it) is that it's harder to debunk. Even if you showed him early Christians who believed that God was immaterial, Jefferson could always respond, "I *said* I do not exactly know when it crept in . . . it must have been before this!" But the only reason it's hard to debunk is that there's not really much of a theory there. It fails to articulate the *who*, *what*, *when*, *where*, *why*, or *how* explaining the creep of this creeping heresy. It's the difference between saying, "Professor Plum killed Mr. Boddy in the drawing room with the revolver" and "Mr. Boddy died." If it can't be easily fact-checked, it's only because it offers so few factual claims. A person can always say, "Christians don't really believe Jesus' teachings," so long as he doesn't bother to explain which teachings.

Over the next four chapters, we'll take a closer look at how the Church worshipped, what it believed about baptism, what the structure of the Church looked like, and which books it considered Gospels. In each case, we'll see that the Catholic teaching was the teaching believed and practiced by the earliest Christians. My goal is not to comprehensively cover every doctrinal question related to the Catholic Church. It's rather to show something of the pattern I am describing here: Protestants (and others) arguing against the historicity of the Church's teaching do so with either inaccurate history or no history at all.

But anyone arguing against Catholic teaching, whether relying on specific historical claims or vaguer *creeping heresy* theorizing, eventually must grapple with two realities: the conservative theological character of the early Church and the short span of time involved.

Problem #1: Early Christianity Was Theologically Conservative

The first "problem" is that early Christianity was theologically conservative. By that, I don't mean that they were *right-wing* (whatever that would mean in the first- or second-century context); rather, they were on guard against any doctrinal innovations. They held fast to the beliefs that were handed on to them and opposed new doctrines. Indeed, simply showing that a doctrine *was* new was considered sufficient to debunk it . . . even if that new doctrine seemed to have biblical support.

This was a matter not of personal preference, but of faithfulness to the system founded by Christ. After all, how could believers in the early Church know what was orthodox Christianity and what was heretical? It would be unreasonable to demand that each member of the flock first decide for himself what orthodoxy looks like and then assess the validity of his shepherds. Not only is such a model unbiblical, but it would have been unworkable. Moreover, many of the early believers were newcomers to the Faith from Jewish or pagan backgrounds. The major heretics in the early days of Christianity, meanwhile, tended to be brilliant, subtle, and persuasive. If they hadn't been, they never would have carried large numbers away from the orthodox flock. St. Irenaeus of Lyons, writing in the second century, warns that "error, indeed, is never set forth in its naked deformity, lest, being thus exposed, it should at once be detected. But it is craftily decked out in an attractive dress, so as, by its outward form, to make it appear to the inexperienced (ridiculous as the expression may seem) more true than the truth itself."[21] So it's not a good enough standard to say a particular teacher's teachings seem believable. As the prophet Jeremiah warns, "the heart is deceitful above all things, and desperately corrupt" (Jer. 17:9). It follows that we cannot rely on our own hearts as the litmus test for orthodoxy.

Instead, Scripture gives us another standard by which to judge a teaching: its antiquity. St. Jude appeals to his readers "to contend for the faith which was once for all delivered to the saints" (Jude 1:3), while St. Paul warns that "the time is coming when people will not endure sound teaching, but having itching ears they will accumulate for themselves teachers to suit their own likings" (2 Tim. 4:3). St. John likewise cautions against anyone whose "progressivism" would lead him beyond the teachings of Christ: "Any one who goes ahead and does not abide in the doctrine of Christ does not have God; he who abides in the doctrine has both the Father and the Son" (2 John 1:9). In other words, Christian theology is explicitly conservative: the old teachings coming down from the apostles are to be trusted, whereas teachers coming in with something new are to be distrusted, even if we happen to like what they have to say.

One consequence of this conservative theology is that the early Christians believed that you could refute a heresy simply by showing where it began. If you *couldn't* point to an unbroken line from the apostles down to the present, that was sufficient evidence to prove the teaching false. Significantly, this approach applied to figure out whether or not a *teaching* was apostolic and whether or not a *church* was apostolic. St. Jerome, writing in the fourth century, captures the idea of this "theological conservativism" well:

We ought to remain in that Church which was founded by the apostles and continues to this day. If ever you hear of any that are called Christians taking their name not from the Lord Jesus Christ, but from some other, for instance, Marcionites, Valentinians, men of the mountain

19

or the plain, you may be sure that you have there not the Church of Christ, but the synagogue of Antichrist. For the fact that they took their rise after the foundation of the Church is proof that they are those whose coming the apostle foretold. And let them not flatter themselves if they think they have Scripture authority for their assertions, since the devil himself quoted Scripture, and the essence of the Scriptures is not the letter, but the meaning. Otherwise, if we follow the letter, we too can concoct a new dogma and assert that such persons as wear shoes and have two coats must not be received into the Church.[22]

Scripture doesn't envision a period in which true Christians will be called to reject the scriptural interpretations that have been handed down to them in favor of new ones. In fact, all of the evidence points in the opposite direction: that those coming along with new interpretations are teaching something heretical. To defeat Marcionism or Valentinianism or (to update the list) Lutheranism, Calvinism, etc., one needs only to show that these sects originate after the time of the apostles, as even their names betray.

This is true despite the fact, as Jerome is quick to point out, that heretics often have scriptural arguments that (at least on a surface level) seem to support their positions. Take the passage to which Jerome alludes. When Jesus sends the Twelve out, his words are recorded in the Gospel of Luke as "Take nothing for your journey, no staff, nor bag, nor bread, nor money; and do not have two tunics" (9:3). But the Gospel of Mark records his words slightly differently: "He charged them to take nothing for their journey except a staff; no bread, no bag, no money in their belts; but to wear sandals and not put on two tunics" (6:8–9).[23] So we can imagine two different denominations arising: one of them, following Mark's version, requires all Christians to walk with staffs and to wear sandals; the other one, following Luke's version, forbids staffs and sandals. Each one, from the perspective of *sola scriptura*, could point to explicit scriptural authority. But neither of these (imaginary) denominations would be grasping the *meaning* of Jesus' words, which wasn't about a legalistic fixation on staffs or sandals or tunics, but was about the Twelve going out in a spirit of total reliance on Christ.

In technical terms, what Jerome is arguing for is what Scripture speaks of as "tradition." Both the Latin *tradere* (the origin of the English *tradition*) and the Greek *paradosis* (the word used for tradition in the New Testament) mean something "handed on."[24] Many Christians want to know: is tradition good or bad? But that's like asking "are teachings good or bad?" To ascertain the answer in both cases, you have to ask: what's being passed on, and where did it come from?

This accounts for the nuanced way in which the New Testament treats the idea of tradition. On the one hand, Jesus rebukes the Pharisees by saying, "You leave the commandment of God, and hold fast *the tradition of men*" (Mark 7:8). In calling it a "tradition of men," Jesus is saying the Pharisees originated and passed down a set of teachings that modified commandments given by God. That's wrong. But Paul writes to the Thessalonians, instructing them to "stand firm and hold to *the traditions which you were taught by us, either by word of mouth or by letter*" (2 Thess. 2:15). So traditions coming from the apostles, or what Catholics call *apostolic Tradition*, are binding, whether they are transmitted orally or in writing. Why the difference? Because in the latter case, the teaching is coming from the apostles, or from Jesus himself. Thus, it is impossible for any Christian to coherently be *anti-Tradition*. After all, as Paul points out,

Scripture itself is tradition. Scripture is the written teachings of the apostles and evangelists, handed on to us "by letter." So the question isn't whether we should accept "tradition" or not, but whether or not a particular tradition is of apostolic or post-apostolic origin.

Why begin here? Because this method of discerning truth from heresy is largely unfamiliar to Christians (particularly Protestants) today. We can see this in three ways. The first is the sometimes explicit rejection of authoritative or binding tradition. For instance, the Baptist theologian Matthew Barrett argues: "Rome challenged Scripture's sufficiency, claiming that an infallible tradition and papal Magisterium is also needed to provide the one, true interpretation of Scripture."[25] In other words, Barrett (and those who hold to this view of Scripture) oppose not only the idea of authoritative extra-biblical teachings, but also the idea of any sort of authoritative and infallible *interpretation* of Scripture, viewing it as a threat to Scripture's "sufficiency."

The second way is that Protestant theologians often devise unbiblical and untraditional tests to distinguish orthodoxy from heresy. The Reformed theologian Tim Challies poses an obvious problem: "two teachers may both claim the authority of the Bible while teaching very different things. How can we know whose interpretation is correct?"[26] The early Christians would have said: "the one who can show he's interpreting things the way they've always been interpreted." But Challies doesn't give that answer. Instead, he offers a five-pronged test to show how we can "distinguish sound doctrine from false":

1. Origin: "Sound doctrine originates with God; false doctrine originates with someone or something created by God."

2. Authority: "Sound doctrine grounds its authority within the Bible; false doctrine grounds its authority outside the Bible."

3. Consistency: "Sound doctrine is consistent with the whole of Scripture; false doctrine is inconsistent with some parts of Scripture."

4. Spiritual growth: "Sound doctrine is beneficial for spiritual health; false doctrine leads to spiritual weakness."

5. Godly living: "Sound doctrine has value for godly living; false doctrine leads to ungodly living."[27]

Failing even one of these five teachings, Challies argues, proves a teaching false. He summarizes his test by saying that "sound doctrine originates with God, is recorded in the word of God, is consistent with the whole revelation of God, and leads to both spiritual health and godly living."[28] But it's not clear that even his test passes his test. That is, where is this fivefold test (and particularly, the idea that all sound doctrine is found in Scripture) "recorded in the word of God"?[29]

More to the point, although Challies's is just one possible litmus test for orthodoxy, it's instructive in what it omits: anything about unbroken apostolic Tradition. A doctrinal novelty can be accepted, as long as the teacher can show that the new teaching is spiritually beneficial, consistent with all of Scripture, and rooted in God or Scripture. But the heretics Jerome describes, proclaiming that we need one tunic (or two), could probably pass each of those five tests. After all, their false teachings are based on an overly literal reading of the words of Jesus in Scripture.

The third reason to begin here is that Protestants will sometimes object that they, too, have traditions handed down. For instance, the Calvinist theologian John Murray insisted that "there is a Reformed tradition. It is enshrined in the Reformed creeds, theology, worship, and practice. We believe it is the purest representation and expression of apostolic Christianity."[30] But remember what we saw earlier: it's not a question of accepting or rejecting *tradition*, but whether a particular tradition is of apostolic origin or not. A tradition dating back to the Reformation is, by definition, a "tradition of men" (Mark 7:8; Col. 2:8) rather than apostolic Tradition. Murray argues not that the Reformers received these teachings in an unbroken line from the apostles, but only that they are the "purest representation and expression of apostolic Christianity." But the whole idea of tradition, by definition, is that it is handed on from one individual (or generation) to the next.

The distinction here should not be overstated. Both the early Christians and later Reformers pored over Scripture, making arguments from exegesis. But the point is simply that the early Christians had a powerful tool that later Protestants lack: an argument from unbroken apostolic Tradition. At this point, my argument is not that the early Christians were right to accept apostolic Tradition in this way (although I believe they were). It's simply that anyone arguing that *heresy crept in* needs to explain how such a thing is possible in an atmosphere in which Christians were opposed to *any* new teaching.

This is not to say that heresy didn't *arise*. Jesus warned his listeners to "beware of false prophets, who come to you in sheep's clothing but inwardly are ravenous wolves" (Matt. 7:15), and St. Peter warned his readers that "there will be false teachers among you, who will secretly bring in destructive heresies" (2 Pet. 2:1). History has repeatedly vindicated these warnings. The argument I am making is a more modest one: that orthodox Christians opposed these heresies when they arose, and that one of the ways they did so is by appeal to apostolic Tradition.

Problem #2: The Timeline Is Too Short

The second problem facing any kind of "creeping heresy" theory is that the timeline doesn't work. As we'll see more specifically in the next four chapters, we can find clear articulations of the Catholic view quickly after the time of the apostles, at which point these Catholic teachings are already being treated as the universal view of Christians. In other words, there's just not enough time for heresy to creep in. Those opposing Catholic doctrine are required to believe in a heresy that didn't creep in, but *sprinted* in, and sprinted in unnoticed by the theologically conservative vanguards of the early Church.

If it helps, consider the debate about evolution. One of the points upon which most evolutionists and young-earth creationists agree is that the Darwinian theory of evolution requires a long time. Researchers at Oregon State University, for instance, argue that "across a broad range of species, the research found that for a major change to persist and for changes to accumulate, it took about one million years."[31] In other words, either evolutionists are wrong about the origin of species, or young-earth creationists are wrong about the age of the earth, since there's no way to account for Darwinian evolution within a 5,000-year timeline. We need not settle that debate in these pages, of course; I raise it simply as an analogy. The Protestant claim is that Christian teaching evolved—or, more accurately, *devolved*.

For Protestants who are unfamiliar with the nearly 1,500 years between St. Paul and Martin Luther, a "creeping heresy" theory might sound plausible. For instance, when we hear that the early Christians held to a certain doctrine in the year 200, many readers might understandably protest, "But isn't that enough time for heresy to have supplanted orthodoxy?" To see why that's *not* enough time, it's helpful to flesh out the timeline with real people. Let's consider just two: St. Polycarp of Smyrna (69–155) and St. Irenaeus of Lyons (130–202).

Polycarp is one of the early Christians we know the most about, primarily from the *Martyrdom of Polycarp*, an account of his death that most scholars accept as being an eyewitness account written within a year of his death in about the year 155.[32] Part of the *Martyrdom* recounts Polycarp's defense before Roman authorities. When the proconsul ordered Polycarp to deny Christ, he responded: "Eighty and six years have I served him, and he never did me any injury: how then can I blaspheme my king and my savior?"[33] Such a declaration simultaneously reveals Polycarp's faith and allows us to date his birth as no later than the year A.D. 69 (depending on whether he was raised as a Christian or converted at a young age).

The account of his martyrdom, which was written from "the church of God which sojourns at Smyrna, to the church of God sojourning in Philomelium, and to all the congregations of the holy and catholic Church in every place," also tells us that Polycarp was "an apostolic and prophetic teacher, and bishop of the Catholic Church which is in Smyrna."[34] In his work *Against Heresies*, Irenaeus, who was a student of Polycarp, gives us more details about his teacher's life:

But Polycarp also was not only instructed by apostles, and conversed with many who had seen Christ, but was also, by apostles in Asia, appointed bishop of the Church in Smyrna, whom I also saw in my early youth, for he tarried [on earth] a very long time, and, when a very old man, gloriously and most nobly suffering martyrdom, departed this life, having always taught the things which he had learned from the apostles, and which the Church has handed down, and which alone are true. To these things all the Asiatic churches testify, as do also those men who have succeeded Polycarp down to the present time.[35]

The seventeenth-century Anglican Archbishop James Ussher argued that when, in the book of Revelation, Jesus tells John to write "to the angel of the church in Smyrna," he means to write to Polycarp (2:8).[36] That is, Ussher argued that John was being instructed to send letters not literally to spiritual beings (where would he send these?) but to the men who served as the bishops and protectors over the seven local churches.[ii] Such a reading would account for the message that Jesus delivers: "Do not fear what you are about to suffer. Behold, the devil is about to throw some of you into prison, that you may be tested, and for ten days you will have tribulation. Be faithful unto death, and I will give you the crown of life" (v. 10). After all, it wasn't angels, but men—Bishop Polycarp and members of his flock— who were imprisoned and martyred.

What can we say about Polycarp and the church of Smyrna, then? Both the biblical evidence and numerous second-century texts point to the orthodoxy and fidelity of both the man and the local church. In addition to the texts already considered (Revelation 2, the *Martyrdom of Polycarp*, and the references to Polycarp in Irenaeus's *Against Heresies*), we also have letters from St. Ignatius of Antioch, to both the church in Smyrna and to Polycarp personally, and a letter from Polycarp to the Philippians. All indications point to a man on fire

---

ii   We'll explore this reading of the Book of Revelation in greater depth in chapter four.

with the love of Jesus Christ, fervent in his orthodoxy, and unafraid to die for his faith. Indeed, the eyewitness account of Polycarp's death describes "a great miracle": when Polycarp was thrown into the fire, the flames would not touch him, and "he appeared within not like flesh which is burnt, but as bread that is baked, or as gold and silver glowing in a furnace," with the fragrance of incense coming forth from the flames.[37] To be sure, a skeptic is free to reject all of this as Christian propaganda (and many scholars do!), but such a conclusion is not based *on* the evidence, but *in spite of it.*

Compared to Polycarp, we know relatively little about the beginning or end of Irenaeus's life. His birth is usually dated between A.D. 120 and 140, probably around 130 or shortly thereafter.[38] Although we remember him as the bishop of Lyons (or Lyon)[39] in modern-day France, he was from Asia Minor (modern-day Turkey). In fact, he was probably from Smyrna itself, which would explain his familiarity with (and repeated references to) the local church there. This would also account for his apparent training in rhetoric (Smyrna was a "major center of sophistic culture and teaching" at the time) and his preference for writing in Greek instead of that "barbarous dialect," Latin.[40] As we saw earlier, Irenaeus describes how in his "early youth," he "saw" Polycarp.[41] He seems to have been (in Eusebius's words) "a hearer of Polycarp,"[42] in the early Christian sense of "disciple."[iii] Later in life, he described his experiences this way:

I remember the events of that time more clearly than those of recent years. For what boys learn, growing with their mind, becomes joined with it; so that I am able to describe

---

iii   Irenaeus uses this same phrase when describing St. Justin Martyr's wayward disciple Tatian as a "hearer of Justin." See Irenaeus, *Against Heresies*, book 1, 28, ANF 1:353.

the very place in which the blessed Polycarp sat as he discoursed, and his goings out and his comings in, and the manner of his life, and his physical appearance, and his discourses to the people, and the accounts which he gave of his intercourse with John and with the others who had seen the Lord. And as he remembered their words, and what he heard from them concerning the Lord, and concerning his miracles and his teaching, having received them from eyewitnesses of the Word of life, Polycarp related all things in harmony with the Scriptures.[43]

Other sources confirm this connection. One of the existing manuscripts of the *Martyrdom of Polycarp* includes these copyist notes at the end: "Caius transcribed from the copy of Irenaeus (who was a disciple of Polycarp), having himself been intimate with Irenaeus. And I Socrates transcribed them at Corinth from the copy of Caius."[44] As for his death, Irenaeus "fades from the annals of history" around the year 190,[45] and his death is usually dated to c. 202 (making him anywhere from about sixty-two to eighty-two at the time of his death).[46]

We'll take a closer look at what Irenaeus said and taught in a moment, but for now notice the plain history (and math): someone claiming that heresy "crept in" sometime between the time of Christ and the year 200 is saying heresy entered the Church and overtook orthodoxy at some point in the adult lifetime of John, Polycarp, or Irenaeus. But there are two sets of objections to this history. First, Mercer University's Thomas B. Slater argues that "Irenaeus stated that he knew Polycarp and that Polycarp knew John the apostle, implying that he has received accurate tradition from an apostle through Polycarp. Although this is possible, many church historians have doubted the veracity of this statement since

Polycarp would have been quite young when John died and Irenaeus would have been very young when Polycarp died."[47] But the evidence suggests that Polycarp was about thirty-one when the apostle John died and (if the c. 130 dating is accurate, or near accurate) that Irenaeus was in his mid-twenties when Polycarp died—plenty old, in each case, to have been disciples under holy mentors. After all, how old was John himself when he lived as a disciple of Christ?[48]

The converse of this argument is the claim that John, Polycarp, and (as we'll soon see) Irenaeus couldn't have *really* lived that long. The atheist and mythicist Richard Carrier, for instance, claims that Polycarp couldn't have met the apostle John, since "average lifespan for an adult at that time was forty-eight,"[49] and the odds are "hundreds or even thousands to one against anyone having lived from the early thirties CE into the reign of Trajan (c. 100 CE), as was being claimed of John."[50] This simply isn't true. Of the hundreds of famous men recorded in the *Oxford Classical Dictionary* who didn't die violent deaths, the *median* lifespan was seventy, with deaths ranging from aged nineteen to aged 107.[51] Caesar Augustus died at seventy-six; his wife Livia died at eighty-six, and her son (and Augustus's successor) Tiberius died at seventy-seven.[52] At least three first-century Roman politicians lived to see ninety or beyond, as did the rhetorician Seneca the Elder (54 B.C.–A.D. 39).[53] So the idea that one of the original disciples died in (at least) his eighties is hardly shocking. After all, Irenaeus's immediate predecessor in Lyons, the bishop Pothinus, was martyred in 177 . . . at the age of ninety.[54]

Nevertheless, as a reader, you're free to believe that the early Christians were (for whatever reason) lying about Irenaeus being a disciple of Polycarp, or Polycarp being a disciple of John, etc. But it's unlikely that they were mistaken, since they were writing too soon after the fact to be ignorant. Treating them as telling the truth poses major problems for the "creeping heresy" theory. Why? Because both Polycarp and Irenaeus were passionate defenders of orthodoxy and opponents of heresy. For instance, Irenaeus recalls an instance in which Polycarp met the heretic Marcion (who argued that the God of the New Testament is good but that the God of the Old Testament is wicked). Marcion said to him, "Do you know me?" to which Polycarp replied: "I do know you, the first-born of Satan." Irenaeus, commenting on this, observed: "Such was the horror which the apostles and their disciples had against holding even verbal communication with any corrupters of the truth."[55]

As for Irenaeus, he is most famous for his *Against Heresies*, written principally against the Gnostic heresy around the year 180. Prior to the discovery of the Nag Hammadi library in 1945, this was the most complete account of what Gnostics actually believed, since Irenaeus offered "a closely argued reading of a range of Gnostic texts" exposing the logical and theological problems with Gnosticism.[56] Irenaeus's work is a model for how to engage heresy: he took the trouble to understand what they thought and to read what they wrote, and then he held those ideas up to critical examination, exposing their logical and theological flaws.

Conclusion

To say that error overtook the Church sometime in the first 200 years is to say that it occurred during the adult lifetime of either St. Polycarp or St. Irenaeus. The argument here is not that heresy was unknown in the first and second centuries. (You don't get a book like *Against Heresies* unless there are heresies out there.) It's that heresy was known *and opposed* and that this opposition is well established. Moreover, one of the ways that heresy was opposed was by appealing to theological conservativism: Irenaeus could point to Polycarp, and Polycarp could point to John.

We can see what this looked like in action from Irenaeus's argument against Florinus, another of Polycarp's followers who had fallen into the Gnostic heresy. Irenaeus wrote to him, saying, "These doctrines, O Florinus, to speak mildly, are not of sound judgment. These doctrines disagree with the Church, and drive into the greatest impiety those who accept them."[57] And how does Irenaeus know that Florinus's teachings are unsound? Because "these doctrines, the presbyters who were before us, and who were companions of the apostles, did not deliver to thee."[58] In other words, both Florinus and Irenaeus know what Polycarp did (and *didn't*) teach, and so it's clear that Gnosticism is a novel heresy.

That's what Bockmuehl means when he says (as we saw in the introduction) that "living personal recollection" back to the apostles was still possible at the close of the second century.[59] And notice that it's not a matter of a handful of holy and orthodox writers (like Polycarp and Irenaeus) living among a sea of heretics. Irenaeus points to "the Church" for doctrinal support, knowing that the Church's teaching agrees with what the apostles taught.

In such a Church, with such guardians of orthodoxy, just how could heresy "creep in" and overtake the Church without anyone noticing?

2

THEOLOGY:

Baptismal Rebirth

WHAT DOES IT mean to be a *born again* Christian? The people at the Barna Group, a Christian research firm, explain what *they* mean by the term:

> "Born again Christians" were defined in these surveys as people who said they have made "a personal commitment to Jesus Christ that is still important in their life today" and who also indicated they believe that when they die they will go to heaven because they had confessed their sins and had accepted Jesus Christ as their savior.[60]

But the *born again* language comes from John 3:3, when Jesus says to Nicodemus, "Unless one is born anew, he cannot see the kingdom of God." ("Born anew" is rendered "born again" in the King James Version of the Bible.) Jesus explains that "unless one is born of water and the Spirit, he cannot enter the kingdom of God" (John 3:5). So does Barna understand our rebirth in the way that Jesus meant it? Or does Jesus mean something else—namely, baptism?

Catholics, Orthodox, and many Protestants (including Lutherans and Anglicans), take this latter view, believing in what's called *regenerative baptism* (*regenerated* just means "born again"). It's the idea that baptism saves you by cleansing you of your sins. But many Evangelicals, particularly Baptists, think this is a false and dangerous belief. In their view, being born again is a matter of personal faith, not baptism, and they tend to deny that baptism is even a sacrament.[61]

So what (if anything) does baptism *do*, exactly? This is an important theological starting place for many reasons. First, it involves a potentially salvific issue, since much of the question is on whether and how baptism saves. Second, this question is inseparably tangled up with a host of other important doctrinal questions: how we're saved, what our relationship is with the Church, whether a person can fall away permanently after being saved, the nature of justification, and so forth. Third, it's got practical consequences as well: should you get your baby baptized? Should your church require members to be baptized?

In attempting to answer these questions, the standard Baptist claim is that the early Christians believed as Baptists do (that baptism is just a symbol) and that the belief that baptism is a means of rebirth is a later corruption. For instance, in an article tracing what he calls "a history of the baptism apostasy," Wayne Jackson writes in the *Christian Courier* that "eventually, as the centuries of the post-Apostolic Age multiplied, an almost magical aura began to be associated with baptism, resulting finally in the doctrine of baptismal regeneration (power in the water itself)."[62] This is a good use of what's called *evasive passive voice.*[63] Instead of explaining *who* introduced this supposed "heresy," or *when*, or *how* it was accepted by the broader Church, Jackson just vaguely claims that it happened multiple (how many?) centuries after the time of the apostles.[iv]

---

iv   It's not encouraging that Jackson misunderstands the theology he means to critique: no one who believes in baptismal regeneration believes in "power in the water itself." (It's not as if swimming in the River Jordan magically turns you into a Christian.) Rather, the grace is in the sacrament.

Nevertheless, the claim is worth investigating. Did the earliest post-apostolic Christians agree with Baptists or Catholics on baptism?

That leads to one final reason why we should take a closer look at the theology of baptism. There's good reason to believe that those early Christians got the doctrine of baptism right in a way that many Christians are getting it wrong today. As the Protestant theologian John D. Castelein[64] points out:

> Remarkably, the apostle Paul includes baptism in the short list of the seven basic realities that unify all Christians (Eph. 4:1–6). There was a time when the shared experience of baptism helped Christians to maintain "the unity of the Spirit through the bond of peace" (v. 3). Today, however, Christians give different answers to the most basic questions about baptism. Christians disagree on (1) the purpose of baptism (the why), (2) the recipient of baptism (the who), and (3) the mode of baptism (the how).[65]

In other words, the early Christians are seemingly united in a sound doctrine of baptism, such that St. Paul could appeal to Christian unity in terms of "one Lord, one faith, one baptism" (Eph. 4:5). Given the lack of basic agreement on the doctrine today, and the fact that some Protestants (including Castelein) get rebaptized because they reject their own baptism as infants, it's safe to say that this "one baptism" unity has largely been lost. If it is ever to be reclaimed, it will be by rediscovering what those early Christians knew. So how do they understand baptism? To get there, we first need to look at what Scripture (in both the Old and the New Testaments) has to say.

What Does Scripture (Seem to) Say About Baptism?

As we'll see shortly, the early Christians seem to have unanimously believed in baptismal regeneration: the idea that God saves us through the rite of baptism, bestowing certain spiritual benefits upon us at the same time. Is there a scriptural case to be made for this view? Protestant readers, in exploring that question, should try to set aside (for now) any objections they might have to the idea that baptism might actually do something. Even if you think the early Christians misread Scripture, first find out what they "misread" and why they read it that way.

As a starting point, let's listen to St. Cyprian of Carthage. Cyprian (c. 210–258) is a bit later than most of the Christian authors we'll be looking at (I'm largely confining myself to looking at the Christians up until 200), but I think he lays out the early Christian theology of baptism clearly, which will help us to understand what we're reading when we encounter some of his predecessors:

> In the sacraments[v] of salvation, when necessity compels, and God bestows his mercy, the divine methods confer the whole benefit on believers; nor ought it to trouble any one that sick people seem to be sprinkled or affused, when they obtain the Lord's grace, when Holy Scripture speaks by the mouth of the prophet Ezekiel, and says, "Then will I sprinkle clean water upon you, and ye shall be clean: from all your filthiness and from all your idols will I cleanse you. And I will give you a new heart, and a new spirit will I put within you."[66]

---

v   Earlier in this letter, Cyprian refers to baptism as the "sacrament of salvation." In speaking now of the sacraments (plural), he probably has in mind the post-baptismal sealing that we now call Confirmation. See Cyprian, Letter 75, ANF 5:400.

Why begin here? Because Cyprian is giving us a view of how the early Christians viewed and practiced baptism. There were three acceptable forms of baptism: by *immersion* (which was the norm), by *affusion* (that is, pouring), or by *sprinkling*, with the latter two forms largely for cases of special necessity.[vi] No matter which way you received the sacrament, God bestows the fullness of his mercy through it. But notice that this theology is explicitly rooted in Scripture, particularly in a prophecy from Ezekiel that Cyprian sees as a promise of saving baptism, administered by "sprinkling" (Ezek. 36:24–28):

> For I will take you from the nations, and gather you from all the countries, and bring you into your own land. I will sprinkle clean water upon you, and you shall be clean from all your uncleannesses, and from all your idols I will cleanse you. A new heart I will give you, and a new spirit I will put within you; and I will take out of your flesh the heart of stone and give you a heart of flesh. And I will put my spirit within you, and cause you to walk in my statutes and be careful to observe my ordinances. You shall dwell in the land which I gave to your fathers; and you shall be my people, and I will be your God.

Contextually, this clearly seems to be a promise of the New Covenant, and a gathering together of the scattered flock. God then promises four things:

---

vi   Canon 758 of the 1917 *Code of Canon Law* says baptism by any of these three forms is valid. In the current (1983) *Code*, "baptism is to be conferred either by immersion or by pouring" (Can. 854). Sprinkling, though still sacramentally *valid*, is no longer permitted.

1. *Cleansing of sin through water*: "I will sprinkle clean water upon you, and you shall be clean from all your uncleannesses, and from all your idols I will cleanse you."

2. *Spiritual rebirth*: "A new heart I will give you, and a new spirit I will put within you."

3. *The gift of the Holy Spirit*: "I will put my spirit within you, and cause you to walk in my statutes and be careful to observe my ordinances."

4. *Entrance into the people of God*: "You will be my people, and I will be your God."

Do these four promises correspond to what the New Testament says about baptism? Let's look.

After Saul's conversion, a man named Ananias came to him; healed him of his blindness; and then said, "And now why do you wait? Rise and be baptized, and wash away your sins, calling on his name" (Acts 22:16). That sounds like the washing away of sins through the baptismal waters. After Jesus tells Nicodemus that only those who are born again will be saved, he says that "unless one is born of water and the Spirit, he cannot enter the kingdom of God" (John 3:5). That sounds like spiritual rebirth. When the crowds on Pentecost "were cut to the heart" at the preaching of St. Peter and asked what they should do, he replied, "Repent, and be baptized every one of you in the name of Jesus Christ for the forgiveness of your sins; and you shall receive the gift of the Holy Spirit" (Acts 2:38). There's the gift of the Holy Spirit. And so "those who received his word were baptized, and there were added that day about 3,000 souls" (v. 41). Added to what? To the Church, the new people of God.

The plain meaning of the New Testament suggests that God's promises through Ezekiel are fulfilled through water baptism. Again, you may think those texts were never meant to be taken at face value and that they were all metaphors for something else. But for now, just notice that the interpretation taken by Cyprian (and, as we'll see soon, everyone else) is a lot more straightforward than the "they didn't *really* mean that" reinterpretations that come from later Protestants. Nor are these the only New Testament passages that seem to point in this direction. Paul stresses baptism as the means by which we are incorporated into Christ (Rom. 6:3–5):

> Do you not know that all of us who have been baptized into Christ Jesus were baptized into his death? We were buried therefore with him by baptism into death, so that as Christ was raised from the dead by the glory of the Father, we too might walk in newness of life. For if we have been united with him in a death like his, we shall certainly be united with him in a resurrection like his.

In Paul's theology, this incorporation is also what makes us children of God: "in Christ Jesus you are all sons of God, through faith. For as many of you as were baptized into Christ have put on Christ" (Gal. 3:26–27). He also speaks of baptism's cleansing power. Speaking to the Corinthians about how "the unrighteous will not inherit the kingdom of God," he adds, "And such were some of you. But you were washed, you were sanctified, you were justified in the name of the Lord Jesus Christ and in the Spirit of our God" (1 Cor. 6:9, 11). The epistle to the Hebrews tells us to draw near to God "with our hearts sprinkled clean from an evil conscience and our bodies washed with pure water" (10:22).

This treats baptism as something that happens at the level of both "our hearts" and "our bodies" (that is, not a merely inward turning toward God, or a merely outward ritual).

Peter, after describing "the building of the ark, in which a few, that is, eight persons, were saved through water," explains (1 Pet. 3:20–22): "*Baptism, which corresponds to this, now saves you*, not as a removal of dirt from the body but as an appeal to God for a clear conscience, through the resurrection of Jesus Christ, who has gone into heaven and is at the right hand of God, with angels, authorities, and powers subject to him." Paul likewise says that "when the goodness and loving kindness of God our Savior appeared, he saved us, not because of deeds done by us in righteousness, but in virtue of his own mercy, by the washing of regeneration and renewal in the Holy Spirit" (Titus 3:4–5). And Jesus says at the close of St. Mark's Gospel, "He who believes and is baptized will be saved; but he who does not believe will be condemned" (16:16).

So how did the earliest Christians understand these passages? What did *they* think Christianity taught about baptism?

What Did the Early Christians Believe About Baptism?

Let's begin with the "big picture" and then take a closer look at several of the earliest Christian witnesses on the theology of baptism. Everett Ferguson, a Protestant elder, biblical scholar, and Church historian, has written what's perhaps the definitive work on the subject, *Baptism in the Early Church: History, Theology, and Liturgy in the First Five Centuries*. Ferguson spends hundreds of pages carefully combing through the evidence to expose the first 500 years' worth of Christians thought about baptism. His findings are neatly summarized on page 854:

Although in developing the doctrine of baptism different authors had their particular favorite descriptions, there is a remarkable agreement on the benefits received in baptism. And these are present already in the New Testament texts. Two fundamental blessings are often repeated: the person baptized received forgiveness of sins and the gift of the Holy Spirit (Acts 2:38). The two fundamental doctrinal interpretations of baptism are sharing in the death and resurrection of Christ, with the attendant benefits and responsibilities (Rom. 6:3–4), and regeneration from above (John 3:5), with its related ideas.[67]

Recall that St. Paul seems to treat the theology of baptism as a basic doctrine upon which the early Church (which could otherwise be so divided) was one. Ferguson's point is that throughout the first 500 years of the Church, we find that same unity on baptism. But what the early Christians are united around is this idea of *regenerative baptism*. A modern time traveler, holding to a standard Baptist or Reformed vision of baptism, would find himself at odds with all Christians everywhere on this basic doctrine during these early years.

Can this really be true? Let's take a closer look, particularly at those living and teaching prior to the year 200.[68] In fact, let's start with a question: why was Jesus baptized (Matt. 3:13–17)? This is a difficult question to answer if baptism is merely a symbolic gesture of our turning away from sin. Southern Baptist Theological Seminary's Jonathan Pennington claims that it's because "Jesus is fulfilling his role as the obedient Son of God by practicing the required righteousness of submitting to God's will to repent." But Pennington is aware that this view sounds obviously wrong ("how does a sinless man repent?"), so he explains: "Jesus repents not in the sense of turning from sin (our repentance necessarily includes this where his does not), but in the sense of dedicating himself to follow God's will fully on earth."[69]

But that's *not* how the earliest Christians understood this event. Their understanding was that this was about not a change in Jesus (either a turning from sin or a dedication to follow God's will), but a change in baptism. But a change from what, and to what?

Ancient Jews practiced a form of convert baptism through the use of a ritual bath called a *mikveh*.[70] Rabbi Maurice Lamm describes it as a "profound symbol" meant "to symbolize a radical change of heart, a total commitment."[71] This symbol, following circumcision, was also the last step to becoming a full member of the Jewish people. As the Talmud explains, "once he has immersed and emerged, he [the convert] is like a born Jew in every sense."[72] As Lamm explains, "as Jews performed immersion at Mt. Sinai to complete the conversion process they had begun with circumcision as they left Egypt, so converts in every age must immerse in a mikveh."[73] In addition to these baptisms, we also find that St. John the Baptist was there in the wilderness, "preaching a baptism of repentance for the forgiveness of sins" (Mark 1:4). Both John's baptism and the Jewish baptisms resemble how Baptists envision Christian baptism: a public and symbolic declaration of repentance and of dedication to God. In fact, there's an encounter between Paul and some Corinthian believers that suggests that the difference between John's baptism and Jesus' is precisely that the former was merely symbolic, whereas the gift of the Holy Spirit is actually given in the latter (Acts 19:1–6):

> While Apollos was at Corinth, Paul passed through the upper country and came to Ephesus. There he found some disciples. And he said to them, "Did you receive the Holy Spirit when you believed?" And they said, "No,

we have never even heard that there is a Holy Spirit." And he said, "Into what then were you baptized?" They said, "Into John's baptism." And Paul said, "John baptized with the baptism of repentance, telling the people to believe in the one who was to come after him, that is, Jesus." On hearing this, they were baptized in the name of the Lord Jesus. And when Paul had laid his hands upon them, the Holy Spirit came on them; and they spoke with tongues and prophesied.

So how do we go from John's baptism to Jesus'? According to St. Ignatius of Antioch and many others who follow him, something changes with Jesus' baptism. Ignatius says (almost in passing) that Jesus "was born and baptized, that by his passion he might purify the water."[74] The purification in question is not that Jesus literally made the Jordan River cleaner, but that he imbued the waters of baptism with a spiritually cleansing effect. Commenting on this passage, William R. Schoedel writes that "it is generally recognized that the more or less magical idea that water was purified by Christ's baptism in the Jordan was known to both the orthodox and the heterodox."[75] Theologically, Schoedel's claim is sloppy: by definition, what Ignatius is arguing for is *miraculous*, not magical, and no more or less ridiculous than the apostle John's claim that Christ sent a blind man to "go, wash in the pool of Siloam" and "he went and washed and came back seeing" (John 9:7). But it's telling that even though Schoedel is unsympathetic to Ignatius's view, he recognizes that it *is* the view held by both orthodox and heretical Christians in Ignatius's day, and that his words "may reflect liturgical practice."[76] (That is, it may be that the reason that there's such a doctrinal consensus may be because the liturgical prayers at the time were explicit on this connection, since we know that this is true of later baptismal prayers). Whether the liturgical connection is true or not, we can say that Christians living in and around 107 seem to have had a clear answer to the question "why was Jesus baptized?," and it wasn't the answer given by modern Baptist theologians like Pennington.

Speaking of the earliest baptismal liturgy, we find the basic outlines in the first-century *Didache*:[77]

> Concerning baptism, baptize thus: having first rehearsed all these things, "baptize, in the name of the Father and of the Son and of the Holy Spirit" in running water; but if thou hast no running water, baptize in other water, and if thou canst not in cold, then in warm. But if thou hast neither, pour water three times on the head "in the name of the Father, Son and Holy Spirit." And before the baptism let the baptizer and him who is to be baptized fast, and any others who are able. And thou shalt bid him who is to be baptized to fast one or two days before.[78]

You may have heard from Baptist sources that affusion (baptism by pouring) didn't exist until the middle of the third century, around the time that Cyprian (whom we heard from above) was writing.[79] The *Didache* shows this claim to be untrue. The text has a strong focus on proper spiritual preparation, combined with a relatively flexible approach to the rite itself. Although there's a preference for immersion in running water, permission is given for other forms of immersion, or by pouring. That's a sharp contrast from *immersion only* Baptists today, who claim things like "true baptism can only be performed in a certain way—by immersion only. Immersion is not merely one of several options: it is the only proper mode consistent with the grammatical evidence, scriptural pattern, and theological implications for what baptism is."[80]

Next, let's look at the so-called *Epistle of Barnabas*. That's the name given to a text from around the year 100.[81] It's anonymous, but it was quickly ascribed to "Barnabas" and was included in a few of the early New Testaments.[82] The scholarly consensus is that it *wasn't*, and never actually claimed to be, authored by the Barnabas mentioned in Acts. Instead, the author seems to have been a Christian layman living in Egypt. (I'll still call him "Barnabas" because that might really have been his name and because it's the only name by which we know him.)

Barnabas refers to Christian baptism as "that baptism which leads to the remission of sins" and traces how he says God took care "to foreshadow the water [of baptism] and the cross" throughout the Old Testament.[83] For instance, Psalm 1 lays out the paths of the just and of the wicked and says the just man "is like a tree planted by streams of water, that yields its fruit in its season, and its leaf does not wither" (v. 3). Barnabas comments: "Mark how he has described at once both the water and the cross. For these words imply, 'Blessed are they who, placing their trust in the cross, have gone down into the water;' for, says he, 'they shall receive their reward in due time': then he declares, 'I will recompense them.'"[84] In other words, Barnabas sees this as a description of the Christian life: placing our trust in the tree of the cross, we are "planted" in our baptisms, enabling us to bear spiritual fruit.

Likewise, Barnabas points to Ezekiel's prophecy of water flowing from the coming temple. The last nine chapters of the book of Ezekiel are a vision of a new temple. Ezekiel is writing during the Babylonian captivity, when Israel had no temple. (The First Temple had been destroyed, and the Second Temple hadn't been built.) But there were clear hints that something deeper was afoot. The temple being described had miraculous properties: for instance, Ezekiel says that "water was flowing down from below the south end of the threshold of the temple, south of the altar" (47:1). These waters flowing from the side of the temple form a life-giving river, and "wherever the river goes every living creature which swarms will live" (v. 9). The vision concludes with Ezekiel saying that "on the banks, on both sides of the river, there will grow all kinds of trees for food. Their leaves will not wither nor their fruit fail, but they will bear fresh fruit every month, because the water for them flows from the sanctuary. Their fruit will be for food, and their leaves for healing" (v. 12).

This seems to be a prophecy, not about a building, but about the Incarnation and Christian discipleship. When Jesus says, "Destroy this temple, and in three days I will raise it up," John explains that he "spoke of the temple of his body" (John 2:19, 21). But John also recounts Jesus' saying that "he who believes in me, as the Scripture has said, 'Out of his heart shall flow rivers of living water'" (7:38). The Scripture Jesus alludes to there seems to be Ezekiel's prophecy, since nothing else comes close. But John points us to one more dimension of the prophecy's fulfillment, at the Crucifixion, when "one of the soldiers pierced his side with a spear, and at once there came out blood and water" (19:34). For his part, Barnabas suggests yet another dimension: that Ezekiel's prophecy foretells "that we indeed descend into the water full of sins and defilement, but come up, bearing fruit in our heart, having the fear [of God] and trust in Jesus in our spirit."[85] The important thing here isn't how persuaded you are by Barnabas's exegesis: the point is rather that his exegesis clearly reveals that *he* believes that baptism is regenerative. Whether or not you're convinced by these and the other scriptural arguments Barnabas offers, his letter bears further witness to the fact that the Christians of the early Church believed (a) that baptism is regenerative and (b) that this is the message taught in both the Old and the New Testaments.

Speaking of prophecies, another important second-century text is the *Shepherd of Hermas*. The so-called *Muratorian Fragment* (itself typically dated to the second century)[86] says that "Hermas wrote the *Shepherd* very recently, in our times, in the city of Rome, while bishop Pius, his brother, was occupying the [episcopal] chair of the church of the city of Rome. And therefore it ought indeed to be read; but it cannot be read publicly to the people in church either among the prophets, whose number is complete, or among the apostles, for it is after [their] time."[87] As you might imagine, we'll return to this when we look at bishops in the early Church. But for now, our concern is twofold: this evidence gives us a rough sense of when the text was written (Pope Pius I reigned c. 140–154), and it also speaks to its reception: it was well respected, and some Christians even (mistakenly) believed it to belong in the New Testament.

Stylistically, the book is a series of visions and their interpretations (the New Testament book to which it is most similar is perhaps Revelation), and much of the text consists of a dialogue between Hermas and an angel. At one point, the angel says to him that "before a man bears the name of the Son of God he is dead; but when he receives the seal he lays aside his deadness, and obtains life. The seal, then, is the water: they descend into the water dead, and they arise alive."[88] As the Presbyterian theologian John V. Fesko observes: "In other words, saving efficacy is tied to the waters of baptism."[89]

At another point, Hermas asks the angel, "I heard, sir, some teachers maintain that there is no other repentance than that which takes place, when we descended into the water and received remission of our former sins."[90] To many modern readers, this is a confusing question, so let's unpack things a bit. Hermas is not saying that "some teachers maintain" that baptism forgives sins and some don't. What we find instead is that "some teachers maintain" that *only* baptism forgives sins. In other words, there's unanimity on the doctrine of baptism, but there's an unsettled question of whether Christians can be forgiven of grave sins committed after baptism. A literal reading of Hebrews 6:4–6 suggests that certain sins after baptism are unforgivable. But there were others, including Tertullian, who saw hope in passages like Ezekiel 18:32 ("For I have no pleasure in the death of any one, says the Lord God; so turn, and live"). Tertullian offers the memorable image of God offering "a shipwrecked man the protection of some plank" in the form of repentance and penance.[91]

Why mention this in a discussion on baptism? Because while this question is still being worked out (which takes a few centuries), many believers are afraid of getting baptized and then sinning. You may have heard the claim that "Baptists can point to an unbroken line of churches since Christ, identified chiefly through congregational polity, believer's baptism, separation from the state, and persecution—the 'trail of blood.'"[92] I've addressed elsewhere[93] why this is such poor history, but let's acknowledge what it gets right: you can find early believers who delay baptism until late in life or would refuse to baptize their infants. The emperor Constantine, for instance, was famously baptized on his deathbed,[94] and St. Augustine, despite being the son of a Christian woman (St. Monica), wasn't baptized as an infant. But that's not because they think baptism is a symbolic ritual to be undertaken by a mature believer. It's because the one point on which seemingly everyone in the second century agrees is that no matter how serious your past sins are, they're washed away in baptism.[vii]

Not long after the *Shepherd of Hermas*, we find St. Justin Martyr's *First Apology*, which dates to around 160. Stylistically, this text is more approachable: Justin is offering an explanation and a defense to the pagan emperor. That includes a description of what the Christians of his day thought about baptism:

> I will also relate the manner in which we dedicated ourselves to God when we had been made new through Christ; lest, if we omit this, we seem to be unfair in the explanation we are making. As many as are persuaded and believe that what we teach and say is true, and undertake to be able to live accordingly, are instructed to pray and to entreat God with fasting, for the remission of their sins that are past, while we pray and fast with them. Then they are brought by us where there is water, and are regenerated in the same manner in which we were ourselves regenerated. For, in the name of God, the Father and Lord of the universe, and of our Savior Jesus Christ, and of the Holy Spirit, they then receive the washing with water.[95]

Justin offers two scriptural passages in support of this practice. He first mentions Jesus' words to Nicodemus in John 3:5: "Truly, truly, I say to you, unless one is born of water and the Spirit, he cannot enter the kingdom of God." Then, to

---

vii If I may use a videogame analogy, think of the *power up* that restores the hero to full health. Smart players will wait to use it until they're almost dead, in order to get the fullest benefit from the aid. But don't wait *too* long, or you'll die. A similar sort of approach was being taken by believers in the first few centuries. But Tertullian and others were right: there was no need to do this, since God is merciful, and he *does* forgive post-baptismal sin through repentance, confession, and penance. (See CCC 1446.)

explain "how those who have sinned and repent shall escape their sins," Justin cites the words of the prophet Isaiah's vision:

> Wash yourselves; make yourselves clean; remove the evil of your doings from before my eyes; cease to do evil, learn to do good; seek justice, correct oppression; defend the fatherless, plead for the widow. Come now, let us reason together, says the Lord: though your sins are like scarlet, they shall be as white as snow; though they are red like crimson, they shall become like wool. If you are willing and obedient, you shall eat the good of the land; but if you refuse and rebel, you shall be devoured by the sword; for the mouth of the Lord has spoken (1:16–20).

Justin cites not only Scripture, but apostolic Tradition, saying, "This [rite] we have learned from the apostles." He also explains why—namely, that since we were born "without our own knowledge or choice," and "brought up in bad habits and wicked training," the rite of baptism exists that we "may obtain in the water the remission of sins formerly committed."[96] Justin even mentions an important detail—why the Christians of the second century referred to baptism as *illumination*:

> And this washing is called illumination, because they who learn these things are illuminated in their understandings. And in the name of Jesus Christ, who was crucified under Pontius Pilate, and in the name of the Holy Ghost, who through the prophets foretold all things about Jesus, he who is illuminated is washed. [97]

So even in the early Christian term for baptism, *illumination*, we find reflected the idea that baptism *does something*.

This idea is found all throughout the second-century descriptions of baptism. In 181, St. Theophilus writes a letter to "my very good friend Autolycus," which is remembered largely because it is the first time in history we find anyone using the word *Trinity* to describe the Godhead.[98] In that same letter, Theophilus gives a reflection on the meaning of the early chapters of Genesis and says of the fifth day of creation:

> Moreover, the things proceeding from the waters were blessed by God, that this also might be a sign of men's being destined to receive repentance and remission of sins, through the water and laver of regeneration—as many as come to the truth, and are born again, and receive blessing from God.[99]

Theophilus's description of the "laver of regeneration" comes from Titus 3:5, and we see clearly that he understands that the spiritual rebirth of water baptism is what Jesus means in John 3 by being "born again."

That leaves us with one last early Christian witness: St. Irenaeus, to whom we were introduced back in chapter one. You may recall that his book *Against Heresies* is usually dated to about the year 180, right around the time that Theophilus is writing to Autolycus about the Trinity. In it, Irenaeus is explicit about how, "giving to the disciples the power of regeneration into God, [Jesus] said to them, 'Go and teach all nations, baptizing them in the name of the Father, and of the Son, and of the Holy Ghost.'"[100] In another text (of which we have only fragments today), we find Irenaeus explaining baptismal theology through a helpful Old Testament reference:

It was not for nothing that Naaman of old, when suffering from leprosy, was purified upon his being baptized, but [it served] as an indication to us. For as we are lepers in sin, we are made clean, by means of the sacred water and the invocation of the Lord, from our old transgressions; being spiritually regenerated as new-born babes, even as the Lord has declared: "Except a man be born again through water and the Spirit, he shall not enter into the kingdom of heaven."[101]

If that first reference doesn't ring a bell for you, Irenaeus is referring to 2 Kings 5. Naaman was a Syrian general and an enemy of Israel. After Naaman contracted leprosy, one of his Israelite slaves told him about the prophet Elisha. So Naaman traveled to Samaria to meet Elisha. Elisha didn't bother meeting with him directly, but instead sent word through a messenger, telling him to "go and wash in the Jordan seven times, and your flesh shall be restored, and you shall be clean" (vv. 9–10). Naaman's response is instructive (vv. 11–14):

But Naaman was angry, and went away, saying, "Behold, I thought that he would surely come out to me, and stand, and call on the name of the Lord his God, and wave his hand over the place, and cure the leper. Are not Abana and Pharpar, the rivers of Damascus, better than all the waters of Israel? Could I not wash in them, and be clean?" So he turned and went away in a rage. But his servants came near and said to him, "My father, if the prophet had commanded you to do some great thing, would you not have done it? How much rather, then, when he says to you, 'Wash, and be clean'?" So he went down and dipped himself seven times in the Jordan, according to the word of the man of God; and his flesh was restored like the flesh of a little child, and he was clean.

What's so special about the water? You will sometimes hear opponents of regenerative baptism act as if the early Christians believed there is something special (or even magical) about the waters themselves. Naaman misses the point in the same way. He comes to Elisha expecting a showy miracle and storms off in a huff because Elisha instead points him to something as ordinary as washing seven times in the Jordan. But Naaman's servants make the proper response: it's irrational to believe in big miracles while disdaining the idea that God might work through small ones. If you believe that God can work in great ways (say, the Resurrection), it's irrational to mock the idea that he might also work in ordinary ones (say, ritual washing).

So why does the miracle work? It isn't the fervor of Naaman's faith (he's openly dubious and almost doesn't obey), and it isn't that there's something particularly special about these waters. It's instead that Naaman obeys the prescribed ritual "according to the word of the man of God." It is a cleansing "by the washing of water with the word" (Eph. 5:26)[viii]. And this cleansing has three effects. First, Naaman is healed of his leprosy, which Irenaeus sees prefiguring our own cleansing from sin. Second, "his flesh was restored like the flesh of a little child," which Irenaeus sees as an obvious symbol of our being "spiritually regenerated as new-

viii The early Christians saw this verse as a reference to baptism. For instance, St. Cyprian of Carthage, writing in the early third century, says that "the blessed apostle sets forth and proves that baptism is that wherein the old man dies and the new man is born, saying, 'He saved us by the washing of regeneration' [Titus 3:5]. . . . For it is the Church alone which, conjoined and united with Christ, spiritually bears sons; as the same apostle again says, 'Christ loved the Church, and gave himself for it, that he might sanctify it, cleansing it with the washing of water.'" See Cyprian, Epistle 73, ANF 5:388.

born babes." Third, it leads him to faith. He returns to the prophet and says, "Behold, I know that there is no God in all the earth but in Israel" (2 Kings 5:15). This faith was not the cause of the miracle, but the result of it. When Naaman is told to "wash, and be clean," he's being given the chance to be spiritually purified, but it's a spiritual cleansing that operates through (literal) water.

It's in *Against Heresies* that we find the clearest witness we have regarding the practice of infant baptism in the early Church. Irenaeus says Christ "came to save all through means of himself—all, I say, who through him are born again to God—infants, and children, and boys, and youths, and old men."[102] Given that Irenaeus has repeatedly expressed his belief that we are "born again to God" through water baptism, the natural meaning of these words is that Christians in his day were baptizing their babies.[103] But it's also here (for perhaps the first time) that we find clearly people *denying* baptismal regeneration—namely, the Gnostics. As Irenaeus explains, "this class of men have been instigated by Satan to a denial of that baptism which is regeneration to God, and thus to a renunciation of the whole [Christian] faith."[104] This denial of regenerative water baptism is based on the Gnostics' warped Christology and their belief that "the baptism instituted by the visible Jesus was for the remission of sins, but the redemption brought in by that Christ who descended upon him, was for perfection; and they allege that the former is animal, but the latter spiritual." And notice how Irenaeus responds to them, calling their rejection of regenerative baptism "a renunciation of the whole faith." This was not a question on which Christians could (or did) disagree; this was a foundational doctrine.

To summarize, then, we find a wealth of Old and New Testament passages that seem to say baptism is regenerative and imparts certain spiritual benefits (particularly, the gift of the Holy Spirit). We find Paul apparently of the belief that the early Christians understand baptism and are unified on this point. And we find the Christians of the first 200 (and, if Ferguson is right, 500) years of Christianity unanimously believing in regenerative baptism and basing their beliefs on Scripture, the testimony of the apostles, apostolic Tradition, and the practice of the Church.

How Might a Protestant Respond?

Broadly speaking, Protestants who reject baptismal regeneration handle the evidence of early Christianity in one of two ways: by arguing that the early Christians (or at least the earliest of those early Christians) don't *really* believe in baptismal regeneration, despite what they appear to say, or by arguing that the early Christians were all wrong.

In this first category, Timothy Kauffman at White Horse Blog maintains, despite all of the above evidence and much more, that "the early Church did not teach baptismal regeneration."[105] He takes a text like Barnabas saying "that we indeed descend into the water full of sins and defilement, but come up, bearing fruit in our heart, having the fear [of God] and trust in Jesus in our spirit"[106] and comes away claiming that Barnabas actually "understood that eternal life comes by faith, and faith comes by the preaching of the word, and it is they who have already received eternal life by faith in the preached word who 'go down into the water,'" even though Barnabas explicitly describes trust in Jesus as following (rather than causing) baptism. He's doing this not because the texts themselves, or the scholarship analyzing them, point in this direction. Neither does. He's doing this because he's committed to the belief that "Roman Catholicism was formed out of a great apostasy that took place in the late 4th century."[107] He simply *cannot* concede that the Christians of the first centuries believe what Catholics today believe about baptism because his theological biases don't allow it.

The most egregious example of Kauffman's treatment of early Christian sources is Tertullian (c. 155–220). Slightly after the pre-200 period we're looking at, Tertullian writes an entire treatise on baptism, called *On Baptism*. Kauffman even admits that "Tertullian spends twenty chapters defending the merits of baptism, its divine origin, the significance of the water, the power to sanctify, remit sins, grant life and secure eternal salvation."[108] It almost seems as if Kauffman will have to give up his presupposition. But Tertullian also describes martyrdom as "a second font" of baptism.[109] He actually has a good argument for it: when Jesus says, "I have a baptism to be baptized with; and how I am constrained until it is accomplished!" (Luke 12:50), he's referencing not water baptism (which he had already undergone), but his upcoming death on the cross. And so Tertullian explains that "this is the baptism which both stands in lieu of the fontal bathing when that has not been received, and restores it when lost."[110] At the time Tertullian is writing, those who wanted to enter the Church underwent a *three-year* catechumenate before being baptized,[111] and Christianity was often persecuted, so the idea of an unbaptized martyr isn't as strange as it may sound. Tertullian's point is basically, don't worry: the martyr who dies without baptism is still saved through this "second font." Likewise, the baptized martyr will find in martyrdom a restoration to the spiritual purity that he possessed on the day of his (water) baptism.

But that's not how Kauffman reads things. He claims that Tertullian "states plainly that the baptism of blood is that of faith in the cross." He doesn't, and it would make no sense to read Luke 12:50 as a way of saying Jesus was preparing himself to have "faith in the cross." But on the basis of mis-reading this one passage in Tertullian's treatise, Kauffman throws out the rest, saying, "Tertullian is tipping his hand, and showing that his own soaring rhetoric is hyperbolic, and he hints at his conviction (which he elsewhere states explicitly) that the water of the baptismal font is merely a signification of the actual baptism that takes place in the heart."[112] But no such thing is occurring. Indeed, Tertullian devotes several chapters of his treatise to responding to the objection "how foolish and impossible it is to be formed anew by water. In what respect, pray, has this material sub-stance merited an office of so high dignity?"[113] He does this, among other ways, by pointing to the Spirit hovering over the waters (Gen. 1:2) as a prefigurement of baptism and the washing in the pool of Siloam as an instance in which "the spirit is corporeally washed in the waters, and the flesh is in the same spiritually cleansed" (that is, in which spiritual cleansing happened through bodily washing).[114] None of these answers makes sense if Tertullian's real response is that "the water of the baptismal font is merely a signification of the actual baptism that takes place in the heart."

I mention this incident because it's egregious. If an author had left behind a few words on baptism, reasonable people could certainly disagree over what those words meant. But Kauffman isn't even trying to understand Tertullian, or the twenty chapters he devotes to baptismal theology, which read nothing like what a Baptist would write. Instead, he isolates a passage, reinterprets it contrary to how everyone else reads it, and uses his own novel interpretation to write off the rest as metaphor. That's just not serious work, or good-faith exegesis, and it suggests that there's literally *no* amount of evidence that Kauffman (and those playing a similar game) won't simply wave away as a metaphor for faith.

Most of those trying to deny that the early Christians were united around the doctrine of baptismal regeneration are less obvious about it, vaguely suggesting that the idea crept in, without worrying about the details (or evidence). On the *Berean Call* radio show, Ron Merryman argues that "slowly but surely water baptism in its essence becomes distorted" after the death of the apostles, so that "water baptism becomes the means of being forgiven of sins. In other words, it's identified with washing away of sins, and then eventually, baptismal regeneration, so that by the time you get to the middle of the fourth century, water baptism is totally destroyed, the significance of it."[115] Thomas Schreiner of the Southern Baptist Theological Seminary claims that "Paul does not sharply distinguish between water baptism and Spirit baptism, for the two were closely associated during the NT era and unbaptized Christians were unheard of. The issue of baptismal regeneration arose in later Church history when baptism was separated from faith, though those who promoted baptismal regeneration rightly saw that baptism was irretrievably tied to initiation into the people of God in the [New Testament]."[116] But when, exactly, is "later in Church history"? Remember, other than a couple of brief digressions into the early third century (with Clement and Tertullian), we've been looking at the Christians of the year 200 and earlier.

Gregg R. Allison and Andreas J. Köstenberger say that "as baptismal regeneration developed in the early Church, the ground for this belief was original sin and the consequent need for cleansing from guilt and corruption if salvation is to occur."[117] For support, they cite a couple of third-century theologians: Origen (c. 184–253) and Cyprian (c. 210–258). But well before Origen or Cyprian (or indeed, any sophisticated treatment of original sin), we find the doctrine fully formed.

So much, then, for the first approach. The second is to concede that the earliest Christians believed in baptismal regeneration (or else ignore the question entirely) and argue that this belief was wrong. Here, it's important to recognize a difference between how (many) Protestants understand baptism and how the early Christians (and modern Catholics) understand it: "for the credobaptists, the primary actor is the individual, which rules out infant baptism," whereas for Catholics, Lutherans, and (many) Calvinists, *God* is the primary actor.[118] In other words, credobaptists (those who believe in "believer's baptism") tend to understand baptism as something we do for God (obeying his "ordinance"), whereas the whole idea of regenerative baptism is that it's something God does for us: "he saved us, not because of deeds done by us in righteousness, but in virtue of his own mercy, by the washing of regeneration and renewal in the Holy Spirit, which he poured out upon us richly through Jesus Christ our Savior" (Titus 3:5–6).

That makes a world of difference.[119] If baptism is something that God does for us, we can rejoice in being saved through it, and we don't need to be legalistic about whether it's by immersion, pouring, or washing, any more than the blind man in John 9 needed to ask how many drops of water needed to touch his body in order to be cleansed. But if baptism is something *we* do for God, two things follow. First, it's easy to become legalistic about it (we want to obey God perfectly, after all), and so you end up with well-meaning Baptists attacking one another about the precise grammatical range of *baptizō* in Greek. Second, the importance of baptism must be downplayed. For instance, John MacArthur argues against baptismal regeneration because "the rest of Scripture unmistakably teaches that salvation is solely by faith."[120] Leave aside whether Scripture really does "unmistakably" teach salvation by faith alone (the lack of belief in this doctrine before the Reformation might call MacArthur's confidence on that point into question), and notice that MacArthur's argument is premised on seeing baptism as relying on ourselves rather than God. Unless you accept that premise (and the early Christians clearly didn't), the rest of the argument doesn't follow.

The same goes for James White's claim that "underlying the idea that man, by an action such as baptism, can bring about his own regeneration, is the rejection of the biblical teaching of sin, and most especially, the truth that sin enslaves man, debilitates man, brings spiritual death to man."[121] He's actually explicit in misunderstanding this: assuming that baptismal regeneration is about "man" bringing about "his own regeneration," when it's actually a belief that God brings about man's regeneration. Think about it this way: if someone misunderstands faith as something we do for God, he will read all the passages about the role of faith in salvation as us saving ourselves. But that conclusion merely begs the question. The same is true here.

This fundamental misunderstanding results in caricatures (presumably unintentional) of what belief in baptismal regeneration entails. R.C. Sproul is characteristic when he claims that "though baptism signifies regeneration, or rebirth, it does not automatically convey rebirth. The power of baptism is not in the water but in the power of God."[122] But that's just Naaman's objection (and the objection that Tertullian spends several chapters answering). Obviously, the water *apart from the power of God* is just water. So Sproul does a fine job of rebutting a position on baptism that no one holds.

And how do these Protestants deal with numerous Old and New Testament passages that seem to explicitly teach baptismal regeneration? The Reformed theologian Dennis W. Jowers claims that "Scripture does mandate rejection of the doctrine of baptismal regeneration in unmistakable, albeit implicit, terms."[123] In other words, if you're expecting opponents of baptismal regeneration to cite some scriptural passage that supports their theology, or describes baptism as a mere symbol of faith, you're going to be disappointed because such evidence doesn't exist. Instead, Jowers makes a series of arguments based on what he calls "unmistakable" "implicit" evidence.

Let's take a closer look at each of his arguments. He first offers "arguments of probability against the doctrine of baptismal regeneration":

> For example, Paul proclaims, "Christ did not send me to baptize, but to preach the gospel" (1 Cor. 1:17). He rejoices that he baptized none of the Corinthians save Crispus and Gaius (1 Cor. 1:14), yet regards himself as the spiritual father of them all (1 Cor. 4:15). Philip demands faith, a fruit of regeneration, from the Ethiopian eunuch as a condition for baptism (Acts 8:37). On numerous occasions, Scripture represents faith as the condition of salvation, without mentioning baptism.[124]

Jowers concedes that "a deft apologist for baptismal regeneration could show arguments such as these to be, at least when considered in isolation, less than absolutely decisive," but I think it's a good deal worse than that. First, he quotes St. Paul's words to the Corinthians. This passage comes up frequently by opponents of baptismal regeneration, and I confess that I'm not sure why. John MacArthur, for instance, claims that Paul's words here are "inexplicable if baptism is necessary for salvation."[125] It's true that Paul's words, read out of context, might sound as though he's downplaying the importance of baptism (although is that really a position opponents of baptismal regeneration want to defend?). But his meaning is perfectly explicable if you read his words in context:

> For it has been reported to me by Chloe's people that there is quarreling among you, my brethren. What I mean is that each one of you says, "I belong to Paul," or "I belong to Apollos," or "I belong to Cephas," or "I belong to Christ." Is Christ divided? Was Paul crucified for you? Or were you baptized in the name of Paul? I am thankful that I baptized none of you except Crispus and Gaius; lest any one should say that you were baptized in my name (1 Cor. 1:11–15).

He's worried about infighting among the Christians of Corinth and is grateful that they can't use "I was baptized by Paul" as a cudgel against each other in that context. Jowers says Paul "rejoices that he baptized none of the Corinthians save Crispus and Gaius" but leaves off *why* Paul says he rejoices: "lest any one should say that you were baptized in my name." If anything, Paul's argument is *stronger* if baptism is the means of salvation, since the Corinthians would have had more cause to boast in who brought them to salvation (as opposed to who helped them to perform a symbolic ritual).

Second, Jowers points out that Paul "regards himself as the spiritual father of them all" despite having baptized only a few. Again, there's no tension there. It isn't as if Catholics call a priest *father* only if he personally baptized them. St. Augustine would later make a point similar to Paul's about the unimportance of the minister of baptism. Noting that those baptized by John the Baptist were rebaptized (Acts 19:3–5), but that there's no indication that this happened to those baptized by Judas, Augustine explains that this is "because if baptism was given by Judas, it was the baptism of Christ; but that which was given by John, was John's baptism. We prefer not Judas to John; but the baptism of Christ, even when given by the hand of Judas, we prefer to the baptism of John, rightly given even by the hand of John."[126] So there's nothing particularly difficult about understanding what Paul is saying here, and none of it conflicts with what the early Christians have to say about baptism.

Third, Jowers relies on Acts 8:37, in which St. Philip responds to the Ethiopian eunuch's question ("See, here is water! What is to prevent my being baptized?") by saying, "If you believe with all your heart, you may." Jowers's treatment of belief as "faith, a fruit of regeneration" begs the question. But there's another difficulty in relying on this verse: it's not in most versions of the Bible, because (in the words of the *Fortress Commentary on the Bible*) it is "clearly not original" and probably "a liturgical gloss with a baptismal formula."[127] The sixth-century *Codex Laudianus* is the first manuscript in which we find this verse.[128] In other words, Jowers is using a passage that scholars say (a) isn't original to the biblical text and (b) derives from a gloss inspired by early Christian baptismal liturgies to argue early Christian baptismal theology.

Fourth, Jowers makes an argument from silence, that "on numerous occasions, Scripture represents faith as the condition of salvation, without mentioning baptism." That's true. Sometimes baptism is presented as an explicit condition for salvation (see Mark 16:16), and sometimes it isn't. But the obvious conclusion from this is that baptism *is* a condition, even if it isn't mentioned each time. For instance, Catholics and

Protestants agree that faith is needed for salvation, but there are times where Jesus speaks of salvation without mentioning faith at all. For instance, in the separation of the sheep and goats, Christ the King will say (Matt. 25:34–40):

> "Come, O blessed of my Father, inherit the kingdom prepared for you from the foundation of the world; for I was hungry and you gave me food, I was thirsty and you gave me drink, I was a stranger and you welcomed me, I was naked and you clothed me, I was sick and you visited me, I was in prison and you came to me." Then the righteous will answer him, "Lord, when did we see thee hungry and feed thee, or thirsty and give thee drink? And when did we see thee a stranger and welcome thee, or naked and clothe thee? And when did we see thee sick or in prison and visit thee?" And the King will answer them, "Truly, I say to you, as you did it to one of the least of these my brethren, you did it to me."

In light of such verses, we could make the same argument Jowers makes: "on numerous occasions, Scripture represents good works as the condition of salvation, without mentioning faith." That's the danger of this type of argument from silence. It's logically unsound and leads to disastrous results.

There's another line of argumentation that Jowers doesn't take, but many opponents of baptismal regeneration do: *impossible case* arguments. In other words, find those who were incapable of water baptism and were still saved, and use that to argue that therefore baptism isn't salvific. The two usual suspects are the good thief (incapable because he was nailed to a cross when he came to believe) and the Gentile converts in Acts 10. In the latter case, they receive the Holy Spirit and then are baptized, the reverse of the usual order depicted in Acts. But these are the first Gentiles to be baptized, and St. Irenaeus points out that St. Peter would not "have given them baptism so readily, had he not heard them prophesying when the Holy Ghost rested upon them," and that "unless the Holy Ghost had rested upon them, there might have been some one who would have raised objections to their baptism."[129] Peter says nearly as much in Acts 10:47: "Can any one forbid water for baptizing these people who have received the Holy Spirit just as we have?"

More has been written on this elsewhere (particularly as relates to the good thief), but impossible cases strike me as obviously weak arguments. A professor may require a paper as a portion of the grade in the syllabus but make an exception for the student whose mother dies during finals week. That's not a contradiction, and it doesn't mean that the paper is now optional. The students are still bound, but the professor is free to act contrary to the syllabus if justice or mercy demands. The *Catechism of the Catholic Church* (CCC) puts it this way: "God has bound salvation to the sacrament of baptism, but he himself is not bound by his sacraments" (1257).

Any thoughtful Christian must deal with such impossible cases. For instance, Scripture is clear about the necessity of faith for salvation. But what about someone who dies during infancy? We can pose subtle theories about the child's "implicit faith," or we can simply say we are bound, and God is not.[130]

So much, then, for the scriptural arguments against baptismal regeneration. Jowers has one more argument, and he's confident that it's his best:

Only one argument, drawn not from scattered texts, but from a central theme of New Testament soteriology, seems adequate to the task of establishing irrefragably the falsehood of the doctrine of baptismal regeneration: viz., that this doctrine cannot be true, because it conflicts with the doctrine of the perseverance of the saints.[131]

In a way, Jowers is right: this *is* his strongest argument. He's absolutely right that baptismal regeneration is incompatible with the Reformed doctrine of "the perseverance of the saints" (sometimes called *once saved, always saved*) because we see obvious cases of people believing, getting baptized, and then falling away. Jesus says that "he who believes and is baptized will be saved" (Mark 16:16), but Simon Magus believes and is baptized (Acts 8:13) but then falls away (vv. 18–24). In fact, we can strengthen Jowers's argument by saying baptismal regeneration is incompatible with a whole host of uniquely Protestant doctrines. If Protestants are right on those doctrines, then the early Christians were universally wrong about baptism from the first two centuries onward. But there's an obvious answer here, too. All of those uniquely Protestant doctrines are based on scriptural texts that have been, and are, understood in a different way by non-Protestants. In other words, it's a question not of Scripture being incompatible with baptismal regeneration, but of the *Protestant interpretations* of Scripture being incompatible.

This explains a curious thing about the arguments against baptismal regeneration. With other doctrines (like justification), both Catholics and Protestants are looking at what Scripture says about justification and trying to make sense of that evidence. But with baptism, Catholics are looking to what Scripture says about baptism, whereas Protestants are frequently looking *elsewhere*, like to their understanding of "New Testament soteriology" or places where the Bible talks about salvation and baptism isn't mentioned. Methodologically, that seems obviously unsound: if you want to know what Jesus teaches about baptism, why not start by listening to him on baptism?

Consider how both the Old and New Testaments describe what appears (at least on its face) to be a promise of baptismal regeneration, and that Paul treats the early Christians as understanding baptism. Then consider how these early Christians clearly describe baptismal regeneration, and treat it as uncontroversial, while the Gnostics who deny it are accused of renouncing "the whole faith."[132] We don't see any evidence that regenerative baptism was some new idea, slowly (or quickly) accepted. It seems to have always been the universal belief, and the second-century Christians even called baptism *illumination* because of this belief.

That leaves two possibilities open: Protestants are right, meaning that the early Christians universally fell into the exact same misunderstanding about baptismal regeneration, seemingly immediately, or the early Christians really did understand baptism, meaning that baptismal regeneration is true and the Protestant doctrines contrary to it are false.

3

WORSHIP:

The Eucharist and the Mass

THE HISTORY of the Catholic Church includes innumerable reform movements. The Reformation, ironically, isn't really one of them. As the historian Eugene Rice explains, "the Protestant Reformation was not strictly a 'reformation' at all," but "a revolution, a full-scale attack on the traditional doctrines and sacramental structure of the Roman Church."[133] To put the distinction simply, the Reformers weren't trying to get bad Catholics to become good Catholics; they were trying to get bad Catholics and good Catholics to stop being Catholic. They were attacking their opponents not for failing to live up to their beliefs (the way a true reformer might), but for having the wrong set of beliefs to begin with. Michael Reeves, in *The Unquenchable Flame: Discovering the Heart of the Reformation*, describes the Reformation as "a revolution, and revolutions not only fight for something, they also fight against something, in this case, the old world of medieval Roman Catholicism."[134] Here's how he describes the faith that the Reformers rejected:

> It was through baptism that people (generally as infants) were first admitted to the Church to taste God's grace.

Yet it was the Mass that was really central to the whole system. That would be made obvious the moment you walked into your local church: all the architecture led towards the altar, on which the Mass would be celebrated. And it was called an altar with good reason, for in the Mass Christ's body would be sacrificed afresh to God. It was through this "unbloody" sacrifice offered day after day, repeating Christ's "bloody" sacrifice on the cross, that God's anger at sin would be appeased.[135]

Reeves makes no pretense of hiding his disgust at Catholicism,[ix] and he gets basic Catholic theology wrong (for instance, the entire point of the "unbloody" and "bloody" distinction is to stress that the Crucifixion *isn't* repeated daily), but he's right to say the Mass is the center of Catholicism, both then and now. We can say, almost literally, that it is the *heart* of Catholicism, for it is here that (if Catholics are right) Christ makes himself present to us, bodily. The Eucharist is "the source and summit of the Church's life and mission."[136] In the words of Pope John Paul II, "the Church draws her life from the Eucharist. This truth does not simply express a daily experience of faith, but recapitulates the heart of the mystery of the Church."[137]

It's for this reason that differences between Catholicism and Protestantism on the Eucharist are the most important doctrinal issue dividing us.[x] When the Reformers rejected the Mass as false worship and even "paganism and idolatry,"[138]

---

ix   For instance, he insists that "the priest was only handling mere bread and wine" and suggests that it "may all have seemed a bit farfetched" to have "imagined" otherwise. Reeves, pp. 18–19.

x   Many Protestants cite the doctrine of justification (particularly on the relationship between faith and "works") as the most important. I am inclined toward C.S. Lewis's view that "it does seem to me like asking which blade in a pair of scissors is most necessary." C.S. Lewis, *Mere Christianity* (New York: HarperOne, 2000), p. 148.

they were rejecting the daily worship that the Christians before them had offered for 1,500 years.[xi] Even today, you can still find variations of the claim the Catholic Mass is really "pagan." For instance, Frank Viola and George Barna claim in their book *Pagan Christianity?* that "the Mass did not originate with the New Testament; it grew out of ancient Judaism and paganism," and that it is "essentially a blending together of a resurgence of Gentile interest in synagogue worship and pagan influence that dates back to the fourth century."[139]

But while Protestants have historically been united in rejecting the Mass, they have not been united on any particular vision of what right worship looks like, or on any particular theology of the Lord's Supper. It is thus simplistic to speak of "the Protestant view" on the matter. But there are at least three major areas in which Catholics and Protestants disagree, and on each of them, Catholics are the ones faithful to the early Church.

1. Did the early Christians believe in the Real Presence of Christ in the Eucharist, and did they view this as a theologically important question for Church communion?

2. Did they view the Mass as a sacrifice?

3. Did they have *open* or *closed* Communion? (That is, did they permit those outside full communion to receive Communion?)

Let's look at each of these in turn.

---

xi   As Rice explains, "Luther struck at the heart of sacerdotal [priestly] power by redefining the sacrament of the Eucharist. He denied that the Mass was a sacrifice. . . . He denied the doctrine of transubstantiation. He denied that the sacrament worked, as medieval theologians had believed, by its own innate virtue and power." *The Foundations of Early Modern Europe, 1460–1559*, p. 157.

The Importance of the Real Presence

At the Last Supper, "Jesus took bread, and blessed, and broke it, and gave it to the disciples and said, 'Take, eat; this is my body.' And he took a cup, and when he had given thanks he gave it to them, saying, 'Drink of it, all of you; for this is my blood of the covenant, which is poured out for many for the forgiveness of sins'" (Matt. 26:26–28). This moment is significant enough that we find it reported by each of the Synoptics, plus St. Paul (Mark 14:22–24; Luke 22:19–20; 1 Cor. 11:23–25). St. John, the only evangelist not to report it directly, instead has the so-called *bread of life discourse*, in which Jesus responds to the question "how can this man give us his flesh to eat?" by declaring:

> Truly, truly, I say to you, unless you eat the flesh of the Son of Man and drink his blood, you have no life in you; he who eats my flesh and drinks my blood has eternal life, and I will raise him up at the Last Day. For my flesh is food indeed, and my blood is drink indeed. He who eats my flesh and drinks my blood abides in me, and I in him (6:52–56).

How literally should we take Jesus? Does he really mean that the bread and wine have become his body and blood? Does he actually mean that his flesh "is food indeed"? There are plenty of reasons within the biblical texts themselves to conclude that the answers to these questions are yes. But for now, I want to make a simpler point: that whether this literal interpretation is true or false, it *is* how the earliest Christians understood Jesus' words.[140]

The Protestant scholar of Church history J.N.D. Kelly summarizes what we might call the "big picture" of early Christian belief: "eucharistic teaching, it should be understood at the outset, was in general unquestioningly realist, i.e., the consecrated bread and wine were taken to be, and were treated and designated as, the Savior's body and blood."[141] We find this literal view present from the start. To get a sense of what Kelly is talking about, let's look at a few specific examples. As you're reading these early witnesses (whether or not you agree with them), notice a few things: how well developed their eucharistic theology is, how universally this theology seems to be accepted, and how central this eucharistic theology is to their faith and to the Church of their day.

Let's start around A.D. 107. St. Ignatius of Antioch is on the way to his martyrdom, and he writes a series of several letters to the churches of Asia Minor. In several of these, he warns about certain heretics[142] who were denying the Incarnation.[143] In technical terms, they were *Docetists*, meaning they taught that Jesus had only *appeared* to come in human form. Docetism is often tied to the heresy of Gnosticism: since Gnostics viewed the flesh as evil, they were repelled by the idea that "the Word became flesh and dwelt among us" (John 1:14). As you might imagine, a denial of the Incarnation also involved rejecting the Real Presence of Christ in the Eucharist. The Eucharist can't be the body and blood of Christ if he didn't really have a body or blood in the first place.

So what does Ignatius have to say about this? According to Protestant apologists like the Christian Apologetics and Research Ministry (CARM)'s Luke Wayne, not much. Instead, he argues:

> The issue is not what these false teachers believe about the physical nature of the bread and wine during Communion. It is what they believe about the nature of Jesus himself and his passion and resurrection. . . . You are not

to avoid these teachers because they might mislead you on the nature of the bread and cup. You are to avoid them because they deny what the scriptures teach about the suffering, death, and resurrection of Christ.[144]

On its face, Wayne's objection is perfectly sensible (particularly for Protestants who have never read Ignatius). If Ignatius were a Protestant, his response to Docetism would have certainly focused only on the implications on "the suffering, death, and resurrection of Christ," since it would not be particularly important what the Docetists believed about the nature of the "bread and wine during Communion." Indeed, Ignatius might even have *agreed* with the Docetists on this point: that while the Incarnation wasn't symbolic, the Eucharist is.

But there's a problem with this view. Ignatius says the opposite of nearly everything Wayne says. Wayne is discussing chapters six and seven of Ignatius's letter to the Smyrnaeans. In chapter six, Ignatius argues that the Docetists cannot be saved by the blood of Christ while rejecting the flesh and blood of the Incarnation.[145] But then, in chapter seven, he turns to the Eucharist. And what does Ignatius have to say about Docetism here? Here's chapter seven in its full, unadulterated[xii] form:

The issue is not what these false teachers believe about the physical nature of the bread and wine during Communion.

---

xii Ignatius's clear shift from discussing the cross (in chapter 6) to discussing the Eucharist (chapter 7) is lost to readers of Wayne's article, because he (hopefully unintentionally) renumbers the material, moving part of chapter 7 into chapter 6. The result is that his new chapter 7 begins halfway through a thought: "therefore those who deny the good gift of God perish in their contentiousness," giving the misleading impression that the "gift" in question is the passion of Christ, rather than the Eucharist. Compare Ignatius, Smyrnaeans 6–7, ANF 1:88–89, with Wayne, "Ignatius of Antioch and Transubstantiation."

They abstain from the Eucharist and from prayer, because they confess not the Eucharist to be the flesh of our Savior Jesus Christ, which suffered for our sins, and which the Father, of his goodness, raised up again. Those, therefore, who speak against this gift of God, incur death in the midst of their disputes. But it were better for them to treat it with respect, that they also might rise again. It is fitting, therefore, that you should keep aloof from such persons, and not to speak of them either in private or in public, but to give heed to the prophets, and above all, to the gospel, in which the Passion has been revealed to us, and the Resurrection has been fully proved. But avoid all divisions, as the beginning of evils.[146]

The issue for Ignatius (or rather, one of the issues) precisely *is* "what these false teachers believe about the physical nature of the bread and wine during Communion." His argument works like this:

1. Because the Docetists deny the Incarnation, they deny the Real Presence of Christ in the Eucharist ("they confess not the Eucharist to be the flesh of our Savior Jesus Christ").

2. Because they "speak against this gift of God," the Eucharist, they "incur death"—that is, damnation.

3. It would be spiritually better for them to acknowledge the truth about the Eucharist, so they can "rise again" in the bodily resurrection.

4. Since the Docetists deny Communion, we can't be in communion with them at all, so avoid them both publicly and privately.

5. Finally, we need to grow in our fidelity to gospel truth and Christian unity (the two things that the Docetists undermine).

Ignatius's arguments make sense only if both he and his readers are understanding Jesus' teaching about the Eucharist literally, including his warning and promise in John 6:53–54, connecting the Eucharist to bodily resurrection: "Truly, truly, I say to you, unless you eat the flesh of the Son of Man and drink his blood, you have no life in you; he who eats my flesh and drinks my blood has eternal life, and I will raise him up at the Last Day." To suggest that Ignatius either isn't focused on the Eucharist (when he's dedicated a chapter to it specifically) or doesn't believe it's really the flesh of Jesus beggars belief.

This is not the only place in which Ignatius spells out his belief in the Real Presence of Christ in the Eucharist,[xiii] but it is a particularly revealing one. Ignatius is clear that Church communion flows from sacramental Communion. In the words of Paul, "because there is one bread, we who are many are one body, for we all partake of the one bread" (1 Cor. 10:17). The converse of this is that the person who rejects the Real Presence rejects the foundation of the Church. That's why Ignatius says it is "fitting" to cut off personal contact with them: they're breaking communion by denying Communion.

---

xiii To the Romans, Ignatius says, "I have no delight in corruptible food, nor in the pleasures of this life. I desire the bread of God, the heavenly bread, the bread of life, which is the flesh of Jesus Christ, the Son of God, who became afterward of the seed of David and Abraham; and I desire the drink of God, namely his blood, which is incorruptible love and eternal life." Ignatius, Epistle to the Romans 7, ANF 1:77. He tells the Ephesians to "obey the bishop and the presbytery with an undivided mind, breaking one and the same bread, which is the medicine of immortality, and the antidote to prevent us from dying, but [which causes] that we should live for ever in Jesus Christ." Ignatius, Epistle to the Ephesians 20, ANF 1:57–58.

Were Ignatius and the Christians of Asia Minor alone in taking this view of the Eucharist? They were not. St. Justin Martyr, writing in Rome around the year 160, includes a description of the second-century liturgy. He explains that "on the day called Sunday, all who live in cities or in the country gather together to one place, and the memoirs of the apostles or the writings of the prophets are read, as long as time permits."[147] After the readings comes the homily, in which the presider "verbally instructs, and exhorts to the imitation of these good things."[148] Then come the prayers of the faithful ("we all rise together and pray"),[149] followed by what we now call the Liturgy of the Eucharist, including the sign of peace,[xiv] presentation of the gifts, eucharistic prayers, and distribution of Communion:

Having ended the prayers, we salute one another with a kiss. There is then brought to the president of the brethren bread and a cup of wine mixed with water; and he taking them, gives praise and glory to the Father of the universe, through the name of the Son and of the Holy Ghost, and offers thanks at considerable length for our being counted worthy to receive these things at his hands. And when he has concluded the prayers and thanksgivings, all the people present express their assent by saying Amen. This word Amen answers in the Hebrew language to *genoito* [so be it]. And when the president has given thanks, and all the people have expressed their assent, those who are called by us deacons give to each of those present to partake of the bread and wine mixed with water over which the thanksgiving was pronounced, and to those who are absent they carry away a portion.[150]

---

xiv Pope Benedict XVI considered moving the sign of peace back to this moment in the liturgy, but this remained only a proposal. See Benedict XVI, *Sacramentum Caritatis* fn. 150.

The references to the "thanksgivings" (*eucharistian*), the presider[151] having "given thanks" (*eucharistēsantos*), and the like are more obviously eucharistic in Justin's original Greek. For instance, the phrase being translated as "the bread and wine mixed with water over which the thanksgiving was pronounced" can also be rendered "the eucharistized bread and wine and water."[152] All of this is drawn out clearly (even in English) in the next chapter, in which Justin says that "this food is called among us *Eucharistia* [the Eucharist]" and explains:

> For not as common bread and common drink do we receive these; but in like manner as Jesus Christ our Savior, having been made flesh by the Word of God, had both flesh and blood for our salvation, so likewise have we been taught that the food which is blessed by the prayer of his word, and from which our blood and flesh by transmutation are nourished, is the flesh and blood of that Jesus who was made flesh. For the apostles, in the memoirs composed by them, which are called Gospels, have thus delivered unto us what was enjoined upon them; that Jesus took bread, and when he had given thanks, said, "This do ye in remembrance of me, this is my body"; and that, after the same manner, having taken the cup and given thanks, he said, "This is my blood"; and gave it to them alone.[153]

Justin then mentions, almost as an aside, that "the wicked devils" have imitated this rite "in the mysteries of Mithras, commanding the same thing to be done." [154]

The liturgy that Justin describes is immediately recognizable as the Mass. Not only are the individual parts the same, but with minor exceptions (like the placement of the sign of peace), even the order is the same. The center of this Mass is not a preacher giving a sermon, but a presider offering up the Eucharist. And how does he understand the Eucharist? That what had been "common bread and common drink" (that is, ordinary bread and wine) ceases to be through the formula of blessing given by Christ, and instead, it is now "the flesh and blood of that Jesus who was made flesh." Even Wayne admits that "this is perhaps the best argument Roman Catholics have for their position," although he nevertheless insists that Justin can't possibly be a believer in the Real Presence since he is against cannibalism (as if Catholics today think cannibalism is okay!). He writes:

> Justin is quite adamant that Christians do not eat human flesh. He was not alone in such comments. His second-century Christian peers also made note of how particularly vile they saw the concept of eating human flesh. When listing accusations he had heard leveled against Christians, Theophilus of Antioch calls the charge of eating of human flesh "the most impious and barbarous of all."[155]

At no point does Wayne seem to consider the obvious point that if the opponents of second-century Christianity are accusing them of cannibalism, that tells us a great deal about those Christians' eucharistic theology. Catholics today routinely have to defend themselves against the charge of cannibalism,[156] while it would be difficult to mistake most Protestant Lord's Suppers as anything more than symbolic.[157] So even in denying the charge of cannibalism, Justin and the second-century Church sound Catholic, not Protestant.

Justin even uses the language of transmutation to describe the transformation taking place, although not where you might expect. That is, he describes *us* as being transmutated by the Eucharist, that our flesh and blood are spiritually united to Christ through receiving Communion. It's not just that the bread and wine change into the body and blood of Christ, but that the body and blood of Christ transform our own bodies. What's going on here? As St. Gregory of Nyssa (c. 335–395) would later explain, Christians believed that since "in no other way was it possible for our body to become immortal, but by participating in incorruption through its fellowship with that immortal body," Jesus "disseminates himself in every believer through that flesh, whose substance comes from bread and wine, blending himself with the bodies of believers, to secure that, by this union with the immortal, man, too, may be a sharer in incorruption."[158] What Christ begins in the Incarnation (uniting divinity and humanity) is done in the individual believer through the Eucharist, and this is how we can be bodily raised to become "partakers of the divine nature" (2 Pet. 1:4).[159] It's for this reason that both Jesus (see John 6:55–58) and so many of the early Christians pass from speaking of the Eucharist to bodily resurrection and back. Ignatius and Justin treat this connection as almost too obvious to mention, leaving modern readers (who've never heard of this connection) to stumble over their writings.

That brings us to the third major witness of what eucharistic theology looked like in the Church before 200: St. Irenaeus. The Patristic historian (and Reformed Protestant) James R. Payton, Jr. rightly calls him "the greatest theologian to arise in the Church since the time of the apostles."[160] As you may recall from chapter one, Irenaeus wrote c. 180 against the Gnostic heresy, a view that rejects the Incarnation and treats the body as evil. As Irenaeus explains:

> But vain in every respect are they who despise the entire dispensation of God, and disallow the salvation of the flesh, and treat with contempt its regeneration, maintaining that

it is not capable of incorruption. But if this indeed do not attain salvation, then neither did the Lord redeem us with his blood, nor is the cup of the Eucharist the Communion of his blood, nor the bread which we break the Communion of his body. For blood can only come from veins and flesh, and whatsoever else makes up the substance of man, such as the Word of God was actually made.[161]

In other words, if you deny the goodness of the body, then you're forced to deny both the reality of Christ's death on the cross and the Real Presence. It's important to recognize the argument being made here by Irenaeus (and by Ignatius before him). In technical terms, it's what we call a *reductio ad absurdum*, or what Aristotle called a *deduction to the impossible*.[162] The argument works by showing that an idea, if taken to its logical conclusion, would produce absurd results. For instance, if someone said, "We should always trust children because they're uncorrupted by sin," you might respond with, "Should we trust them when they claim that monsters live under their beds?" That's a *reductio ad absurdum*. But notice that it works only if both sides agree that a particular thing is absurd or impossible. If the person you're speaking to believes in monsters, your argument is logically sound but rhetorically unpersuasive.[163] Both Ignatius and Irenaeus lived in a world in which showing "X idea is logically contrary to believing in the Real Presence" is sufficient to debunk X idea (in this case, Docetism). Protestants who deny the Real Presence find themselves in a strange place, unable to agree with either the Gnostics or their Christian opponents.

Irenaeus continues by arguing that Christ "has acknowledged the cup (which is a part of the creation) as his own blood, from which he bedews our blood; and the bread (also a part of the creation) he has established as his own body, from which he gives increase to our bodies."[164] This is the same argument but in reverse: since we know that Christ turns created matter (bread and wine) into his body and blood, we must therefore conclude that creation isn't evil. He then says:

> When, therefore, the mingled cup and the manufactured bread receives the Word of God, and the Eucharist of the blood and the body of Christ is made, from which things the substance of our flesh is increased and supported, how can they affirm that the flesh is incapable of receiving the gift of God, which is life eternal, which [flesh] is nourished from the body and blood of the Lord, and is a member of him?—even as the blessed Paul declares in his epistle to the Ephesians, that "we are members of his body, of his flesh, and of his bones." He does not speak these words of some spiritual and invisible man, for a spirit has not bones nor flesh; but [he refers to] that dispensation [by which the Lord became] an actual man, consisting of flesh, and nerves, and bones—that [flesh] which is nourished by the cup which is his blood, and receives increase from the bread which is his body.[165]

Irenaeus is explicit here: the bread and the "mingled cup" (wine with water poured into it) receive the Word of God, and the Eucharist "is made." The wording there is significant: he's suggesting that some actual change is taking place. We don't just start calling bread *Communion* for a while during the liturgy. God turns the wine and bread into something that they weren't before: "the blood and the body of Christ." Like Ignatius before him, Irenaeus refers to this as "the gift of God"[xv] and points out that this is all meant of a true body

---

xv Remember Wayne's confusion about Ignatius, supposing that the "gift of God" meant the cross and not the Eucharist. Irenaeus's use of the same phrasing for the Eucharist should eliminate any ambiguity.

(with flesh, and nerves, and bones!), not "some spiritual and invisible man." After stressing the literalism of his eucharistic theology, he refers to the Eucharist as "the bread which is his body." This is an important point for certain Protestant objections, which we'll address at the end of the chapter: there's nothing inconsistent in calling Jesus the bread of life and believing that the bread literally becomes his body.

Irenaeus's explanation concludes with an argument similar to what we heard from both Justin Martyr and Ignatius, about how receiving the Eucharist is key to the ultimate incorruption and resurrection of the body:

> And just as a cutting from the vine planted in the ground fructifies in its season, or as a corn of wheat falling into the earth and becoming decomposed, rises with manifold increase by the Spirit of God, who contains all things, and then, through the wisdom of God, serves for the use of men, and having received the Word of God, becomes the Eucharist, which is the body and blood of Christ; so also our bodies, being nourished by it, and deposited in the earth, and suffering decomposition there, shall rise at their appointed time, the Word of God granting them resurrection to the glory of God, even the Father, who freely gives to this mortal immortality, and to this corruptible incorruption.[166]

Elsewhere, he makes this same point in the context of what it looks like to give proper sacrifice to God:

> For we offer to him his own, announcing consistently the fellowship and union of the flesh and Spirit. For as the bread, which is produced from the earth, when it receives the invocation of God, is no longer common bread, but

the Eucharist, consisting of two realities, earthly and heavenly; so also our bodies, when they receive the Eucharist, are no longer corruptible, having the hope of the resurrection to eternity.[167]

With each of these three Christians—Ignatius, Justin, and Irenaeus—we have a rather sophisticated eucharistic theology from remarkably early in the life of the Church. The latest of these three, Irenaeus, writes around the year 180.[168] By way of reference, the first time we see the word *Trinity* used is in 181,[169] so this eucharistic theology is well established even while these same Christians are parsing through the nuances of trinitarian theology. If you knew little about the early Christians, it might be easy to imagine that their belief in the Real Presence was because of superstition and ignorance or some connection to paganism. What we find instead is that their eucharistic theology is inseparably interwoven with their beliefs about Jesus' incarnation, passion, and resurrection, as well as our own bodily resurrection. When we find later forms of paganism, like Mithraic rituals, practicing things that remind us of the Eucharist, it's because (as Justin notes) they've copied them from Christianity, not the other way around.

No less remarkable is the lack of serious debate that we see about the Eucharist. What I mean is that these are not just three theologians, but three eyewitnesses to a much broader belief system. Ignatius doesn't tell the Smyrnaeans that they *ought* to believe in the Real Presence, but writes with the understanding that they already *do*—and that he can point to the Gnostics' rejection of the Real Presence as grounds to treat them as excommunicated. Justin says not how the Mass *ought* to look, but how it *does* look. And Irenaeus treats belief in the Real Presence as such a universally accepted doctrine that he argues the following:

Then, again, how can they [the Gnostics] say that the flesh, which is nourished with the body of the Lord and with his blood, goes to corruption, and does not partake of life? Let them, therefore, either alter their opinion, or cease from offering the things just mentioned. But our opinion is in accordance with the Eucharist, and the Eucharist in turn establishes our opinion.[170]

Given the radical nature of Jesus' eucharistic teaching, we might expect more controversy than we find. After all, the first hearers of Christ's eucharistic teaching responded, "This is a hard saying; who can listen to it?" (John 6:60), and it is understandable that many modern Protestants have the same reaction. But the early Christians seem to have not only accepted this "hard saying," but built their lives (and their theology, and their ecclesial communion) around it.

The Sacrifice of the Mass

On the question of the *Real Presence*, Protestants adopt a wide variety of views. But there's one doctrine in particular in which we see all (or almost all) of the Protestant Reformers arrayed on one side, and all of the early Christians on the other: the question of whether or not the Mass is a sacrifice.

Radical Reformers like the Anabaptist Balthasar Hubmaier argue that the "Mass is not a sacrifice, but a remembrance of our Lord's death."[171] So does Ulrich Zwingli, the father of the Swiss Reformation: "The Mass is not a sacrifice, but rather a commemoration of the sacrifice and confirmation of the salvation which Christ has won for us."[172] But so did more conservative Reformers, like Martin Luther and John Calvin. This rejection of the sacrifice of the Mass continues among Protestants today, whether it's Gregg Allison gently describing it as the "culminating expression" of the "incongruity" between how Catholics and Protestants approach "the worship of God and the salvation he offers,"[173] or it's John MacArthur lambasting it as "a denial of the singular sacrifice of Christ on the cross, because the Mass is an offering of Christ repeatedly by an illegitimate priesthood on an illegitimate altar for a useless and ungodly purpose."[174]

This position puts Protestants at odds with the whole of pre-Reformation Christianity, a fact the Reformers readily admitted. Martin Luther laments that "there is no belief in the Church more generally received or more firmly held than that the Mass is a good work and a sacrifice."[175] John Calvin likewise claims that Satan (somehow) "not only obscured and perverted, but altogether obliterated and abolished" the Lord's Supper when he "blinded almost the whole world into the belief that the Mass was a sacrifice and oblation for obtaining the remission of sins."[176] Luther explains that the Church "universally believed" this for good reason, since it agrees with the witness of the early Christians and the liturgical text itself:

> With this opinion the words of the canon of the Mass appear to agree, such as—"These gifts; these offerings; these holy sacrifices"; and again, "this oblation." There is also a very distinct prayer that the sacrifice may be accepted like the sacrifice of Abel. Hence Christ is called the victim of the altar. To this we must add the sayings of the holy Fathers, a great number of authorities, and the usage that has been constantly observed throughout the world.[177]

Calvin also points to the liturgical texts to show that "this is not merely the common opinion of the vulgar, but the very act has been so arranged as to be a kind of propitiation, by which satisfaction is made to God for the living and the dead. This is also expressed by the words employed, and the same thing may be inferred from daily practice."[178] In other words, this wasn't a matter of illiterate, superstitious medieval peasants misunderstanding what Christianity taught. Ordinary believers and great theologians believed the same thing, and it was what they prayed each time they went to (or celebrated) Mass. That is, the Reformers were railing against not some "monstrous late medieval distortion of doctrine,"[179] but the entire system of Christian worship for the preceding 1,500 years. To accept the Protestant argument is to believe that the whole Church, from the time of the early Christian martyrs onward, was deceived by Satan when it thought it was offering sacrificial worship to God.

On what basis do the Reformers justify such a radical stance? Luther argues that "there is nothing about a work or sacrifice" in the "plain meaning"[xvi] of Christ's words and deeds.[180] That is, his case is built on an argument from (alleged) silence. As for those early Christian witnesses, Luther says that "it would be safer to deny their authority altogether, than to grant that the Mass is a work or a sacrifice, and thus to deny the word of Christ and to overthrow faith and the Mass together."[181] Zwingli offers a stronger argument against the sacrifice of the Mass, one familiar to many modern readers: that the Mass cannot be a sacrifice, because "Christ has sacrificed himself once and for all eternity as a true and sufficient sacrifice for the sins of all believers."[182] The epistle to the Hebrews says Jesus "has no need, like those high priests, to offer sacrifices daily, first for his own sins and then for those of the people; he did this once for

---

xvi Bear in mind (as we'll see at the close of this chapter) that the Reformers could never actually agree on the "plain meaning" of Jesus' words.

all when he offered up himself" (7:27). So how can this be harmonized with the idea of Christ being offered daily in the eucharistic sacrifice?

The answer to Luther's and Zwingli's objection requires understanding Jewish sacrificial meals. Certain sacrifices *required* those offering the sacrifice to eat of it. For instance, the peace offering "shall be eaten on the day of his offering; he shall not leave any of it until the morning" (Lev. 7:15). If the peace offering was a free-will offering, the one offering it had an additional day to eat it. Still, "if any of the flesh of the sacrifice of his peace offering is eaten on the third day, he who offers it shall not be accepted, neither shall it be credited to him; it shall be an abomination, and he who eats of it shall bear his iniquity" (v. 18). The point here is that there are two distinct aspects to the sacrifice: (1) slaying and offering the animal and (2) eating the animal. Failing to eat the sacrifice within the mandated time period rendered it unacceptable, an abomination. But the killing and the eating of the animal were two dimensions to one sacrifice, not two distinct sacrifices.

We can see this perhaps most clearly with the Passover sacrifice. The Passover liturgy consisted of two aspects: the slaying of the lamb on 14 Nisan (Preparation Day) and the eating of the lamb at the Passover meal on 15 Nisan (Exod. 12:6, 8).[xvii] Preparation Day prefigures Good Friday, a connection St. John makes explicit in John 19:14. This is the once-for-all sacrifice of which Hebrews 7 speaks. But if "Christ, our paschal lamb, has been sacrificed" (1 Cor. 5:7), when and how do we participate in that sacrificial meal?

---

xvii   The Jewish day begins at sundown, which is why Preparation Day and the Feast of Unleavened Bread are on separate days, while they would be on the same day on our own calendars.

As St. Luke says, "the day of Unleavened Bread, on which the Passover lamb had to be sacrificed" (Luke 22:7), is Holy Thursday, at the Last Supper. But even though John describes Preparation Day as a sacrifice, and Luke describes the Passover meal as a sacrifice, these aren't two separate sacrifices: they're two aspects of the same Passover sacrifice.

When Jesus offers his Passover, he *is* the Lamb (hence the conspicuous lack of any references to a lamb in any of the four Gospel accounts of the Last Supper). But Jesus is also the priest of his own sacrifice: "I lay down my life, that I may take it again. No one takes it from me, but I lay it down of my own accord. I have power to lay it down, and I have power to take it again" (John 10:17–18). But if Christ is our "great high priest" (Heb. 4:14), where do we see him offering himself? At the Last Supper, when he says, "This is my body which is given for you" (Luke 22:19) and "This is my blood of the covenant, which is poured out for many" (Mark 14:24). The Jewish context of these words is the sealing of the covenant with Moses, when Moses "sacrificed peace offerings of oxen to the Lord" and then applied them to the people by throwing the blood upon them while declaring, "Behold the blood of the covenant which the Lord has made with you in accordance with all these words" (Exod. 24:5, 8).

To sum up, eating the Passover lamb didn't "re-sacrifice" the lamb slain on Preparation Day. It was rather the way in which a believer participated in the sacrifice and applied it to himself. And if a person ate the peace offering over the span of two days, he wasn't "re-sacrificing" the peace offering, but continuing to participate in it. And so when Jesus says at his Passover, "Do this in remembrance of me" (Luke 22:19), he's not telling them to crucify him repeatedly, but telling them to repeatedly participate in the sacrificial meal.

St. Paul draws this sacrificial eucharistic theology out in his first letter to the Corinthians. He employs a fascinating threefold parallel: proving that the Eucharist is a sacrifice by comparing it to Jewish and even pagan sacrifices. He begins by describing "the cup of blessing which we bless" as "a participation in the blood of Christ" and "the bread which we break" as "a participation in the body of Christ" (1 Cor. 10:16). So how is it a "participation"? He explains (vv. 18–21):

> Consider the practice of Israel; are not those who eat the sacrifices partners in the altar? What do I imply then? That food offered to idols is anything, or that an idol is anything? No, I imply that what pagans sacrifice they offer to demons and not to God. I do not want you to be partners with demons. You cannot drink the cup of the Lord and the cup of demons. You cannot partake of the table of the Lord and the table of demons.

Paul's analogy is shocking: he's just compared the Lord's Supper to both the Jewish sacrificial system and the demonic sacrifices offered by pagans. Jews become "partners in the altar" by eating the sacrificial offering, and pagans become partners with demons by partaking of the "table of demons" and drinking from "the cup of demons," eating and drinking the sacrificial offerings. (The "table" here is not a dinner table, but an *altar*). These are the two analogies that Paul uses to explain how he can say that "we who are many are one body, for we all partake of the one bread" (1 Cor. 10:17). But notice that these analogies make sense only if the Eucharist is also a sacrificial offering, such that we become "partners in the altar" when we "partake of the table of the Lord."

As we've already seen, Christians always understood the Eucharist in this sacrificial way until the Reformation, a fact that even the Reformers were forced to concede. In support of their eucharistic theology, the early Christians frequently cited Malachi 1:10–12:

> I have no pleasure in you, says the Lord of hosts, and I will not accept an offering from your hand. For from the rising of the sun to its setting my name is great among the nations, and in every place incense is offered to my name, and a pure offering; for my name is great among the nations, says the Lord of hosts. But you profane it when you say that the Lord's table is polluted, and the food for it may be despised.

What was significant about this Old Testament text? It predicted that the Jewish sacrificial system would be set aside ("I will not accept an offering from your hand") in favor of a new sacrificial system in which even Gentiles ("the nations") would be able to offer incense and a "pure offering" to God. This is also the first explicit biblical reference to "the Lord's table." Before this, we had heard of both Jews and pagans eating food sacrifices (Exod. 34:15; Lev. 7:15–16; etc.), but this is the clearest Old Testament prophecy that this will also be the case in the New Covenant. (This is the backdrop for Paul's description of altars as "tables" in 1 Corinthians 10.)

The first time we see Malachi cited in this way is the first-century *Didache*, perhaps even predating parts of the New Testament. The work is a sort of catechism, summarizing "the teaching of the twelve apostles," and includes these instructions:

> On the Lord's Day of the Lord come together, break bread and hold Eucharist, after confessing your transgressions that your offering may be pure; but let none who has a

quarrel with his fellow join in your meeting until they be reconciled, that your sacrifice be not defiled. For this is that which was spoken by the Lord, "In every place and time offer me a pure sacrifice, for I am a great king," saith the Lord, "and my name is wonderful among the heathen."[183]

St. Justin Martyr likewise cites Malachi as proof both of the cessation of the Jewish sacrificial system and of the fact that "God, anticipating all the sacrifices which we offer through this name, and which Jesus the Christ enjoined us to offer, i.e., in the Eucharist of the bread and the cup, and which are presented by Christians in all places throughout the world, bears witness that they are well-pleasing to him."[184]

So does St. Irenaeus, when he explains that the prophecy shows "that the Lord instituted a new oblation in the New Covenant."[185] But Irenaeus makes an additional scriptural connection, seeing the Malachi prophecy fulfilled in Jesus' words about worshipping God "in spirit and truth" in John 4. When the Samaritan woman says to Jesus, "Our fathers worshiped on this mountain; and you say that in Jerusalem is the place where men ought to worship" (John 4:20), Jesus responds by saying that "the hour is coming when neither on this mountain nor in Jerusalem will you worship the Father," and that "the hour is coming, and now is, when the true worshippers will worship the Father in spirit and truth" (John 4:21, 23).

There's a common[186] Protestant misreading of this passage that views Jesus as dispelling the idea that prayer "has to happen in a certain way, at a particular time, and only at a church."[187] But both Jews and Samaritans already knew that that was false. Even the hypocrites knew that; Jesus observes that they "love to stand and pray in the synagogues and at the street corners" (Matt. 6:5). The Old Testament is replete with examples of the faithful praying in all manner of places. So what is the Samaritan woman asking Jesus about? *Sacrificial* worship. To this day, the Samaritans offer the Passover sacrifice on Mount Gerizim, while the Jews offer it in Jerusalem.[188] Jesus is letting her know that those systems are coming to an end, in favor of something new (thus fulfilling Malachi's prophecy). Irenaeus concludes:

> And therefore the oblation of the Eucharist is not a carnal one, but a spiritual; and in this respect it is pure. For we make an oblation to God of the bread and the cup of blessing, giving him thanks in that he has commanded the earth to bring forth these fruits for our nourishment. And then, when we have perfected the oblation, we invoke the Holy Spirit, that he may exhibit this sacrifice, both the bread the body of Christ, and the cup the blood of Christ, in order that the receivers of these antitypes may obtain remission of sins and life eternal.[189]

These are far from the only early Christian witnesses to the fact that the Eucharist was understood as a sacrifice from the earliest days. (For instance, St. Clement, writing around A.D. 96, refers to the "offerings" made by the bishop, and St. Ignatius in c. 107 calls on the church in Philadelphia to "have but one Eucharist" at the "one altar.")[190] But I hope they will suffice to show the point. Viola and Barna, whom we heard from at the start of this chapter, blame St. Cyprian of Carthage (210–258) for introducing this idea of the Eucharist as sacrifice, but it's hard to see how this could be the case, given that Cyprian *wasn't born yet.*[191]

Nor were these authors alone. As both Luther and Calvin point out, the liturgical texts themselves treat the Eucharist as a sacrifice. In short, this was not some fringe theory, or the private musings of a handful of bishops or theologians, or of half-converted pagans coming into the Church. This is the unbroken theology of 2,000 years of Christianity, affirmed in every Mass daily and rooted in the teaching of both the Old and New Testaments.[xviii]

Closed Communion

A third dimension of eucharistic theology in which we find early Christianity united against later Protestant innovations is on the question of *open* or *closed* Communion. In other words, should those who aren't members of the church or denomination be permitted to receive communion? For instance, the United Methodist Church teaches that "the Lord's Supper in a United Methodist congregation is open to members of other United Methodist congregations and to Christians from other traditions," explaining that "the United Methodist Church recognizes that it is only one of the bodies that constitute the community of Christians. Despite our differences, all Christians are welcome at the table of the Lord."[192] Indeed, some Methodist theologians have gone farther, insisting that even the unbaptized be able to partake of the Lord's Supper.[193] But Protestants attending a Catholic (or Orthodox) liturgy will find that they are *not* invited up to receive Communion. This has been the source of some controversy lately within Catholicism as well as Protestantism, with some Catholic theologians arguing that Protestants should be allowed to receive Communion in the Catholic Church[194] and Catholic and Protestant leaders in Germany even announcing plans for intercommunion, ignoring objections from the Vatican.[195]

---

xviii I use "Mass" here in the broader sense of divine liturgy, not strictly to refer to the Roman form of the liturgy.

But this issue is a particularly keen problem for the Baptist communion, since Baptists don't recognize infant baptisms as real baptisms.[196] This creates a theological problem for the Lord's Supper: can Baptists invite other supposedly *unbaptized* Protestants—that is, Protestants who were baptized as babies—to the Lord's Supper? Officially, the Southern Baptist Convention teaches *no*: Baptists stress their belief that Christian baptism requires "the immersion of a believer in water in the name of the Father, the Son, and the Holy Spirit" and "is prerequisite to the privileges of church membership and to the Lord's Supper."[197] But in practice, only about a third of Southern Baptist pastors follow their denomination's teaching on this subject. A majority, when surveyed, reported that they offer communion to "anyone who has put faith in Christ," regardless of whether the person is baptized or not.[198]

This position, called *open communion*, dates back at least to the seventeenth-century Puritan John Bunyan (most famous for his book *Pilgrim's Progress*), who argued that communion should be open even to unbaptized believers, since "a failure in such a circumstance as water baptism, doth not unchristian us," as there really is "no difference between that believer that is, and he that is not yet baptized with water" other than an "outward ceremony of the substance which he hath already."[199] The modern debate over open communion and Bunyan's writings show how poor baptismal theology leads to poor eucharistic theology. Bunyan unwittingly captures this problem in a single expression: "the church is a church without water-baptism."[200] If baptism doesn't do anything significant in terms of one's salvation or church membership, why should being unbaptized be a bar to receiving communion?

The question of open communion is largely a symptom of deeper theological differences in how we understand what (if anything) happens in the Lord's Supper. Tellingly, the Methodist theologian Mark Stamm's book arguing for open communion is entitled *Let Every Soul Be Jesus' Guest: A Theology of the Open Table.*[201] If the Lord's Supper is just about having a meal with Jesus, it would seem only fitting to open it to anyone and everyone. After all, we find Jesus in the Gospels "eating with sinners and tax collectors" (Matt. 9:10–11; Mark 2:15–16; Luke 5:29–30). But on the other hand, the Last Supper wasn't a big open table. For *that* occasion, "he sat at table with the twelve disciples" (Matt. 26:20).[202] The Last Supper was also a Passover meal, and the Passover meal was "closed" to uncircumcised: "when a stranger shall sojourn with you and would keep the Passover to the Lord, let all his males be circumcised, then he may come near and keep it; he shall be as a native of the land. But no uncircumcised person shall eat of it" (Exod. 12:48).

If the Lord's Supper isn't *just* the new Passover, but also where we receive the body and blood of Christ, this closed nature of Communion makes even more sense. As St. Paul warns, "any one who eats and drinks without discerning the body eats and drinks judgment upon himself" (1 Cor. 11:29). Offering Communion to those who don't believe in (and thus, cannot discern) the body and blood of Christ in the Eucharist is a false mercy if it means that you're encouraging people to eat and drink judgment upon themselves.

Those advocating for "open communion" (particularly for the unbaptized) have drifted far from the teachings of early Christianity. The first-century *Didache* says to "let none eat or drink of your Eucharist except those who have been baptized in the Lord's name. For concerning this also did the Lord say 'give not that which is holy to the dogs.'"[203] We've already heard from Ignatius about refusing communion (and thus, Communion) with heretics like the

Docetists. He likewise warns the Philadelphians to "keep yourselves from those evil plants which Jesus Christ does not tend, because they are not the planting of the Father."[204]

But the clearest explanation of closed communion comes from St. Justin Martyr, who explains that the Eucharist is that food "of which no one is allowed to partake but the man who believes that the things which we teach are true, and who has been washed with the washing that is for the remission of sins, and unto regeneration, and who is so living as Christ has enjoined."[205] In other words, in order to receive Communion, you need to (1) believe the teachings of the Catholic Church, (2) be baptized, and (3) be in a state of grace. Communion is accordingly closed to those who reject Catholic teaching, are unbaptized, or are living in a manner contrary to what Christ enjoins.

How Might a Protestant Respond?

Remember that (as is often the case) there's no such thing as *the* Protestant position on this doctrine. Most Protestants reject the Real Presence, nearly all reject the sacrificial nature of the Mass, and there are debates within Protestantism about open and closed communion. But there's no one coherent eucharistic theology throughout Protestantism, in the way that there was a coherent theology throughout the early Church.[206]

This problem goes back to the Reformers. As R.C. Sproul explains, "The Reformers declared their total confidence in what they called the *perspicuity* of Scripture. What they meant by that technical term was the clarity of Scripture. They maintained that the Bible is basically clear and lucid. It is simple enough for any literate person to understand its basic message."[207] In fact, the Reformers went even beyond this; Luther's argument was not that the "basic message" was clear, but that "nothing whatsoever is left obscure or ambiguous, but all that is in the Scripture is through the Word brought forth into the clearest light and proclaimed to the whole world."[208] The Catholic side was arguing that the Church is needed for interpreting otherwise confusing passages of Scripture, of the sort that St. Peter talks about in 2 Peter 3:15–16. The Protestant response was that this interpretative role of the Church is unnecessary because there is *nothing* ambiguous or obscure in the Bible.

But then the Reformers get to the question of the Eucharist, and each interprets Scripture "clearly" in a way that contradicts both early Christianity and the other Reformers. As the Calvinist historian Alister McGrath explains:

> Luther and Zwingli were unable to agree on the meaning of such phrases as "this is my body" (which Luther interpreted literally and Zwingli metaphorically) and "at the right hand of God" (which—with apparent inconsistency on both sides—Luther interpreted metaphorically and Zwingli literally). The exegetical optimism of the early Reformation may be regarded as foundering on this rock: Scripture, it seemed, was far from easy to interpret.[209]

Little progress has been made on this question in the half-millennium since the Reformation began, and this remains one of the largest barriers to Lutheran-Reformed communion.[210] In the preface to his book *Understanding Four Views on the Lord's Supper*,[211] John Armstrong writes that "earnest and faithful Christians . . . disagree over the *meaning* of the Supper as well as the *importance* of it. They disagree over *who* should take it and *when*. And they strongly disagree over *what happens* to the elements themselves when they are prayed over and taken by the people of God."[212]

Given this, one way that Protestants may respond to this chapter is by agreeing with at least large chunks of what the early Christians have to say. But what about those who disagree? There are (at least) five approaches that you might take.

The first approach is to say that St. Ignatius, St. Justin, St. Irenaeus, and the rest are all misunderstood, and that they don't *really* mean to say what they appear to say, and that their eucharistic theology actually agrees with Protestantism. If you lean in this direction, let me suggest three things. First, notice the manner in which these early Christians speak about the Eucharist, and ask yourself if they sound more like Catholics or Protestants. Second, consider the fact that even many Protestant scholars and theologians concede that they were (as Kelly puts it) eucharistic "realists." Why is that? Third, remember that I'm only highlighting three of the most prominent Christians of the first two centuries of the Church; there are numerous others I could have chosen.[213] So how plausible is it that this many otherwise careful theologians all managed to express themselves so poorly, and in such consistently similar ways? Finally, beware of bar-raising: of demanding that the "other side" produce evidence, and when they do, continually demanding *more* evidence, or more specific evidence, or looking for ambiguities to explain their evidence away.[xix]

I've singled out Wayne a bit in this chapter because I think he's a textbook case for how *not* to handle the evidence.[214] He claims that the New Testament "never makes

---

xix I am not suggesting here any kind of precise standard for what accounts for "sufficient evidence," only warning against a certain kind of attitude toward the truth. An easy test to ask is whether you hold "your side" and "the other side" to the same evidentiary standards.

or even alludes to" the claim that the Eucharist is a sacrifice (in fact, St. Paul does in 1 Corinthians 10, as I mentioned above), but then he says, "even if it were called a sacrifice, that still wouldn't be enough to prove the Roman Catholic point!"[215] When the *Didache* and Justin Martyr clearly *do* describe the eucharistic sacrifice, he responds that this doesn't prove it's a *propitiatory* sacrifice, because they didn't happen to specify that point. That's bar-raising, and no amount of evidence can persuade a person committed to such an approach. As the old adage says, "there's none so blind as those who will not see."

The second approach is to concede but minimize. Wayne does this as well, as a sort of backup position. Perhaps sensing that his explanations for why the early Christians mentioned above are not *really* Catholic are a bit implausible, he adds a sort of general disclaimer that it doesn't matter even if they are. For instance, "Ignatius was not an inspired author. His words are not God-breathed. He is fallible and perfectly capable of error. If Ignatius taught transubstantiation, then so what?"[216] In other words, Ignatius is just one guy, and he's fallible! But then Wayne does the same for others, like Justin Martyr: "Justin is not an arbiter of some infallible, apostolic tradition that the Spirit never inspired the apostles themselves to right [*sic*] down. Justin is a fallible man like you and me."[217] At a certain point, it's like insisting that your sixth beer isn't going to get you drunk because "it's just one beer." Ignatius and Justin aren't theological outliers in the early Church; they're describing the apparently universal beliefs and practices of their day.[218] It's not a question of whether Justin Martyr is infallible—no one claims he is. It's a question of whether the apostolic Tradition—to which he and Irenaeus and Ignatius and the *Didache*, etc. witness—is.

The third approach is to concede but shrug. Many Protestants today differ from their sixteenth-century forebears not in that they believe *differently,* but in that they believe *less.* The Reformers at least recognized that the eucharistic doctrines were important to get right, whereas many modern Protestants treat the question as trifling. In *What Divides Protestants and Catholics on the Eucharist?,* written from a Reformed Protestant perspective, Bradford Littlejohn says of the religious violence over eucharistic theology that followed the Reformation: "It may be difficult for us now to appreciate how such a seemingly arcane dispute could have been a life-or-death issue. But it is important to remember that the debate over transubstantiation stood at the strategic intersection of many other high-stakes doctrinal issues."[219] That is, the only way Littlejohn can show his Protestant readers why eucharistic theology even matters is that it used to matter, since it was "another battleground of the Reformation's great war against the belief that Jesus works through the *church outside of us.*"[220] That speaks to a sea change within Protestantism of which Catholics are often unaware. The *Heidelberg Catechism* (1563), one of the most important Protestant confessions, calls transubstantiation "a condemnable idolatry,"[221] and it's easy for Catholics to assume that their Protestant neighbors are as passionately opposed to transubstantiation as devout Catholics are in affirming it. Instead, the neighbors may just not see what the big deal is.

For instance, the Baptist theologian Timothy George calls questions about "transubstantiation, consubstantiation, how are the elements changed, what do you do with them when people have finished consuming them" mere "liturgical niceties."[222] But consider the last of those supposed "niceties": after the service has ended, what should happen with the leftover elements of the Lord's Supper? From a Catholic perspective, "the sacred species are reserved after Mass," both to be brought to those unable to make it to Mass (especially the sick) and to permit "the practice of adoring this great sacrament and offering it the worship due to God."[223] This practice of bringing the Eucharist to those unable to make it to Mass is also found in Justin's description: he talks about the deacons taking a portion of the "the eucharistized bread and wine and water" to those who are absent.[224] On the other hand, many Protestants "feel no compunction about simply throwing the leftover bread into the trash and pouring left-over wine/juice down the kitchen sink."[225]

So is the leftover Eucharist Jesus, or garbage, or something else? That seems like an important question, doesn't it? If Catholics are wrong, we're committing idolatry; if Protestants are wrong, they're rejecting the fullest presence of Christ here on earth and (according to the earliest Christians) the means by which he intends to impart bodily redemption to us.

The fourth approach is to divide the early Christians into *literalist* and *spiritualist* camps. I mentioned above the Protestant historian J.N.D. Kelly, who said eucharistic teaching "was in general unquestioningly realist" in the early Church. For the specific period he is looking at (325–451), Kelly argues that ordinary laypeople believed in the Real Presence in this "realist" way, while fourth-century theologians were split between "the figurative or symbolical view, which stressed the distinction between the visible elements and reality they represented," and "a new and increasingly potent tendency" to "explain the identity as being the result of an actual change or conversion in the bread and wine."[226]

The problem with this *two camps* theory is twofold. First, there's no apparent fighting over eucharistic theology between these two "camps." But second, the same author will speak of the Eucharist at one moment using "literal" language and at another moment using "spiritual" language (for instance, calling the Eucharist the "figure" or "type" or "similitude" of Christ's body and blood).[227] Kelly offers an unsatisfying solution to this problem, saying simply that "these interpretations, mutually exclusive though they were in strict logic, were often allowed to overlap."[228] But anyone familiar with the great theologians of the early Church should realize at once how unlikely it is that there was such a glaring logical contradiction in their theology and that none of them noticed it.

Another way of resolving this supposed contradiction is to use the spiritual-sounding language to explain away the literal-sounding language. Nathan Busenitz (an elder at John MacArthur's "nondenominational" megachurch and a dean at The Master's Seminary) claims that "many of the church fathers . . . clarified their understanding of the Eucharist by describing it in symbolic and spiritual terms."[229] He then uses this "clarification" to explain away the words of those theologians who spoke only in literal terms, saying, "We have good reason to view the words of Ignatius and Irenaeus in that same light."[230]

In fairness to both Busenitz and Kelly, they're dealing with confusing (even seemingly contradictory) evidence, particularly as we move from the pre-200 period to later theologians who spend more time talking about the symbolic significance of the Eucharist. But there's a better solution. As William Crockett explains in *Eucharist: Symbol of Transformation*:

> In the ancient world, a symbol had almost the opposite meaning of that which it has in modern culture. . . . Ancient thought does not distinguish in the way in which

modern popular thinking does between symbol and reality. In antiquity, the symbol is the presence of that which it represents and mediates participation in that reality.[231]

In John 9, Jesus heals a man born blind and uses the occasion as an opportunity to talk about the Pharisees' spiritual blindness (vv. 39–41). The physical healing was a true healing, but it was also a symbol or sign of the invisible healing that Jesus was offering. Likewise with the healing of the paralytic in Matthew 9: Jesus sees a paralyzed man and (recognizing his deepest wound) says, "Take heart, my son; your sins are forgiven" (v. 2). Only when the scribes challenge this invisible, spiritual healing does Jesus heal the man's paralysis, so that the scribes "may know that the Son of Man has authority on earth to forgive sins" (v. 6).

There are two things to note here. First, like many Protestant theologians, Busenitz equates (and conflates) *symbolic* and *spiritual*. When he sees the *Didache* describe the Eucharist as "spiritual food and drink," for instance, he points to this as an argument against the Real Presence. But in Jesus' ministry, the outward actions, like the healing of the paralytic and the blind man, pointed toward a deeper inward action. To say Jesus healed the paralytic *spiritually* means something quite different from saying that he healed him *symbolically* (in either the ancient or the modern sense of the word).

Second, this idea is key for understanding sacramental theology, including on the Eucharist. Baptism *symbolizes* cleansing (by using water, which we use for cleaning things) but also really does cleanse us. The Eucharist looks (sort of) like flesh and blood, but it also really is. In technical terms, sacraments are "efficacious signs" (CCC 1131), meaning that they *do* what they symbolize.

When the early Christians used the language of *symbol* to describe this reality, "the distinction was not that between what we might call mere image or picture and reality, but between two different forms in which the reality existed."[232] In other words, there's no contradiction in believing that (1) the Eucharist is the body and blood of Jesus Christ, (2) his bodily presence in the Eucharist is nevertheless not the same as the mode of his presence when he walked the earth (or when he will return in glory), and (3) the Eucharist is also a visible symbol of Jesus' body and blood.[xx] The Eucharist *is* symbolic; it's just not *merely* symbolic. It's also really the flesh and blood of Christ. That's what the Catholic Church believes, and it's what we find all over the writings of the earliest Christians, which is why the same theologians say things that (to a Protestant) sound contradictory, and why we don't see any fighting between the two supposed "camps" of literalists and spiritualists. They're simply describing two halves of the same reality!

The fifth and final approach a Protestant might take is to say, in essence, "yes, the entire early Church believed in the Real Presence, in the sacrifice of the Mass, and in closed Communion, but I think they were all wrong." We'll get to *that* view, too, but not just yet.

---

xx We often don't think of the symbolism, because it fits neatly, but imagine if Christ had called for us to use sewage for baptism, or garbage for the Eucharist. In those cases, the mismatched signs would have drawn our attention to this dimension.

4

BEHAVIOR:

Do Nothing Without the Bishop

WHAT DOES the Church founded by Christ look like? And what did the various local churches founded by the apostles look like? The question is of tremendous theological importance. For starters, if Christ created the Church with the intention that it should possess a certain structure, it would be good for us to know what that structure *is*. But there are also important Protestant and Catholic questions wrapped up in the question of church structure.

On the Protestant side, many (if not most) of the divisions within Protestantism relate to the structure of the Church. The chief difference among Episcopalians and Presbyterians and Congregationalists isn't about a particular theological issue (on most questions, you'll find splits *within* each denomination and agreement *across* denominations). Instead, the church-dividing issue has historically been the question of church structure: what does a "biblical" structure of church governance look like? The epistle to the Hebrews says to "obey your leaders and submit to them" (13:17), but how can we submit to them if we don't know who they are?

On the Catholic side, meanwhile, the Church claims that "the pope, bishop of Rome and Peter's successor, 'is the perpetual and visible source and foundation of the unity both of the bishops and of the whole company of the faithful'" (CCC 882). Jesus establishes the Church with St. Peter in a unique position of authority (Matt. 16:17–19; Luke 22:24–32; John 21:15–17; etc.), Peter converts the first Roman Christians on Pentecost (Acts 2:10) and then personally governs the capital city's church (1 Pet. 5:13), and his successors carry on his ministry. But many Protestants (and liberal Catholics, and some secular scholars)[xxi] question the idea that any of this authority continues after Peter's death. According to this theory, the bishop of Rome *can't* be Peter's successor, because there was no such thing as a "bishop of Rome" for about a century after Peter's death. In *The Rise of the Papacy*, Robert Eno argues that the evidence suggests that "in the first century and into the second, there was no bishop of Rome in the usual sense given to that title" and asks: "If there were no bishop of Rome, in what sense can one speak of a Petrine succession?"[233] Kenneth J. Collins and Jerry L. Walls, in *Roman but Not Catholic: What Remains at Stake 500 Years after the Reformation*, likewise argue that papal infallibility cannot be true, since the episcopacy and apostolic succession "appeared sometime in the second century at the earliest, not the first century, where Rome needed it for the establishment of its papal office in Peter."[234]

So what do Scripture and the early Christians have to say about these questions? Specifically, we'll look at two

---

xxi For the sake of clarity and ease, I refer to the various theories about the gradual emergence of a distinct episcopacy as the *Protestant theories*, but it's worth acknowledging that some of the most notable proponents of the theories are, in fact, secular scholars or liberal Catholics.

questions: (1) did the early Christians inherit the structure of the churches from the apostles or invent it? and (2) was there an unbroken lineage of bishops of Rome from the time of Peter onward, or was that a later invention?[xxii]

The Dangers of Biblical "Reverse Engineering"

You will sometimes find Protestant authors claiming that the structure of the early Church is "clear" from the New Testament evidence. For instance, the nineteenth-century author Philip Dixon Hardy (1794–1875) confidently asserts that "the New Testament clearly intimates the existence of two orders of ministers in the Church—the deacons and the presbyters; and it is no less clear that the apostles ordained of this latter order one in each church, to be chief presbyter, with power to appoint ministers in conjunction with the other presbyters."[235] According to this view, the New Testament leaves us a clear instruction manual to follow in the details of church-building—or at least that we can "reverse engineer" the Church by looking at how the New Testament authors describe it. That is to say, just as we might learn how a clock works by opening one up and taking it apart, we can figure out how the Church works by opening up the New Testament evidence and parsing it out carefully. But there are several difficulties with holding this view.

First, the New Testament descriptions typically don't distinguish *offices* from ministries or spiritual gifts.[236] St. Paul says that "God has appointed in the Church first apostles, second prophets, third teachers, then workers of miracles,

---

xxii This does not answer every possible objection about the nature of the bishop of Rome's authority in the early Church, but it at least answers many of the most popular objections.

then healers, helpers, administrators, speakers in various kinds of tongues" (1 Cor. 12:28), and elsewhere that God's gifts "were that some should be apostles, some prophets, some evangelists, some pastors and teachers, for the equipment of the saints, for the work of ministry, for building up the body of Christ" (Eph. 4:11–12). From the text alone, how do we know which of these are "offices" and which are informal ministries or personal charisms?[xxiii]

Second, even when the New Testament authors *do* mention a term like *bishop, presbyter,* or *deacon,* they don't explain what those offices are, likely because they (correctly) assume that their original audiences know what those terms mean. The Bible doesn't so much *describe* the structure of the Church as *mention* it, in the way a modern author might mention "Senator So-and-So" without explaining what a senator is (or does). We can see this clearly with the twelve apostles. The Gospels and the book of Acts *describe* how Jesus calls twelve men to be his disciples and ultimately his apostles. They serve as the most important part of the early Church's visible structure. But you would never know that there were twelve apostles from reading the epistles—that is, the letters of Paul, James, Peter, John, and Jude. Paul, the only one of the five who *wasn't* part of the original Twelve, mentions that after Christ arose, "he appeared to Cephas, then to the Twelve. . . . then he appeared to James, then to all the apostles" (1 Cor. 15:5, 7). Paul gives no explanation of who or what "the Twelve" are, and a reader left with only this evidence would reasonably infer from this that whatever "the Twelve" are, they're not apostles, since those are mentioned separately two verses later.

xxiii For instance, it's clear that the apostleship is an office: Peter explicitly refers to it as such (Acts 1:20), and Paul seems to say the same (Col. 1:25). Paul also refers to "the office of bishop" (1 Tim. 3:1) but doesn't include "bishop" by name in either the Corinthian or Ephesian list.

Third, the Greek words for *bishop, presbyter*, and *deacon* are common Greek words meaning *overseer, elder*, and *servant*, respectively. Sometimes, these words are used in a technical sense to refer to the *office*, but they're also frequently used in a less formal sense.[xxiv] Take *deacons*, for example. Paul clearly describes an office (or at least ministry) of *deacon* distinct from that of *bishop* in 1 Timothy 3. But he uses the same word (*diakonos*, "servant") to describe Jesus (Rom. 15:8), himself (Eph. 3:7), St. Timothy (1 Thess. 3:2), and a Christian woman named Phoebe (Rom. 16:1). John uses this word to describe the servants at the wedding feast of Cana (John 2:9), and in Mark 9:35, Jesus calls the Twelve and says to them, "If any one would be first, he must be last of all and servant [*diakonos*] of all." So it's not just that the word isn't always used in a technical sense; it's not clear that it's *ever* used in a technical sense, outside 1 Timothy 3 and perhaps Philippians 1:1. In the book of Acts, seven men are called to assist in the daily "distribution" (*diakonia*) to widows (Acts 6:1–6), in a role that appears to be the diaconate,[237] but these men are never directly referred to as deacons. So the deacons in the New Testament aren't called deacons, and the people referred to in the New Testament as deacons aren't.[xxv]

Fourth, it's not clear from the New Testament evidence alone which of these roles in the Church (be they offices or ministries) are meant to be permanent and which are unique

---

xxiv To take an example from English, when Supreme Court justice Samuel Chase was impeached in 1805, "the man presiding over that trial was Vice President Aaron Burr, who was dodging charges in New Jersey for fatally shooting Alexander Hamilton in a duel the previous summer." Ronald G. Shafer, "The impeachment trial presided over by Alexander Hamilton's killer," *Washington Post*, February 13, 2021. A non-native speaker might struggle with the idea that the vice president *presided*, since the same word is doing double duty for both the office (the vice presidency) and the action (chairing an impeachment trial).

xxv It's possible that some of those called "deacons" *are* deacons, but in no case is that clear from the biblical evidence itself.

to the first generation. When the apostle Judas is replaced, Peter refers to his vacant office as an *episkopē*, which the King James Version of the Bible accurately translates as a "bishoprick" (Acts 1:20). But the apostleship is more than being a bishop, and Peter specifies that his replacement must be "one of the men who have accompanied us during all the time that the Lord Jesus went in and out among us, beginning from the baptism of John until the day when he was taken up from us—one of these men must become with us a witness to his resurrection" (vv. 21–22). That suggests that apostleship was intended only for the first generation of Christians, inseparable from being a witness of the earthly ministry and resurrection of Christ. But what about "prophets," "teachers," "evangelists," and "pastors"? Which of these is meant to be lasting, and which is meant to be temporary? And how do the permanent roles change with the death of the apostles?[238]

Finally, Protestants who find the structure of the Church "clear" from the New Testament nevertheless disagree with one another about just what that structure clearly is. The Southern Baptist Convention claims that "a New Testament church of the Lord Jesus Christ is an autonomous local congregation of baptized believers" and that "its scriptural officers are pastors and deacons."[239] The *Book of Church Order*, part of the constitution of the Presbyterian Church in America, claims that "the ordinary and perpetual classes of office in the Church are elders and deacons" but that "within the class of elder are the two orders of teaching elders and ruling elders," and "only those elders who are specially gifted, called and trained by God to preach may serve as teaching elders."[240] According to this Presbyterian view, "elder," "bishop," "pastor," and "teacher" are all the same thing, different ways of describing "one and the same office."[241] United Methodists take a slightly different view from either of these: they have the "offices of bishop and district superintendent," with bishops "elected from the elders and set apart for a ministry of servant leadership, general oversight and supervision," although they deny that this constitutes a distinct order, calling it simply a "special ministry."[242] Episcopalians and most Anglicans believe in a threefold ministry (bishop, priest, deacon), with distinct rites of ordination for each.[243] Meanwhile, Lutherans have historically held that "according to divine authority, there is no difference between bishops and pastors or ministers," such that "all clergymen are bishops and priests alike."[244] The Protestant Reformer John Calvin teaches that "there are four orders of office instituted by our Lord for the government of his Church. First, pastors; then doctors; next elders; and fourth deacons. Hence if we will have a church well-ordered and maintained we ought to observe this form of government."[245]

So you can find Protestants claiming that the biblical model of ordained Christian ministry consists of one order; or two; or two, but with two distinct types of elders; or two, plus bishops and superintendents with unique ministries; or three; or four.[246] How could such an astonishing diversity of views (even among those who pride themselves upon being "Bible Christians") exist if the New Testament evidence is as explicit as is sometimes pretended?

What the New Testament Shows

So what *can* we say about the New Testament evidence? As we've seen, the New Testament authors, particularly St. Paul, speak of "bishops," "elders," and "deacons." Generally (but not always),[247] the term *bishop* is used in the singular, and "elders" and "deacons" are mentioned in the plural. So, for instance, Paul speaks to St. Timothy about the qualifications for "a bishop," singular (1 Tim. 3:2), but for "deacons," plural (v. 8), and he later talks about "the elders," plural (5:17–22). Nevertheless, no New Testament author mentions "bishops" and "elders" in the same breath, which is why many Protestants think these are two names for the same office.[xxvi] So are the New Testament authors (for some reason) calling the same office by two different names, *bishop* and *elder*? Or are these two different offices?

For the reasons I outlined above, I don't think the answer to that question will come simply from looking at how the words *bishop*, *elders*, and *deacons* are used, since the usage is fluid. For instance, St. John introduces himself as "the elder" (2 John 1:1; 3 John 1:1) even though he's an apostle. St. Peter likewise exhorts "the elders among you, as a fellow elder" (1 Pet. 5:1)—but this may be a way of emphasizing Christ's own authority as "the Shepherd and Guardian [*episkopos*, "bishop"] of your souls" (2:25). Peter's writings may still be a clue that there was one bishop and multiple elders, but since he's using the terms in a non-technical sense, the case is not 100 percent clear.

If you were to say, "I don't see the word *Trinity* in the Bible," any well-formed Catholic or Protestant would respond by saying the *reality* is taught in Scripture even though the

---

xxvi There are other ways of reading this evidence. For instance, the ministry of the early deacons was specially tied to that of the bishop (just as the first deacons' ministry was connected with that of the apostles in Acts 6:1–16), which would account for Paul's decision to speak of the bishop and deacons together in 1 Timothy 3 before addressing "presbyters" in 1 Timothy 5:17–22. As late as the fourth century, we find deacons claiming superiority over priests because of this connection. See David G. Hunter, "Rivalry between Presbyters and Deacons in the Roman Church: Three Notes on Ambrosiaster, Jerome, and *The Boasting of the Roman Deacons*," *Vigiliae Christianae*, vol. 71, no. 5 (2017), pp. 495–510. To make sense of the deacons' argument, imagine office politics: the CEO's personal assistant may wield more power than the organization chart would suggest.

wording hadn't been invented yet. So, too, the question here isn't whether the New Testament authors already use the words *bishop*, *elder*,[xxvii] and *deacon* as we use them today. The question is whether the *reality* of those offices existed in the Church of their day. To answer that, we should look at how the churches of the Bible actually operate. In other words, it's a question of not just what the New Testament authors say, but what they show us about daily life in the churches of the first century.

The church we see most clearly is the church in Jerusalem, which always seems to have a single leader. For the first eleven chapters of the book of Acts, that leader is Peter, but after Peter's arrest (and miraculous release from prison), he seems to turn the reins over to St. James. In Acts 12:17, Peter describes to the assembled Christians "how the Lord had brought him out of the prison. And he said, 'Tell this to James and to the brethren.' Then he departed and went to another place."[248] After this, we find Peter moving around the empire, while James seems to be the local "overseer" (which is what *bishop* means) at Jerusalem. At the Council of Jerusalem in Acts 15, both Peter and James appear to be occupying important leadership roles, which is what we would expect if Peter is the head of the global Church while James is the head of the local church.

Many Protestants point to this leadership of James (particularly at the Council of Jerusalem), thinking it disproves papal authority, apparently never considering the implications of James's role for their own visions of church structure. For instance, A.T. Robertson writes that "James, not Peter, seems to be the master spirit at Jerusalem."[249] Witness Lee claims that "the foremost leading one in the church

---

xxvii The English word *priest* comes from the Greek *presbyter*, which literally means "elder."

at this time was not Peter, but James the brother of the Lord,"[250] and D.A. Carson says James's role at the Council of Jerusalem in Acts 15 suggests that he is "by this time apparently the chief elder of the Jerusalem church."[251] But this is perfectly consistent with both the Catholic claim and the testimony of the early Christians. St. Jerome writes in the fourth century that James was "at once ordained by the apostles bishop of Jerusalem."[252] Normally, that testimony would be too late to be of much use to us, but Jerome quotes Hegesippus from the second century, who says that "after the apostles, James the brother of the Lord surnamed the Just was made head of the church at Jerusalem."[253] If the apostles meant to create churches headed by co-equal presbyters (instead of a single bishop), why wasn't their own local church structured that way?

Nor was the church in Jerusalem alone in being structured in this way. The book of Revelation opens with Jesus' message "to Ephesus and to Smyrna and to Pergamum and to Thyatira and to Sardis and to Philadelphia and to Laodicea" (1:11), seven churches in the western part of what is now Turkey, churches that were close to Patmos, the island where tradition holds that the apostle John had been exiled. But the messages to the seven churches begin: "To the angel of the church in [city] write . . ." (see Rev. 2:1, 8, 12, 18; 3:1, 7, 14). So who are these seven "angels" over the seven churches?

A choice is generally offered between (1) heavenly guardians of the churches, and (2) human representatives of them, generally their bishops. Three other principal variants deserve consideration: (3) that the "angels" are personifications of the churches; (4) that they are literally human "messengers"; and (5) that the term is used in some complex and elusive way or at differing levels, so that we cannot expect to assign it a lexical equivalent that tells the whole story.[254]

There are clues within the text that these seven addressees aren't literally angels. After all, how can John be expected to write and deliver a letter to angels? Second, the messages include things like Jesus telling one angel that "the devil is about to throw some of you into prison" (2:10) and another "remember then from what you have fallen, repent and do the works you did at first" (v. 5). But how could a purely spiritual being like an angel get arrested or repent after growing lukewarm?

Nor should these angels be understood simply as the "personifications of the churches." Immediately before this, John sees "seven golden lampstands," with Christ in the midst of them holding seven stars (1:12–16). Jesus explains that "the seven stars are the angels of the seven churches and the seven lampstands are the seven churches" (v. 20). If the angels simply *are* the churches, then the lampstands, stars, angels, and churches all refer to the same thing, while Christ explicitly distinguishes them.

Instead, the "angels" (the term means "messengers" in Greek) seem to refer to specific individuals in each church, to whom John is addressing the revelations. That leaves us with theories (2) and (4): either the angels are bishops, or they're literal messengers. But they don't appear to be simply messengers: they are upheld as seven stars in the hand of Christ and praised or rebuked for the spiritual state of their respective churches. The problem with theory (4), then, is that Jesus would be (almost literally) "shooting the messenger." Instead, the best reading is that these are the seven local *bishops*. In the book of Malachi, we read that "the lips of a priest should guard knowledge, and men should seek instruction from his mouth, for he is the messenger of the Lord of hosts" (2:7), so it's not unprecedented to refer to the spiritual representative of the people as God's *messenger* or *angel* (again, the same word in Greek).

Colin Hemer objects to this interpretation on the basis that "the individual could scarcely be held responsible for the character of the church, and there is no unambiguous evidence for the idea of episcopal authority in the churches of the Revelation, though it looms large in Ignatius twenty years later."[255] But the Bible clearly teaches that the leaders of the church *are* responsible for its spiritual state. The verse from Hebrews that I quoted above continues: "Obey your leaders and submit to them; for they are keeping watch over your souls, *as men who will have to give account*" (13:17). That accounting is exactly what we seem to see in Revelation. So it makes more sense to read the one being judged as the bishop, rather than a random messenger. And although Hemer is right that the evidence of these churches having bishops may not be "unambiguous," it's worth considering that the next time we hear from (or about) these churches is in the letters of Ignatius, c. 107, at which point each of them *is* unambiguously headed by a single bishop and seems to believe that it always was. (Don't worry—we'll get to that soon.)

Finally, look at what Paul has to say about the churches in Crete and Ephesus.[xxviii] Paul says to St. Titus, "This is why I left you in Crete, that you might amend what was defective, and appoint elders in every town as I directed you" (Titus 1:5). Titus's role appears to be that of a bishop. He's supposed to "appoint elders," and he's also supposed to "teach what befits sound doctrine" (2:1) and "declare these things; exhort and reprove with all authority. Let no one

---

xxviii Notice that Ephesus appears to be headed by a single overseer both in Paul's writings
and in the book of Revelation.

disregard you" (v. 15). Whatever authority the elders have in Crete, it's clear that they're answerable to Titus, whose authority they are not free to disregard. Likewise, Paul recounts to Timothy how "I urged you when I was going to Macedonia, remain at Ephesus that you may charge certain persons not to teach any different doctrine" (1 Tim. 1:3) and gives him these instructions for his overseeing of the elders (5:17–22):

> Let the elders who rule well be considered worthy of double honor, especially those who labor in preaching and teaching; for the Scripture says, "You shall not muzzle an ox when it is treading out the grain," and, "The laborer deserves his wages." Never admit any charge against an elder except on the evidence of two or three witnesses. As for those who persist in sin, rebuke them in the presence of all, so that the rest may stand in fear. In the presence of God and of Christ Jesus and of the elect angels I charge you to keep these rules without favor, doing nothing from partiality. Do not be hasty in the laying on of hands, nor participate in another man's sins; keep yourself pure.

So whether or not Paul uses the words *bishop* and *elder* interchangeably (as many Protestants claim he does in this letter), it's clear that he sees the elders as accountable to a higher local authority—namely, Timothy, who is charged with overseeing the elders, rebuking erring individuals when necessary, and ordaining them.

To sum up so far, the New Testament writers are not entirely clear (or even consistent) in how they use terms like *bishop*, *elder*, and *deacon*, but each of the churches they describe seems to be governed by a single individual, whether that be Peter or James in Jerusalem, the "seven angels" overseeing the seven churches of Asia Minor, Titus in Crete, or Timothy in Ephesus. We can see this yet more clearly by looking at the writings of the early Christians.

The Big Picture of Early Church Governance

Leon Morris paints the "big picture" neatly in an entry in the *Evangelical Dictionary of Theology*:

> Nowhere is there evidence of a violent struggle as would be natural if a divinely ordained congregationalism or presbyterianism were overthrown. The same threefold ministry is seen as universal throughout the early Church as soon as there is sufficient evidence to show us the nature of the ministry.[256]

All of the evidence from the first few centuries of Christian writers either explicitly points to a threefold structure (one bishop, assisted by elders and deacons) in the early Church or is too vague to draw any reliable conclusions (usually because the author wasn't directly writing about church governance). Sometimes, the evidence is murkier than we would like. But other times, we get a good look at a local church, and we invariably find that it's governed by a single bishop, assisted by elders and deacons. Often, we even know the names of these early bishops, elders, and deacons. Catholics can accept all of the evidence, while Protestants have to reject all of the clear Catholic evidence and rely instead on arguments from silence.

David J. Stagaman notes that "by the early third century Hippolytus can take for granted that monoepiscopacy exists everywhere in the Church,"[257] which can be explained in only one of two ways: either because the monoepiscopacy is what the apostles established or because every church on earth changed its structure from whatever the apostles instituted to something else. And by this time, there are literally hundreds of churches. The historical theologian Margaret Miles points out that "in North Africa, one of the few places for which evidence exists, lists of hundreds of third-century bishops are extant; every small town had a bishop."[258]

Michael Kruger, who claims that "the first-century church was largely led by a plurality of elders/presbyters," is forced to argue that "at some point during the second century, churches began to be ruled by a singular bishop (as opposed to a plurality of elders)."[259] In other words, those arguing for the Protestant view have to tell a story of change. How and why did all of these churches abandon the apostolic structure of the Church (including those churches *personally founded by the apostles*)? And here, Protestants encounter several problems. For one thing, there's no actual evidence of this change occurring. You would think a church overthrowing an apostolic institution would make some kind of waves, yet we see no hint that the early Christians think this change occurred. In fact, they *deny* that their church changed structures, proudly pointing to the fact that they're preserving what they received from the apostles (in contrast to the early heretics, who cannot make such a claim).

The Divine Origins of the Episcopacy

As we'll see soon, the Protestant theories about the early Church require accepting three presuppositions:

1. That the early Christians felt free to change the structure of the churches bequeathed them by the apostles;

2. That there were various types of church governance in the early Church; and

3. That for pragmatic reasons, every local church eventually decided on three-tiered governance headed by a single bishop (the technical term for this is *monoepiscopacy*).

But when we let the early Christians speak for themselves, we discover that they *didn't* feel free to change the structure of the Church or adopt the structure they thought best. Around the year 96, St. Clement of Rome writes a letter to the church in Corinth (a letter normally called 1 Clement, although it's the only authentic letter we have of his). The letter begins:

> The church of God which sojourns at Rome, to the church of God sojourning at Corinth, to them that are called and sanctified by the will of God, through our Lord Jesus Christ: Grace unto you, and peace, from Almighty God through Jesus Christ, be multiplied.
>
> Owing, dear brethren, to the sudden and successive calamitous events which have happened to ourselves, we feel that we have been somewhat tardy in turning our attention to the points respecting which you consulted us; and especially to that shameful and detestable sedition, utterly abhorrent to the elect of God, which a few rash and self-confident persons have kindled to such a pitch of frenzy, that your venerable and illustrious name, worthy to be universally loved, has suffered grievous injury.[260]

This tells us three important things. First, Clement is writing on behalf of the church of Rome. This will be an important and controversial point, as we'll see a bit later.

Second, the Corinthians have written to Rome (i.e., to Clement) in order to resolve an internal dispute, giving us an indication of the authority that the church of Rome and its bishop already possess at this time. And third, the problem facing the Corinthians is "sedition," which Clement calls "shameful and detestable" and "utterly abhorrent to the elect of God."

Clement's response is to lay out a Christian vision of authority, tracing how Christ "was sent forth by God, and the apostles by Christ," with the apostles in turn appointing "the first fruits" of their labors "to be bishops and deacons of those who should afterward believe."[261] Quite understandably, that line (removed from context) sounds as though Clement is saying there are only two tiers to the post-apostolic Church: bishops and deacons. But immediately before this, he describes how "it behooves us to do all things in [their proper] order, which the Lord has commanded us to perform at stated times":

> For his own peculiar services are assigned to the high priest, and their own proper place is prescribed to the priests, and their own special ministrations devolve on the Levites. The layman is bound by the laws that pertain to laymen. Let every one of you, brethren, give thanks to God in his own order, living in all good conscience, with becoming gravity, and not going beyond the rule of the ministry prescribed to him.[262]

Clement appears to be comparing the New Testament structure of the Church to the Old Testament structure of high priest, priest, Levite, layman. Deacons are the new Levites, elders are the priests of the New Covenant, and bishops are the new high priests. Other early Christians would make this same parallel: an ordination rite from the early 200s explicitly describes the bishop as ordained to "feed thy holy flock, and discharge the office of an high priest to thee."[263] A working group of Anglican theologians acknowledged that the early Christians thought of their threefold structure as the fulfillment of the threefold structure found in Judaism but dismissed this connection, saying,

> But the Old Testament typology did not create the three-fold Christian ministry. That is a structure which owes its origins to the second century Church's inheritance from the sub-apostolic generation, in which an originally two-tiered ministry of bishop-priest and deacon passed into the three-tiered ministry to meet practical needs; with the presiding bishops representing apostolicity.[264]

All of this would have certainly been news to Clement, who connects the two structures in the first century. And notice that Clement rejects the idea that we are free to change the governance of the church "to meet practical needs."[xxix] He views it instead as a matter of *reception*: we receive the structure of the Church from the apostles, who receive their authority from Christ, who receives his own mission from the Father.

One reason the connection to the Old Testament priesthood is important is that it shows that the early Christians were thinking about Christian ordination in terms of priesthood. Many Protestants today reject what they consider the "unbiblical clergy-lay distinction,"[265] but Clement explicitly acknowledges the distinction between "the priests" and

---

xxix It's significant that these Anglicans were assembled as a working group to explore the possibility of women's ordination. Once you accept the idea that the God-given structure of the Church can be changed to meet the "practical needs" of the day, why not continue to change it?

"laymen." He also gives us a helpful framework in thinking about how the early Christians (particularly converts from Judaism) might have viewed their own clergy.

But if Clement *does* believe in a threefold structure, paralleling the Old Testament priesthood, why does he refer to it simply as "bishops and deacons"? It's impossible to say for sure, but it's worth noting that the Old Testament does the same thing. That is, there is a threefold structure (high priest, priest, Levite), generally described simply as "priests and Levites" (1 Chron 13:2; 2 Chron. 8:15, 11:3; Ezra 3:12, 10:5; Neh. 12:1, 13:30; etc.), which could easily give the false impression that there were only two orders.[xxx]

Ignatius of Antioch

In any case, the fact that there were three orders, and not two, is abundantly clear from Clement's contemporary, St. Ignatius of Antioch. On the way to his martyrdom in c. 107, Ignatius writes seven letters. As we're about to see, he's explicit (repeatedly) about the existence of the threefold structure of the Church.

Indeed, Ignatius is so early, and so obviously Catholic, that Protestants don't know what to do with him. For years, Protestants simply denied that Ignatius really wrote the letters ascribed to him (at the time, an understandable view, since there *were* forgeries ascribed to Ignatius). The Reformer John Calvin wrote that "nothing can be more nauseating,

---

xxx Hebrews 5 talks about the unique ministry of the high priest, and when the high priest Caiaphas says that "it is expedient for you that one man should die for the people, and that the whole nation should not perish," John says that "he did not say this of his own accord, but *being high priest that year he prophesied* that Jesus should die for the nation, and not for the nation only, but to gather into one the children of God who are scattered abroad" (John 11:50–52). So the high priest had a ministry (and perhaps a charism?) distinct from that of other priests.

than the absurdities which have been published under the name of Ignatius; and therefore, the conduct of those who provide themselves with such masks for deception is the less entitled to toleration."[266] Jaroslav Pelikan, a Lutheran who later became Eastern Orthodox, explains that "because this text showed such an advanced stage of doctrinal development in its emphasis on the hierarchical nature of the Church and made such explicit reference to the authority of the bishop, certain Protestant scholars insisted that [the seven letters attributed to Ignatius] could not have been written by Ignatius." Ironically, Pelikan observes, "it was Protestant historical scholarship that vindicated the authenticity of the seven epistles,"[267] such that there is no longer any serious scholarly question on this point. We can say with a good deal of historical certainty that Ignatius wrote seven "nauseatingly" Catholic letters around the year 107 . . . which is a real problem for Protestants who think Catholicism didn't exist yet.

Just what does he say in these letters? Let's start with what he *doesn't* say. Paul Anderson, a prominent New Testament scholar and influential member of the Society of Biblical Literature, claims that Ignatius "calls for the appointing of a single bishop in every church—one who will maintain unity within the community as a function of being entrusted with Petrine keys to the kingdom."[268] But this is sheer fiction. Ignatius doesn't "call for" a single bishop to be appointed in each city. He instead describes churches in which individual bishops are *already governing* each church, and he simply encourages the faithful to be obedient to the bishop they already have. And he doesn't cite the "Petrine keys to the kingdom"; there are literally no references to the "keys" in any of his writings. That's not a small difference. If I say, "Obey your parents," I'm not proposing that you should choose a mother and a father. Yet Ignatius is routinely described as if he were arguing that these churches *should* have a bishop, when he's in fact aware that they *do* have bishops.

To the Magnesians, he commends "Damas your most worthy bishop," "your worthy presbyters Bassus and Apollonius," and "my fellow-servant the deacon Sotio."[269] He doesn't try to sell the Magnesians on the threefold structure of the Church; he simply reminds them "not to treat your bishop too familiarly on account of his youth, but to yield him all reverence," submitting "to him, or rather not to him, but to the Father of Jesus Christ, the bishop of us all."[270] He also gives an important justification for *why* the trifold structure of the Church exists: "Your bishop presides in the place of God, and your presbyters in the place of the assembly of the apostles, along with your deacons."[271] Cyril Hovorun writes that "the earliest promotor of the mono-episcopal order in the church was Ignatius of Antioch," who "believed that the more church authority was consolidated in one person's hands, the more it could help the church solve the new problems that it faced in the second century."[272] But that's not Ignatius's argument at all. He's not making some kind of pragmatic cost-benefit analysis to persuade people to give authority to the bishop. He's instead observing that the bishop already *has* authority and explaining that the basis for this is theological: there's one bishop because he's an image (and representative) of the one God.

Ignatius praises the Ephesians for the fact that "your justly renowned presbytery, worthy of God, is fitted as exactly to the bishop as the strings are to the harp," so that "in your concord and harmonious love, Jesus Christ is sung."[273] His counsel is that, since "we ought to receive every one whom the master of the house sends to be over his household, as we would do him that sent him," we should therefore "look upon the bishop even as we would upon the Lord himself."[274]

Their bishop is "Onesimus, a man of inexpressible love, and your bishop in the flesh, whom I pray you by Jesus Christ to love, and that you would all seek to be like him."[275] F.F. Bruce and other scholars have suggested that this may be the same Onesimus whose freedom from slavery St. Paul defended decades earlier in the letter to Philemon. That would explain how Paul's private letter to Philemon made it into the New Testament, since "if indeed it was this Onesimus who became bishop of Ephesus, then, wherever and by whomsoever the first collection of Pauline letters was made, he could scarcely fail to get to know about it, and would make sure that this letter found a place in the collection."[276] While we can't know for sure if this is the same Onesimus,[277] it's a good reminder that the Christians to whom Ignatius is writing include people who knew the apostles intimately and would know if Ignatius (or Onesimus) was inventing some new unapostolic doctrine of the Church.

Ignatius encourages the Trallians to "continue in intimate union with Jesus Christ our God, and the bishop, and the enactments of the apostles."[278] It's to these Christians that Ignatius most clearly spells out his view (which the Trallians apparently share) that you literally don't have a church without the threefold hierarchy:

In like manner, let all reverence the deacons as an appointment of Jesus Christ, and the bishop as Jesus Christ, who is the Son of the Father, and the presbyters as the sanhedrim of God, and assembly of the apostles. Apart from these, there is no church. Concerning all this, I am persuaded that you are of the same opinion.[279]

This is a critical point that many modern scholars misunderstand. Eamon Duffy writes that "neither Peter nor Paul founded the church at Rome, for there were Christians in the city before either of the apostles set foot there."[280] But Ignatius, like any Christian who's read Acts 2, already knew that there were Roman Christians converted (by Peter, incidentally) before Peter or Paul arrived at Rome. The mistake that Duffy makes is assuming that "Christians in the city" is all you need for there to be a "church." Ignatius reveals that this *isn't* what the early Christians believed: they thought that you needed a bishop and elders and deacons, since "apart from these, there is no church."[xxxi] This also neatly debunks the Protestant myth that in "the early second century, multiple forms of ministry continued, though with greater emphasis on official leadership roles. In some churches, elders ruled; in others, bishops; in some instances, leaders were appointed; in yet others, they were elected."[281] Ignatius shows us that this simply wasn't the case.

Ignatius reminds the Philadelphians how "when I was among you, I cried, I spoke with a loud voice: Give heed to the bishop, and to the presbytery and deacons," and he encourages them to take heed to "have but one Eucharist. For there is one flesh of our Lord Jesus Christ, and one cup to [show forth] the unity of his blood; one altar; as there is one bishop, along with the presbytery and deacons, my fellow-servants."[282] Not only does this show the link between the bishop and the eucharistic sacrifice, but it also is a good reminder that Ignatius knows these Christian churches intimately.

---

xxxi As I mentioned in *Pope Peter*, Yale Divinity School's Miroslav Volf argues that "where two or three are gathered in Christ's name, not only is Christ present among them, but a Christian church is there as well." Yet Christ clearly distinguishes in Matthew 18:16–17 between "two or three witnesses" and "the Church." Miroslav Volf, *After Our Likeness* (Grand Rapids: Wm. B. Eerdmans Publishing Co., 1998), p. 136; Joe Heschmeyer, *Pope Peter* (El Cajon: Catholic Answers, 2020), p. 44.

That's an important reminder, because you will sometimes encounter scholars saying things like "Ignatius' direction of duties addressed to Polycarp, whom he assumes
to be the *episkopos*, is particularly interesting."[283] What that
description gets wrong is the idea that Ignatius is just making "assumptions" about churches he doesn't know personally. That is plainly wrong in the case of Polycarp and the
church of Smyrna. Ignatius mentions to the Magnesians that
he's writing them *from Smyrna*, and he sends along Bishop
Polycarp's greetings.[284]

He later writes to this Smyrnaean church, encouraging
its members to "follow the bishop, even as Jesus Christ
does the Father, and the presbytery as you would the
apostles; and reverence the deacons, as being the institution of God. Let no man do anything connected with the
Church without the bishop."[285] This is also the first time
in history we hear the phrase "Catholic Church," as Ignatius says: "Wherever the bishop shall appear, there let the
multitude [of the people] also be; even as, wherever Jesus
Christ is, there is the Catholic Church."[286] He also writes
to Polycarp personally, thanking God for the fact that "I
have been thought worthy [to behold] your blameless face,
which may I ever enjoy in God," and encouraging him "by
the grace with which you are clothed, to press forward in
your course, and to exhort all that they may be saved."[287]
Ignatius gives his own words of encouragement: "My soul
be for theirs that are submissive to the bishop, to the presbyters, and to the deacons, and may my portion be along
with them in God!"[288]

That leaves us with the last of Ignatius's letters: his letter
to the Romans. This is the letter that has received the worst
treatment at the hands of scholars. Within the span of a single
page, Raymond Brown argues that "to explain Ignatius'

insistence on and defense of the threefold order, one must posit that the single-bishop model appeared in Antioch and Asia Minor ca. 100"[289] but also that "the signal failure of Ignatius (ca. 110) to mention the single-bishop in his letter to the Romans (a very prominent theme in his other letters) and the usage of *Hermas*, which speaks of plural presbyters (Vis. 2.4.2) and bishops (Sim. 9.27.2), make it likely that the single-bishop structure did not come to Rome till ca. 140–150."[290] So if Ignatius tells a group of Christians to obey their bishops, that must mean that bishops are a novelty. And if he *doesn't* tell them to obey their bishops, that must mean that bishops are a novelty that hasn't arrived yet. No matter what Ignatius does or doesn't say, it "proves" Brown's thesis. Duffy likewise argues that unlike his other letters, Ignatius's "letter to the Roman church . . . says nothing whatever about bishops, a strong indication that the office had not yet emerged at Rome."[291]

But none of this is true. First, there's really no mystery as to why Ignatius's letter to the Romans is different from his other letters. The other bishop (Polycarp) and churches (Smyrna, Ephesus, Tralles, Philadelphia, and Magnesia) to whom Ignatius writes were people he had gotten to know personally while stationed in Smyrna, while awaiting transport to Rome, where he was to be fed to the lions. In those letters, "Ignatius wrote as a friend to friends, in a personal affair and in a cordial manner."[292] The letter to the Romans, in contrast, is "the most formal and impersonal of Ignatius's correspondences,"[293] because Ignatius is writing to a group of Christians he doesn't personally know, asking them not to intervene to prevent his martyrdom. In other words, both the "genre" of the letter and the audience are unique.

It's simply untrue that Ignatius's letter "says nothing whatever about bishops." Ignatius encourages the Romans not to intercede to stop his martyrdom, but instead to "sing praise to the Father, through Christ Jesus, that God has deemed me, the bishop of Syria, worthy to be sent for from the east unto the west."[294] He also asks them to "remember in your prayers the church in Syria, which now has God for its shepherd, instead of me. Jesus Christ alone will oversee it, and your love [will also regard it]."[295] That is, Ignatius writes with the understanding that the Romans know there's only one bishop per church, such that Ignatius can be called *the* bishop of Syria, and that the church of Syria will be bereft of episcopal oversight without him. It's true that Ignatius doesn't talk about *the Romans'* bishop. But he also never mentions elders or deacons. So how does that show that their church was governed by a panel of elders?

In any event, the view that the Roman church *wasn't* headed by a bishop doesn't make sense, given Ignatius's reverence for that church. As Brown notes:

> Ignatius' greeting "to the church that presides in the chief place of the country of the Romans" is more fulsome and laudatory than that to any other church. The church of Rome is "worthy of honor, worthy of felicitation, worthy of praise, worthy of success, worthy of holiness." . . . In particular, it is a church "pre-eminent in love" (see also 2:2, 3:2), a church that has never been jealous, indeed a church that has taught others (3:1).[296]

Whether the Roman church's pre-eminence was a matter of authority or simply example, it's clear that Ignatius is saying Rome is (at the very least) a model church. But remember Ignatius's words to the Trallians that they should reverence the bishop, elders, and deacons since "apart from these, there is no church."[297] If the church of Rome lacked a bishop, it wouldn't be a model church. It would be, in Ignatius's eyes, no church at all.[xxxii]

Bishop Lists and Apostolic Succession

So far, we've seen how the Bible seems to be describing a governance structure in which one individual holds final authority in each local church. We've also seen St. Clement talk about the structure of the Church given to us by the apostles, seemingly comparing it with the threefold high priest, priest, Levite structure of Judaism. And we've seen both *that* there are three orders within each of the early churches (bishop, elder, deacon) and *why* (monoepiscopacy being rooted in the theology of monotheism). But there's one final piece to add to the puzzle: bishop lists and the theology of apostolic succession.

We hear about such lists from Hegesippus (c. 110–180), who mentions that "on my arrival at Rome, I drew up a list of the succession of bishops down to Anicetus, whose deacon was Eleutherius. To Anicetus succeeded Soter, and after him came Eleutherius."[298] We know that Pope Anicetus was bishop of Rome from c. 157 to 168, so we have a rough date for his original list. (Most of Hegesippus's writings are lost, so we don't know if he actually provides the list). But he says something that suggests that these bishop lists were the norm: "But in the case of every succession, and in every city, the state of affairs is in accordance with the teaching of the Law and of the prophets and of the Lord."[299]

---

xxxii A simple analogy may suffice: imagine that you found the letters of a pastor. In six of the letters, he talks about God's plan for marriage involving a husband and a wife, and in the seventh letter, he praises the Roman family for their model marriage. Would a reasonable interpretation be that the Romans must be a same-sex couple, given the pastor's "signal failure" to specify whether *their* marriage is between a man and a woman?

So why did the Christians of his day care about tracing a list of the order of bishops in a church like Rome or Antioch or Jerusalem? One answer to this comes from our old friend St. Irenaeus. The heresy of Gnosticism (from *gnosis*, "knowledge") is based on the idea that Jesus and the apostles had one set of teachings for the crowds and another secret set of "higher" teachings known only to the specially initiated. How can you rebut such an error? If you bring up an argument from Scripture or from Tradition, they'll say these were just the public teachings, but they know better.[300] The cause might seem hopeless, but Irenaeus offers a clever solution. He points out that "if the apostles had known hidden mysteries, which they were in the habit of imparting to 'the perfect' apart and privily from the rest, they would have delivered them especially to those to whom they were also committing the churches themselves."[301] In other words, we can put this whole idea of "secret teachings" to a simple test. If the apostles were going to share secret teachings with anyone, surely they would share them with their chosen successors. And surely those men would in turn share the teachings with *their* successors, and so on. So if Gnosticism were true, we should find that the leaders of the Church were committed Gnostics. Since they aren't, that's a good sign that Gnosticism is false.

This was a smart way of refuting Gnosticism, and it's also a good test for our own beliefs. Think of it this way: if you're presenting evidence of a crime in court, how do you prove that this evidence was gathered at the crime scene and that the defendant isn't being framed? Through what's called the *chain of custody*:

The chain of custody is the most critical process of evidence documentation. . . . The chain of custody needs to document every transmission from the moment the evidence is collected, from one person to another, to establish that nobody else could have accessed or possessed that evidence without authorization.[302]

You need to know whom you got it from, and where he got it from, all the way back to the scene of the crime. Likewise, modern financial transactions increasingly use blockchain technology, which works like a sort of automated chain of custody: you can show that a bitcoin is yours because it has permanently embedded information about all of its previous transactions from its origins until it arrived in your digital wallet.[xxxiii] But it's not just evidence and electronic currency: What Irenaeus shows us is that *ideas* work like this. If Irenaeus knows he got a teaching from Polycarp, who got it from John, who got it from Jesus, then he knows it's reliable. But if we can't trace an idea back to the apostles and their students, that's a red flag that it's not to be believed.

If you believe that the apostles taught that the Lord's Supper was merely symbolic, or that baptism *doesn't* save, or that bishops and elders are the same office, you should be able to show whom they taught these things *to* . . . and if none of their followers remembers them teaching any such thing (and, in fact, insist that they taught the opposite), that's a strong indication that your belief is unfounded.

Of course, it's possible for a student to misunderstand his teacher, or even to go astray. But in that case, we should see

---

xxxiii The analogy between apostolic succession and blockchain technology is not as absurd as it may seem: Irenaeus compares orthodoxy to "a rich man [depositing his money] in a bank, lodged in her hands most copiously all things pertaining to the truth." Irenaeus, *Against Heresies*, book 3, ch. 4, ANF 1:416. We should be able to show that we are withdrawing our beliefs from the deposit of the Faith and not getting counterfeit ones from elsewhere.

the others immediately speaking out to protest the introduction of heresy. Indeed, that's exactly what we *do* see: as we saw back in chapter one, a student of St. Polycarp named Florinus embraced Gnosticism, and Irenaeus responded to him by pointing out that they both learned from Polycarp (who wasn't a Gnostic), and "these doctrines, the presbyters who were before us, and who were companions of the apostles, did not deliver to thee."[303] Similarly, if Catholic beliefs about the Eucharist, baptism, and the Church are contrary to what the apostles taught, we should expect to find early Christian writers denouncing these beliefs as heretical novelties.

So that's the basic idea of apostolic succession, as well as the basic idea of this book: if you want to know if a particular belief was taught in the first or second century, look to the Christians (and particularly the leaders of the Church) from that time. But since it "would be very tedious, in such a volume as this, to reckon up the successions of all the churches," Irenaeus chooses to look at the succession of bishops of just one church, "the very great, the very ancient, and universally known church founded and organized at Rome by the two most glorious apostles, Peter and Paul."[304] Why Rome? Because "it is a matter of necessity that every church should agree with this church, on account of its pre-eminent authority."[305] Irenaeus then traces how Peter and Paul, "having founded and built up the church, committed into the hands of Linus the office of the episcopate," followed by Anacletus, Clement,[xxxiv] Evaristus, Sixtus, Telesphorus, Hyginus, Pius, Anicetus, Soter," until finally, "Eleutherius does now, in the twelfth place from the apostles, hold the inheritance of the episcopate."[306]

---

xxxiv The same Clement who wrote 1 Clement, as Irenaeus explains.

Irenaeus is writing all this about 114 years after the death of the apostles.[307] To put that in perspective, if you're reading this book in 2022, you're about 114 years removed from the introduction of the Ford Motor Company's Model T and a bit more than 114 years removed from the Wright brothers' famous flight at Kitty Hawk. Chances are, if I said to you that the Model T had a built-in CD player, or that the Wright brothers broke the sound barrier in their plane, you would know at once that those details couldn't be true.[xxxv] Likewise, if Protestants are right that the papacy was no more than a few decades old at the time Irenaeus traced its history, surely, his readers would have noticed such glaring factual errors . . . and certainly, the Gnostics would have loved throwing Irenaeus's argument from apostolic succession back in his face!

There's one more important early source on this score. Tertullian, writing around the year 200,[308] shows us how the apostolic succession lists functioned in early Christianity. First, he points out that the heretics *don't* have apostolic succession. Their founders lived long after the apostles, and "persons are still living who remember them—their own actual disciples and successors—who cannot therefore deny the lateness of their date."[309]

But if there be any [heresies] which are bold enough to plant themselves in the midst of the Apostolic Age, that they may thereby seem to have been handed down by the apostles, because they existed in the time of the apostles, we can say: Let them produce the original records of

---

xxxv If you prefer a different example, in 1908 (114 years ago), the philosopher Dietrich von Hildebrand was a young student at the University of Munich, and his widow Alice is still alive today. See Alice von Hildebrand, *The Soul of a Lion: Dietrich von Hildebrand* (San Francisco: Ignatius Press, 2000), p. 65*ff*.

their churches; let them unfold the roll of their bishops, running down in due succession from the beginning in such a manner that [that first bishop of theirs] shall be able to show for his ordainer and predecessor some one of the apostles or of apostolic men—a man, moreover, who continued steadfast with the apostles.[310]

These are what Tertullian calls "these two tests by our apostolic church": can a church trace its lineage to the apostles, and does the church agree with what the apostles taught?[311] If Irenaeus was the only witness to apostolic succession, Protestants could write him and his list off as untrustworthy. But Irenaeus clearly is not alone. Tertullian tells us that "this is the manner in which the apostolic churches transmit their registers."[312] You will often read Protestants who say the early Christians "assumed" that there had always been a bishop.[xxxvi] But Tertullian's references to unfolding "the roll of their bishops" and "the original records of their churches" show that these churches didn't just *claim* to be founded by the apostles, but kept careful written records to that effect— a sort of apostolic chain of custody.

It's one thing to think the Christians of this period believed some myths and legends that weren't grounded in historical fact. It's another to accuse them all of doctoring evidence, falsifying written records to make it appear that there was an unbroken chain of bishops. Rejecting apostolic succession, then, requires more than dismissing Hegesippus

---

xxxvi Peter Lampe, for instance, writes off Hegesippus's list by saying that during his trip to Rome, "Hegesippus *tried to convince himself* that this passing down [of the Faith] had indeed occurred in the different cities of the world." Lampe, p. 404 (emphasis added). But the evidence doesn't support the idea that Hegesippus, Irenaeus, Tertullian, etc. were simply imagining (or inventing) apostolic succession; rather, it's evident that this was the public teaching of the Church.

and Irenaeus and Tertullian; it requires treating each of the apostolic churches as untrustworthy and unreliable.

How Might a Protestant Respond?

On what basis do modern Christians reject the evidence of second-century Christians about their own churches? The Protestant theory[xxxvii] consists of the three basic prongs: (1) the original structure of the churches was two-tiered, without a bishop; (2) something happened; (3) the Christians opted for a new three-tiered governance structure instead of the one they'd been given. But how strong is the evidence for each of these prongs?

Prong #1: Did Jesus and the Apostles Establish Two-Tiered Churches?

As I've argued throughout this chapter, the answer to that is *no*: the biblical evidence might look two-tiered on the surface (just like in Judaism), but a closer read reveals that it is describing a three-tiered structure (just like in Judaism), and there's a mass of clear evidence from the early Christians that their churches were set up as three-tiered from the apostles.

But why might someone believe otherwise? There are two Bible verses in particular that are worth addressing. First, St. Paul writes "to all the saints in Christ Jesus who are at Philippi, with the bishops and deacons" (Phil. 1:1). Second, he says to the elders of Ephesus to "take heed to yourselves and to all the flock, in which the Holy Spirit

---

xxxvii Again, please bear in mind that many of those arguing for the "Protestant theory" in the twentieth century were liberal Catholic priests and scholars who rejected their Church's claim about her origins.

has made you guardians" (Acts 20:17, 28). The word for "guardians" there is *episkopos*, which can be translated "bishops." You can see why that *looks* two-tiered. But the early Christians (many of whom spoke Greek) knew that words like *episkopos* and *diakonos* are used throughout the New Testament in a loose, non-technical way. St. John Chrysostom (c. 347–407) comments on the Philippians passage: "What is this? Were there several bishops of one city? Certainly not; but he called the presbyters so. For then they still interchanged the titles, and the bishop was called a deacon."[313] John's point can be lost on us English-speakers, but the bishop he's referring to is St. Timothy, whom Paul refers to as "Timothy, our brother and God's servant [*diakonos*] in the gospel of Christ" (1 Thess. 3:2), and whom he encourages to "fulfil your ministry [*diakonia*]" (2 Tim. 4:5). Taken at the surface level, Paul is calling Timothy a "deacon," but he's also telling him to "charge certain persons not to teach any different doctrine" and giving instructions for properly ordaining and overseeing elders (1 Tim. 1:3, 5:17–22), which are the jobs of a bishop, not a deacon. And of course, if Timothy is the bishop of Ephesus, then it follows that Acts 20 is describing the elders as "guardians" and not as "bishops" of Ephesus.[xxxviii]

Besides the biblical evidence, many Protestants are persuaded by the weight of scholarly authority. For instance, Jerry Walls argues that "there is a strong scholarly consensus that the classic belief that Peter was the first pope is a pious myth, and indeed, there was not even a monarchical bishop in Rome—let alone anyone who was recognized as having jurisdiction over the entire Church—until sometime in the

---

xxxviii In Revelation 2:1, Christ also addresses "the angel of the church in Ephesus," which indicates that there was a single bishop.

latter half of the second century, if not later."[314] Walls clearly has in mind people like Eamon Duffy, who says:

> The tradition that Peter and Paul had been put to death at the hands of Nero in Rome about the year AD 64 was universally accepted in the second century, and by the end of that century pilgrims to Rome were being shown the "trophies" of the apostles, their tombs or cenotaphs, Peter's on the Vatican Hill, and Paul's on the Via Ostiensis, outside the walls on the road to the coast.[315]

But Duffy nevertheless insists that "we have no reliable accounts either of Peter's later life or of the manner or place of his death," since the accounts that we do have "are pious romance, not history."[316] Markus N.A. Bockmuehl likewise writes that "no one working from the first-century evidence alone can fail to be struck by the disparity between the unanimous teaching of the Church, both East and West, and the lack of any 'strictly historic proof' that Peter was ever in Rome."[317]

So are Peter's ministry and martyrdom in Rome simply the stuff of "pious legend" or "pious romance"? Not at all. To give a sense of the evidence: Peter says he's writing from "Babylon" (1 Pet. 5:13), which both the early Christians and most modern scholars recognize as a reference to Rome.[318] Christ prophesies "by what death [Peter] was to glorify God" (John 21:18–19). St. Clement of Rome uses the martyrdoms of Peter and Paul as "noble examples furnished in our own generation."[319] And St. Ignatius says to the Romans (admittedly, about seven years too late to count as "first-century evidence"), "I do not, as Peter and Paul, issue commandments unto you. They were apostles; I am but a condemned man: they were free, while I am, even until now, a servant,"[320] a remark implying that Peter and Paul *did* command the Romans. Indeed, the Christians of Rome knew the precise spots where Peter and Paul were killed and built shrines (and later, basilicas) there; in which the bodies of the two saints can be found to this day.[321]

So it's not really that there's a lack of evidence. Indeed, the fact that the details of Peter's ministry and martyrdom in Rome are "universally accepted in the second century," and in both the East and West, *is* evidence of their authenticity. Yet we still find scholars like Michael Goulder arguing that Peter instead "probably died in his bed in Jerusalem about AD 55" without ever having visited Rome.[322] Goulder admits that 1 Peter 5 points to Peter's having been in Rome, but he doubts that Peter actually wrote it; he admits that John 21 shows Jesus foretelling Peter's death by crucifixion, but he thinks that this was just "John's belief that he had been crucified," a belief he drew "not from independent tradition but by inference from the synoptics."[323]

So yes, if you're prepared to dismiss 1 Peter, the Gospel of John, and the earliest Christian witnesses, you can deny Peter's connection to Rome. At that point, you're free to make up whatever story you'd like, without apparently needing evidence, about how he *really* died. In Goulder's story, he died in bed in Jerusalem in A.D. 55. In Fred Lapham's story, Peter "was executed by Herod Agrippa shortly after the death of James."[324] But in either case, does anyone in the whole history of Christianity record this pivotal moment? No one does. Does the church of Jerusalem claim this site of the death of the chief apostle and build a church there (one sure to draw in pilgrims)? It does not. Do the followers of the apostles, the faithful who sought just to have Peter's shadow fall upon them (Acts 5:15), preserve his body in Jerusalem? They do not. As Bockmuehl says, "the tradition connecting

Peter with Rome is early and unrivaled"[325]—that is, from the beginning, everyone knew that Peter ministered and died at Rome, and nobody claimed otherwise.

What this reveals is not a deficiency in the evidence; it's plenty clear that Peter was martyred in Rome by Nero sometime after the Great Fire of A.D. 64. Instead, it reveals a problem with much of "critical" scholarship, which blithely dismisses the early Christians' testimony about their own time and place while uncritically accepting novel theories without any serious historical support. It's not that these scholars are finding early evidence that forces them to reject the Catholic tradition in favor of some other conclusion. It's that the evidence all points to the Catholic position, and they're *dismissing* the evidence in favor of theories that are often totally unsupported and appear to be simply inventions. This is a widespread problem in New Testament scholarship, as the historian Paula Fredriksen describes:

In recent scholarship, Jesus has been imagined and presented as a type of first-century shaman figure; as a Cynic-sort of wandering wise man; as a visionary radical and social reformer preaching egalitarian ethics to the destitute; as a Galilean regionalist alienated from the elitism of Judean religious conventions (like Temple and Torah); as a champion of national liberation and, on the contrary, as its opponent and critic—on and on. . . . Debate continues at a roiling pitch, and consensus—even on issues so basic as what constitutes evidence and how to construe it—seems a distant hope.[326]

My point isn't just that this is bad scholarship, or that this approach is unlikely to arrive at the truth (although both of those things are plainly true), but that it's incoherent for

Protestants to rely on such scholarship, particularly when the scholarly conclusions are contingent on rejecting the New Testament books (in this case, 1 Peter and John) as false.[xxxix]

That leaves one final reason Protestants may believe in a two-tiered structure to the early Church: arguments from silence. As we've seen, the early Christians spoke a great deal about how each church had a bishop, elders, and deacons. But some authors *don't* mention all three offices explicitly. Arguments from silence are not automatically wrong, but here, there's not that much silence. And when we do find someone referring to "elders and deacons" or "bishops and deacons" or just "elders," it's from works that aren't specifically about church governance, or where the reference is too vague to be of much use. Duffy, for instance, writes that Clement's letter to the Corinthians suggests "that at Corinth as at Rome the church at this time was organised under a group of bishops or presbyters, rather than a single ruling bishop."[327] When pressed, he concedes that there is "admittedly not much in I Clement to go on in deciding how the churches at Rome and Corinth were ordered."[328]

An honest assessment of the evidence suggests that it falls into two basic categories: (1) evidence that explicitly supports the Catholic position or (2) evidence that is ambiguous and could be read in either a Catholic or Protestant direction. This first prong of the Protestant case requires rejecting everything in (1) and consistently interpreting (2) as somehow *proof* of the Protestant position (rather than simply *compatible with* it).

What's remarkable is how weak this case is. For instance, we know from one of Ignatius's letters that the church

---

of Magnesia in c. 107 had a bishop named Damas, elders named Bassus and Apollonius, and a deacon named Sotio,[329] just as we know that all of the apostolic churches kept careful lists of who their bishops (allegedly) were. Protestants arguing for a two-tiered church structure are strikingly vague in contrast: what were the names of some of these co-ruling elders? Where and when did the first bishop usurp authority in the church, and who was he? Who supported or opposed this shift? If Protestants are right, this shift happened in *every church on earth*. Surely, it's not too much to expect clear evidence of this *somewhere*, right?

Prong #2: Did Some Event Cause the Early Christians to Reject the Structure of Their Churches?

To get from two-tiered to three-tiered governance, *something* must have happened to the early Church. But what? Adherents of the Protestant view can't agree; instead, as with Prong #1, there's a good deal of creative storytelling.

The Baptist theologian Laurie Guy claims that "advocates of ecclesial democracy and/or plural leadership may regret the emergence of a dominating mono-episcopacy. The development was probably necessary, however, if the Church was to remain strong and united, a major force in society."[330] Eamon Duffy writes that this change happened "by the end of the first century" and "was at least in part a response to the wildfire spread of false teaching—heresy."[331] Johannes Brosseder likewise claims that the episcopacy "owed its first development as a mono-episcopate to the battle against Gnosticism."[332] Karen Jo Torjesen offers Ulrich Volp's theory that the episcopacy emerged after "the presiding elder achieved city-wide recognition through collecting food, clothing, and gifts, providing for burials, and caring for the poor."[333] Cyril Hovorun (as we've seen) blames St. Ignatius, who he claims "believed that the more church authority was consolidated in one person's hands, the more it could help the church solve the new problems that it faced in the second century."[334]

J.P. Meier claims that in Antioch, "it was only natural that the college of Christian teachers and prophets" would "reorganize and unify itself to counter the Gnostic doctrine more effectively," but also that "civil persecution may have been another reason for consolidation of leadership in the face of crisis," since even "local sporadic outbursts against Christians may have pushed the Church towards increasing consolidation of authority."[335]

The Lutheran theologian Peter Lampe, meanwhile, tells an even more imaginative story about the church in Rome. He claims that "in the first half of the second century, a 'minister of external affairs' was responsible for the correspondence with other cities."[336] His whole theory turns on this, and his evidence for it is that, in the *Shepherd of Hermas*, there are instructions to "write therefore two books, and you will send the one to Clemens and the other to Grapte. And Clemens will send his to foreign countries, for permission has been granted to him to do so."[337] This Clemens (or Clement) is clearly a scribe. His job isn't to decide what to write, but to take dictation and make copies. But Lampe is convinced he was the external affairs minister, an office in the Church (about which the early Christians were strangely silent) apparently so influential that "the shipments of aid to congregations in other cities probably also passed through his hands."[338] (Doesn't the church secretary *always* have a massive budget?) Lampe admits that this requires presupposing that "there must have been in Rome a central collection place for offerings to such shipments: a central fund—*apart* from the cash funds of the individual communities administered by the bishops of these congregations and used to care for the needy *in the city*."[339] But if you are willing to speculate that there must have been a "minister of external affairs" in charge of all correspondence with other churches, and that he must have also had exclusive control over a large budget, all that's left is granting Lampe's theory that this minister of external affairs "gains ever more 'prominence,' until at the latest with Victor (c. 189–99) a powerful *monarchos* has developed."[340] In summary, "the role of 'external minister' was predestined to flow into a monarchical episcopacy in the second half of the second century."[341]

So the event needed for Prong #2 is . . . *something*: Gnosticism, Roman persecution, a desire for greater unity, a desire for more social clout, the influence of Ignatius of Antioch, a usurping external affairs officer, fill in the blank. But whatever you can come up with, the event has to be large enough that it caused people to despair of the apostolic structure of the Church, almost overnight. In Meier's story about Antioch, for instance:

> At any rate, ca. 100, one particularly gifted prophet-teacher came forth from the Antiochene college of prophets and teachers to take the "first seat" (*prōtokathedria*) so deprecated by Matthew (Matt 23:6; the evangelist was more a prophet than he knew). This chief teacher and prophet (preacher), presiding over the college from which he emerged, received the designation "bishop" or "overseer" (*episkopos*). The remaining teachers and prophets were called "elders" or "presbyters" (*presbyteroi*), and their group or college was called a *presbyterion*. . . . Ironically, the term Matthew wanted to mark the greatest leader in the church, "servant" (*diakonos*, Matt 23:11) was relegated

to the assistants (deacons) who stood on the third and lowest rung of the hierarchical ladder.[342]

So Protestants think something (no one knows what!) caused the early Christians not only to abandon the structure of the Church bequeathed them by the apostles, but to do so in favor of a structure that the evangelists "deprecated" and rejected. And this apparently happened not only in Antioch, but also in Rome and every church. Yet precisely at the moment in history in which they were allegedly making this shift, we find Clement talking about how the structure of the Church is something *received* and not invented and Ignatius talking about the theological reasons for the trifold structure.

Prong #3: Did the Christians Switch Governance?

Obviously, the third prong follows from the first two. The apostles set up the churches with elders and deacons; something (heresy, Ignatius, social standing, persecution, etc.) put a strain on that structure; and so . . . they changed it, instituting bishops.

It's easy to breeze by this detail, but we shouldn't. If you're a Protestant, imagine what would happen if your denomination announced that, from now on, there will be a single pope governing the whole church. Would people simply meekly accept this? And then imagine that they told you that it had always been this way: that from the time of the Reformation, your denomination had always had a pope. Might not someone . . . protest? Indeed, we would logically expect schism. As I mentioned at the start of the chapter, if anything has historically been a cause for schism among Protestant denominations, it's the question of church governance. Yet, as Michael McGuckian points out, the Protestant theory of the early Church lacks "historical plausibility" because the evidence we should expect to find simply doesn't exist:

> The notion of a church choosing its church order is unheard of in Christian tradition until the sixteenth century with the Reformation in Switzerland, and the choice between presbyteral and episcopal government is church-dividing to this day. Is it plausible to suggest that it would not have been equally divisive in the first decades of the Church's life, and could have taken place without leaving any trace whatever?[343]

It's not just that we have no evidence that there was a switch in church governance. It's that, with the bishop lists and the theology of apostolic succession, we have positive evidence that there was *no* switch. Protestants might object that the Church covered the evidence up, but there's no evidence of a cover-up, either. We *do* have evidence of important conflicts within the Church, on everything from Christology to which books belong in the Bible. It's not that it's impossible for Christians to have changed their minds, or for an idea to have gained gradual acceptance. It's that on this one issue, the Christians living in the 100s are emphatic that (1) they haven't changed the structure of the Church, (2) they don't have the authority to do so, and (3) they have the written records showing that they can trace their bishops back to the apostles. Secular scholars (and the Protestant apologists who rely upon them) deny these conclusions in spite of the evidence—and not because of it.

5

WRITINGS:
The Four Gospels

MANY PROTESTANTS believe that the sixty-six-book Bible they use is the same as the Bible used in the early Church, but it isn't. This is an understandable mistake, as certain popular Protestant authors peddle outright falsehoods about where the Bible comes from. That full story, with all of its twists and turns, is beyond the scope of this book. But I want to focus on a small part of that story: how do we know that we have the right four Gospels? Unlike the other doctrines we've examined so far, related to baptism, the Eucharist, and bishops, this is an area in which Catholics and Protestants tend to agree. But why?

Even here, we have to address some of the popular falsehoods. For instance, the Reformed theologian John MacArthur contrasts what he claims is "the view of the Roman Catholic Church" with the "biblical view":

The view of the Roman Catholic Church is that the Bible is an authoritative collection of writings. However, that authority was conferred on the books of Scripture by the Church itself. The biblical view understands that the canon is a collection of divinely authoritative writings. . . . It is not a church or the people of God that determines which books to make authoritative. Rather, the people of God *recognize* the inspired nature that these writings already possess. Rightly understood, the canonization of Scripture is a process not of conferring but of recognizing authority.[344]

In other words, MacArthur is claiming that the Catholic Church teaches that the books of the Bible *became Scripture* once the Church recognized them as canonical. But that's blatantly false. The Catholic Church actually rejects that view, affirming what MacArthur calls "the biblical view." Here's the First Vatican Council, in its own words, describing the inspiration of the biblical books:

These books the Church holds to be sacred and canonical not because she subsequently approved them by her authority after they had been composed by unaided human skill, nor simply because they contain revelation without error, but because, being written under the inspiration of the Holy Spirit, they have God as their author, and were as such committed to the Church.[345]

So Catholics and Protestants actually agree on the question: when the Church recognized the books of the Bible as inspired, it's because they were already inspired by God.[xl] But does that mean that the Church's role is dispensable? Not at all. MacArthur inadvertently shows why in his book *Why Believe the Bible?* by describing what he says were the four tests "used by the early Christian Church to determine New Testament Scripture":

---

xl   Likewise, when the Church declares that a saint is in heaven, or that a miracle has occurred, it's because those things have *already happened*. The Church is not claiming that its declaration is sending the saint to heaven or causing the miracle.

1. "Was the book authored by an apostle or someone closely associated with an apostle?"

2. "Did the writing square with apostolic doctrine?"

3. Was it "read and used in the churches"?

4. Was it "recognized and used by the next generations after the early Church, especially by the Apostolic Fathers"?[346]

Lee Martin McDonald (president emeritus of Fuller Seminary) gives a similar list to MacArthur's,[xli] explaining that "the most common criteria employed in the canonical process include apostolicity, orthodoxy, antiquity, and use."[347] However, I hasten to add McDonald's warning that no surviving evidence "suggests that all churches used the same criteria in selecting their sacred collections. Likewise, no evidence suggests that each separate criterion weighed equally with others in deliberations about canon."[348] Instead, these are simply the types of questions that the early Christians were asking as they determined whether a particular book belonged in their Church (and eventually, their Bible).

Test #1: Apostolicity

As the biblical scholar Robert H. Gundry explains, apostolicity is the single most important test of canonicity:

---

xli   You might notice that neither MacArthur nor McDonald claims, as some modern Protestants do, that Christians can figure out which books to accept and which to reject because some of them are *self-authenticating*, or that the internal evidence of Scripture reveals which books belong in the Bible. I think it will quickly become clear why that approach wouldn't work.

Various criteria for canonicity have been suggested, such as edifying moral effect and agreement with the oral tradition of apostolic doctrine. But some edifying books failed to achieve canonical status. So also did some books that carried forward the oral tradition of apostolic doctrine. More important—in fact, crucial—was the criterion of apostolicity, which means authorship by an apostle or by an apostolic associate and thus also a date of writing within the apostolic period.[349]

Orthodoxy isn't enough.[350] In the words of Michael Kruger, "a book must be orthodox to be apostolic, but orthodoxy does not *make* a book apostolic."[351] What else is needed? It also needs to have been written by an apostle, or else "by someone who got his information directly from an apostle," and penned during the Apostolic Age (when the living apostles could ensure that the Gospel was free of errors).[352] But how do we know that the four Gospels really were written by apostles (St. Matthew and St. John) or the associates of apostles (St. Mark and St. Luke)?[353] As the skeptic Bart Ehrman argues,

The four Gospels that eventually made it into the New Testament, for example, are all anonymous, written in the third person *about* Jesus and his companions. None of them contains a first-person narrative ("One day, when Jesus and I went into Capernaum . . .") or claims to be written by an eyewitness or companion of an eyewitness. Why then do we call them Matthew, Mark, Luke, and John? Because sometime in the second century, when proto-orthodox Christians recognized the need for *apostolic* authorities, they attributed these books to apostles (Matthew and John) and close companions of apostles (Mark, the secretary of Peter; and Luke, the travelling companion of Paul). Most scholars today have abandoned these identifications, and recognize that the books were written by otherwise unknown but relatively well-educated Greek-speaking (and writing) Christians during the second half of the first century.[354]

Let's unpack this, bit by bit. First, Ehrman is right that the four Gospels are anonymous: the closest we get to declarations of authorship are hints that the fourth Gospel is by (or at least based on the teachings of) the apostle John.[355] That obviously makes it harder to prove their authorship, but ironically, it is a point in favor of their antiquity and authenticity. The famed Protestant scholar F.F. Bruce says that "it is noteworthy that, while the four canonical Gospels could afford to be published anonymously, the apocryphal Gospels which began to appear from the mid-second century onwards claimed (falsely) to be written by apostles or other persons associated with the Lord."[356]

A few years after writing the passage I quoted above, Ehrman echoed F.F. Bruce's point on his blog. The New Testament epistles and the book of Revelation begin with their authors identifying themselves (which is to be expected, since these are "genres in which this is typically done"), but "the Gospel writers saw themselves as writing in a genre that did not require a self-identification of an author." Like Bruce, Ehrman sees the contrast between the false Gospels and the canonical Gospels:

Later [false] Gospel writers were very intent indeed on showing that *their* message, as opposed to the message of other Gospels, was the right, true, and apostolic message to be believed as authoritative. To provide an authoritative account for their own book, in light of the fact that there were other books with other messages floating around, the later authors produced forgeries, *claiming* to be an apostle (Peter, James, Thomas, Philip, etc.) when in fact they were not. That wasn't a problem with the earlier Gospels. When Mark wrote his Gospel, he felt no need to establish that *his* book, as opposed to others, was apostolic. There *were* no others. So too Matthew and Luke: they were continuing a Gospel tradition, started with Mark, that was widely seen in their circles as authoritative, and so did not need to authorize their message by pretending to be an apostle when they were not.[357]

A second-century forger creating a false Gospel would pretend to be an apostle or a companion of an apostle. But if the four canonical Gospels are so old that they didn't need to distinguish themselves from false Gospels, and if they were universally accepted as authentic, then we can understand why the evangelists see no need to provide their credentials.

On what basis, then, do we call them the Gospels of Matthew, Mark, Luke, and John?

You might imagine that the Christian authors of the first and early second centuries regularly referred to the evangelists by name in referencing the Gospels, but that really wasn't the case. Instead, you get things like the *Didache* saying, "But your prayers and alms and all your acts perform as ye find in the Gospel of our Lord."[358] That sounds like a reference to Matthew 6:1–9, but the author doesn't quote the Gospel directly, much less name it as "the Gospel of Matthew." He simply refers generally to "the Gospel of our Lord" and expects readers to know what he's referencing.

The earliest attestation of authorship comes from Papias (c. 60–130), the bishop of Hierapolis. According to St. Irenaeus, Papias was "a hearer of John and a companion of Polycarp."[359] Papias's own writings are now lost, but he's quoted by the Church historian Eusebius in the early fourth century (at a time when his writings were still available). There are a few relevant fragments of Papias's writings that Eusebius preserves. First, we get a hint to Papias's methods.

If, then, any one came, who had been a follower of the elders, I questioned him in regard to the words of the elders,—what Andrew or what Peter said, or what was said by Philip, or by Thomas, or by James, or by John, or by Matthew, or by any other of the disciples of the Lord, and what things Aristion and the presbyter John,[xlii] the disciples of the Lord, say. For I did not think that what was to be gotten from the books would profit me as much as what came from the living and abiding voice.[360]

In other words, he lived in an age in which the apostles were dying off, as well as those who had heard the apostles. And so Papias made it a point to listen to those who were eyewitnesses (or "earwitnesses") to the apostles, rather than relying only on the information available in writing.

Of the Gospel of Matthew, Papias says, "So then Matthew wrote the oracles in the Hebrew language, and every one interpreted them as he was able."[361] It's a tantalizing line for several reasons, not least of which is that the Gospel of Matthew as we know it today is in Greek, whereas Papias seems to be saying Matthew originally wrote in Hebrew (or Aramaic).

---

xlii Scholars have debated extensively the identity of "the presbyter John." Some have argued that he simply means the apostle John (seeing as John refers to himself as *presbyteros* in 2 John 1:1 and 3 John 1:1), or that Papias is claiming that a different John wrote 2 and 3 John from him who wrote the Gospel of John. (Eusebius takes something like this second view.) But given that this "presbyter John" is grouped with Aristion (a Christian whom we never hear of outside Papias's writings), it's also possible that he was simply another moderately famous (but now forgotten) elder in the early Church, who had seen Christ and the apostles.

Of the Gospel of Mark, Papias gives this description:

This also the presbyter said: Mark, having become the interpreter of Peter, wrote down accurately, though not in order, whatsoever he remembered of the things said or done by Christ. For [Mark] neither heard the Lord nor followed him, but afterward, as I said, he followed Peter, who adapted his teaching to the needs of his hearers, but with no intention of giving a connected account of the Lord's discourses, so that Mark committed no error while he thus wrote some things as he remembered them. For he was careful of one thing, not to omit any of the things which he had heard, and not to state any of them falsely.[362]

Papias's wording leaves it ambiguous as to whether it was Peter or Mark who "adapted his teaching to the needs of his hearers . . . with no intention of giving a connected account of the Lord's discourses,"[xliii] but it does make clear that the Gospel of Mark is based on Peter's preaching and teaching.

In a similar vein, there's a probable reference to the Gospel of Mark as the "memoirs of Peter" in the following passage from St. Justin Martyr from the *Dialogue with Trypho* (c. 155–160): "when it is said that [Jesus] changed the name of one of the apostles to Peter; and when it is written in the memoirs of him that this so happened, as well as that he changed the names of the two brothers, the sons of Zebedee, to Boanerges, which means sons of thunder."[363] The expression "memoirs of him" is ambiguous: it could mean Jesus' memoirs or Peter's memoirs. It's most likely the latter, since Justin refers to the Gospels as the "memoirs of the apostles" thirteen times

---

xliii This may account for differences in Mark's chronology compared to the Gospels of Matthew and Luke.

in this same section, and never refers to them as the "memoirs of Jesus." But if that's right, what does Justin mean about the "memoirs of Peter"? Some scholars believe it's a reference to the so-called *Gospel of Peter*, while others recognize it (I think correctly) as a reference to Peter's role in the formation of the Gospel of Mark.[364] After all, Jesus doesn't give the nickname *Boanerges* in the *Gospel of Peter*; he gives it in the Gospel of Mark (specifically, Mark 3:17). Justin's repeated description of the Gospels as the "memoirs of the apostles" reveals the importance of apostolicity to the Christians of his day (that is, they are reading not just any books about Jesus, but the ones they believe originated with the apostles).

Additionally, there are the so-called "anti-Marcionite prologues" to the Gospels. Latin versions of the Bible had short introductory sections explaining who the author of the work was, to whom it was addressed, and the like. (You'll often see something similar in modern Bibles.) In the early twentieth century, scholars discovered prologues to the Gospels of Mark, Luke, and John. (The Gospel of Matthew didn't have one, or else it's been lost.) The difficulty is, since they're brief and we don't know who wrote them or why, we can't accurately date them: scholars originally believed that these dated back to the second century, in response to the heresy of Marcionism,[xliv] which would make them among the earliest witnesses to the authorship of the Gospels. However, subsequent scholars tend to date them to the third or fourth century, too late to be of much help to us.[365]

All of the evidence we've looked at thus far is complicated for one reason or another. We no longer have Papias's books, so we're getting Papias through the sometimes unreliable

---

xliv They're often called the "anti-Marcionite prologues" for this reason, even by scholars who deny that they were written in response to Marcion.

historian Eusebius.[366] And Papias's own accounts are messy, based on relaying what he heard from the "elders" (which could mean either leaders or literally old Christians here). Justin is probably showing us that the Gospel of Mark is based on the preaching of Peter, but he doesn't actually *name* Mark (someone going off this evidence alone might think Peter wrote the Gospel himself), and his reference to "his memoirs" could mean three different things. The "anti-Marcionite prologues" are clearer about authorship, but of an unclear date.

That brings us to the *Muratorian Fragment*. As you may recall from chapter two, we can date it fairly reliably to the latter half of the second century, perhaps around the year A.D. 170,[367] because of its reference to the *Shepherd of Hermas*: "Hermas wrote the *Shepherd* very recently, in our times, in the city of Rome, while bishop Pius, his brother, was occupying the [episcopal] chair of the church of the city of Rome."[368] Since we know that Pius was bishop of Rome in the 140s, the *Muratorian Fragment* must be early enough to consider that pontificate "very recent." In any case, the *Muratorian Fragment is* a fragment, and so we pick up the list of Gospels halfway through:

> . . . at which nevertheless he was present, and so he placed [them in his narrative].
>
> The third book of the gospel is that according to Luke. Luke, the well-known physician, after the ascension of Christ, when Paul had taken with him as one zealous for the law, composed it in his own name, according to [the general] belief. Yet he himself had not seen the Lord in the flesh; and therefore, as he was able to ascertain events, so indeed he begins to tell the story from the birth of John [the Baptist].

The fourth of the Gospels is that of John, [one] of the disciples. To his fellow disciples and bishops, who had been urging him [to write], he said, "Fast with me from today for three days, and what will be revealed to each one let us tell it to one another." In the same night it was revealed to Andrew, [one] of the apostles, that John should write down all things in his own name while all of them should review it.[369]

Presumably, this once identified all four evangelists. What we have today still provides clear references to the Gospels of Luke and John.

It's not until we get to about the year 180 that we find an author naming each of the four evangelists. Irenaeus seems to be the first, writing:

Matthew also issued a written Gospel among the Hebrews in their own dialect, while Peter and Paul were preaching at Rome, and laying the foundations of the Church. After their departure, Mark, the disciple and interpreter of Peter, did also hand down to us in writing what had been preached by Peter. Luke also, the companion of Paul, recorded in a book the gospel preached by him. Afterward, John, the disciple of the Lord, who also had leaned upon his breast, did himself publish a Gospel during his residence at Ephesus in Asia.[370]

Around 181, St. Theophilus of Antioch explains to his friend Autolycus how the Word can be both God and begotten of God by saying, "Hence the holy writings teach us, and all the spirit-bearing [inspired] men, one of whom, John, says, 'In the beginning was the Word, and the Word was with God,' showing that at first God was alone, and the Word in him."[371] It's a clear attestation to John's authorship of the fourth Gospel, and seemingly independent of Irenaeus, given that the two testimonies are given on opposite ends of the empire (modern-day Syria and France, respectively) within about a year of one another.

That's roughly the state of the evidence up to the close of the second century, along with several early-third-century texts referring to the evangelists by name. So how big of a problem is it that we don't get all four evangelists identified clearly until Irenaeus? Or to put it another way, how much should we trust these second-century authors?

In this area, Protestants tend to rally to the defense of the second-century Christians. D.A. Carson writes that "even if Irenaeus, toward the end of the second century, is amongst the strongest, totally unambiguous witnesses, his personal connection with Polycarp, who knew John, means the distance in terms of personal memories is not very great."[372]

Timothy Paul Jones rightly points out that the tradition is unanimous on this point. With certain books (particularly the epistle to the Hebrews), the early Christians disagreed over who the author was. For the four Gospels, everyone who answers the question answers it the same way.[373] No one claims, for instance, that the Gospel of Luke was really written by St. Paul, even though that might seem to give the Gospel more weight.

On the other hand, reject the reliability of the Christians of the late second century, and what are you left with? Not much. David Alan Black, of Southeastern Baptist Theological Seminary, laments that "because it has long been popular to devalue the Patristic evidence and the ecclesiastical background of the Gospel," modern scholars have been devoting their attention "to attempts to solve it solely through the study of the internal evidence."[374] In other words, instead of listening to the unanimous witness of the early Christians, many scholars try to solve the problem from Scripture alone. As Black explains,[xlv] that sort of approach will get you nowhere:

> But far from achieving their objective in this way, the result of over two hundred years of endeavor has been frustration and stalemate, and not a few critics have come to the conclusion that the problem is insoluble—and so it is, without the two other criteria [of external evidence and the historical likelihood of the hypothesis adopted]. For internal criticism deals with anonymous and unidentifiable editors and sources and never comes down to flesh-and-blood realities, to known persons and situations.[375]

To get a sense of this "frustration and stalemate," put the question this way: if Matthew, Mark, Luke, and John *didn't* write the four Gospels, who did? Skeptical scholars can't decide. The historian Paula Fredriksen asks a simpler question: "Who wrote the Gospels, Jews or Gentiles?" She answers, "No one knows, although scholars, on the basis of internal evidence, will venture various 'ethnic' identifications."[376] Fredriksen claims that "the author of Matthew is universally regarded as Jewish," but in fact, scholars over the last century have taken every possible position (that the author is the apostle Matthew, or an anonymous Palestinian Jewish Christian, or a Hellenistic Jewish Christian, or a Gentile Christian).[377] She speaks of a growing consensus for the view that the author of John was a Jewish Christian but adds that "any answer is speculative" for Mark, and "arguments for

---

xlv Black's specific focus is on the so-called Synoptic Problem (Why are Matthew, Mark, and Luke so similar? Why are they different? And in what order were they written?), but his critique applies to the question of Gospel authorship more broadly.

Luke can go either way." Indeed, Fredriksen herself originally argued that these two evangelists were Gentiles and now argues that they were Jewish.[378] So even on the question of whether the evangelists were Gentiles or Jews, we find unstable consensuses at best and naked guessing at worst.

Some skeptical scholars have rejected the idea that the Gospels had individual authors at all, or that there was such a thing as an "original author."[379] For instance, the University of Pennsylvania's William L. Petersen states: "To be brutally frank, we know next to nothing about the shape of the 'autograph' Gospels; indeed, it is questionable if one can even speak of such a thing. This leads to the inescapable conclusion that the text in our critical editions today is actually a text which dates from no earlier [than] about 180 CE, at the earliest."[380] Rather than fixed texts, Petersen claims that there were simply "clusters" of saying or episodes of what we would later call the Gospels,[381] that people added to (and removed from) these clusters, and that they became fixed as books only somewhere in the second half of the second century.[382] But Bethel's Michael W. Holmes rightly points out that Petersen's conclusions don't follow from his arguments, for "if nothing is known about the early text of the Gospels, then how can it be determined that they do not match our critical texts?"[383]

As Howard Jackson notes regarding the Gospel of John, much of critical scholarship imagines "a long line of redactors" for the Gospel text, and "it does not seem to matter much that outside the pericope of the woman taken in adultery there is not the slightest shred of evidence in the manuscripts or anywhere else . . . which attests to any redactional activity for the Fourth Gospel."[384] But it's not just that the skeptical theories are based on massive guesswork and a total lack of hard evidence. It's that the manuscript evidence that we *do* have points to the opposite conclusion. With two notable exceptions,[xlvi] the differences among ancient Gospel manuscripts are relatively minor. Shouldn't there be massive variations, as different communities added and removed entire stories from the Gospels? And what happened to the earlier, now discarded clusters that Petersen imagines?[385]

In short, there are good scholarly reasons to trust that the early Christians know who wrote the four Gospels, not least of which is that they *don't* blindly accept claims of apostolicity. They reject plenty of false Gospels purporting to be written by the apostles, and they raise questions of authenticity and apostolicity even of the books that they ultimately accept.[xlvii] If we choose to trust them, we have a basis for affirming the apostolicity of Matthew, Mark, Luke, and John. If we choose *not* to trust them, we're left in a morass of uncertainty, without anything reliable that we *can* say about the authorship and transmission of the Gospels.

Test #2: Orthodoxy

The second test that MacArthur mentions involves the *contents* of the Gospels: that the early Church accepted them because they were orthodox.

---

xlvi   The two major textual variants are the ending of Mark's Gospel (the original ending may have been lost, and we find a few different endings in ancient manuscripts) and the story of the woman caught in adultery (many scholars believe that this was originally an independent text that was later incorporated into the Gospel of John).

xlvii For instance, Eusebius writes that St. James "is said to be the author of the first of the so-called catholic epistles. But it is to be observed that it is disputed; at least, not many of the ancients have mentioned it, as is the case likewise with the epistle that bears the name of Jude, which is also one of the seven so-called catholic epistles. Nevertheless we know that these also, with the rest, have been read publicly in very many churches." Eusebius, *Church History*, book 2, ch. 23, NPNF 2/1:128. Notice that in that short description, Eusebius makes clear that the early Christians were asking questions about apostolicity, traditional acceptance, and liturgical usage of the books.

Now, there are three ways of understanding this idea. The first is to accept or reject a book because you like or dislike the contents. Martin Luther, in his preface to the book of Revelation, writes, "Let everyone think of it as his own spirit leads him. My spirit cannot accommodate itself to this book. For me this is reason enough not to think highly of it: Christ is neither taught nor known in it."[386] Such an approach is inherently and obviously subjective: your spirit and my spirit may like or dislike different books, but that doesn't necessarily tell us anything about whether or not those books are divinely inspired. It's unlikely that the early Christians would ever have produced a New Testament canon if they had taken this approach.

The second is to compare the book in question to the Scripture that the Jews already had: the Old Testament. St. Luke praises the nobility of the Jews of Beroea, for they "received the word with all eagerness, examining the Scriptures daily to see if these things were so" (Acts 17:11). This approach is better, but it still has its limits: Jesus' listeners are right to proclaim, "What is this? A new teaching!" (Mark 1:27), so you can't expect to find the fullness of the New Testament already present in the Old Testament.

The third way is the one to which MacArthur (wisely) points: does the writing "square with apostolic doctrine"?[387] In the example of the Beroean Jews in Acts 17 who "received the word with all eagerness," it's easy for us to read that as "received the New Testament." But that's not what Luke says: instead, he's describing how "the word of God was proclaimed by Paul at Beroea" (v. 13). In other words, long before the four Gospels (or any New Testament books) were written, the apostles and other eyewitnesses were proclaiming "that which was from the beginning, which we have heard, which we have seen with our eyes, which we have looked upon and touched with our hands, concerning the word of life" (1 John 1:1).

The early Christians knew this orally proclaimed gospel, and it served as a check against any false doctrines or false Gospels. This is an important point to remember because we often think of Christianity as starting with texts, when it didn't. Indeed, one of the major contrasts between Jesus and, say, Muhammad or Joseph Smith is that Jesus doesn't write anything. There's an error that some Protestants hold that the apostles' *writings*, and *only* their writings, were inspired. For instance, a Baptist pastor named Tim Lewis claims that the *New Hampshire Baptist Confession* of 1833 teaches error when it says, "We believe that the Holy Bible was written by men divinely inspired." According to Lewis, "God inspired the '*graphe*' or Scriptures, not the men. While the Holy Spirit carried along the human penman (2 Pet. 1:21), the men themselves were never inspired."[388]

That's an obvious misreading of Scripture: you need only to open the book of Acts to find the apostles when they "were all filled with the Holy Spirit and began to speak in other tongues, as the Spirit gave them utterance" (2:4); or how St. Peter and St. John were brought before the Sanhedrin, where "Peter, filled with the Holy Spirit, *said* to them . . ." (4:8); or how they "went to their friends" and told them about this, and decided to pray, until they "were all filled with the Holy Spirit and spoke the word of God with boldness" (vv. 23, 31). God doesn't just inspire words. He inspires *people* who then communicate that inspiration.

But I think the more common error is simply to think of Christianity primarily as a religion of *writings*. Karen Swallow Prior begins an essay for *Christianity Today* by saying, "Christianity is a religion of the Word. Christians are a 'People of the Book.' These distinctives have defined the

Christian faith from the beginning, even before the age of print that brought us books."[389] That's just not so, and the *Catechism* points this out: "The Christian faith is not a 'religion of the book.' Christianity is the religion of the 'Word' of God, a word which is 'not a written and mute word, but the Word which is incarnate and living'" (108). Does that distinction matter? It does.

Here's the popular Baptist theologian John Piper's take:

> Let me just try to say this gently. One of the things that separate Protestants and Roman Catholics is the way you think about authority of the Bible in relationship to the Church. Protestants like to say that the Bible created the Church, and Catholics tend to say the Church created or confirmed the Bible. In other words, the Bible has its authority because the Church councils gave it their authority, and thus align Church authority, [the] pope especially . . . the office that he holds and [the] Bible are together in the Roman Catholic Church. Protestants order it like this: Bible and Church. That's where I am, and I think that's what happened, that the Bible pressed itself upon the Church and the Church didn't create a canon. It recognized a canon.[390]

Piper is making the same false claim that MacArthur made earlier: this idea that Catholics think the Church gave Scripture its authority (despite the Church explicitly teaching the opposite). But he's still giving us a helpful framework. I think he is largely right to say Protestants tend to think of the Bible coming first and creating the Church, whereas Catholics talk about the Church coming first and the Bible being written (on the human level) by leaders of that Church and largely *to* the Church.

One has only to open the Bible to see that the Catholic side to this is right. The book of Acts speaks of "the church in Jerusalem" (8:1), "the church throughout all Judea and Galilee and Samaria" (9:31), "the church at Antioch" (13:1), and of St. Paul and St. Barnabas appointing "elders for them in every church" (14:23), before the two of them were "sent on their way by the church" back to Jerusalem (15:3), where "they were welcomed by the church and the apostles and the elders" (15:4). All of this occurs before the writing of the New Testament. And when the New Testament *is* written, much of it is written to these previously existing local churches: "to the church of God which is at Corinth" (2 Cor. 1:1), "to the churches of Galatia" (Gal. 1:2), "to the church of the Thessalonians" (1 Thess. 1:1), etc.

Writing to the church of the Thessalonians, Paul warns them "not to be quickly shaken in mind or excited, either by spirit or by word, or by letter purporting to be from us, to the effect that the day of the Lord has come" and instructs them to "stand firm and hold to the traditions which you were taught by us, either by word of mouth or by letter" (2 Thess. 2:2, 15). Paul sees the twofold threat of false preaching and fake epistles and reminds them that their safeguard is Tradition, transmitted both in written and unwritten forms.

When the early Christians rejected books because they didn't match what they had heard from the apostles, they were simply heeding the safeguards entrusted to them by the apostles. The Christians in the first and early second centuries were nourished not just by the writings that would later form the New Testament, but also by the living testimony of the apostles and then those who had sat at their feet. Recall Papias's description: "I did not think that what was to be gotten from the books would profit me as much as what came from the living and abiding voice."[391] As Everett Ferguson explains, there were several ways that Christians in the second century could see if a proposed teaching (or proposed New Testament book!) squared with apostolic doctrine:

> At the core of all these developments [in the second century] was one central concern: Where can we find the apostolic message? Christians clung to the apostles' teaching about Jesus as the standard for determining what was true and what was not. Those who taught a different message from what the local bishop and elders taught appealed to a secret tradition going back to one of the apostles. Over against this claim to "secret teaching," their opponents pointed to the public succession of leaders and teaching in the established churches. The theologian Tertullian summarized this argument: Truth is what "the churches received from the apostles, the apostles from Christ, Christ from God," and all other doctrine is false. Such concerns led to a "canon" of accepted apostolic writings (the New Testament), a summary of the message these writings contained (the Rule of Faith), a confession of faith (the Apostles' Creed), and an apostolic succession of bishops and elders.[392]

Of the four chief ways (New Testament writings, the Rule of Faith, the creeds, and apostolic succession), the one that most likely needs explaining is the Rule of Faith, or *regula fidei*. In the words of the Protestant theologian and biblical scholar Theodor Zahn, the term is "used so frequently in early Christian literature from the last quarter of the second century that an understanding of it is necessary to a correct idea of the religious conceptions of that period."[393] It's something distinct from Scripture: Zahn points out that the early Christians "never considered as the Rule of Faith the Bible or any part of it."[394] In fact, when these early Christians talk about "the canon," they're talking about not a list of books of the Bible, but the contents of "the baptismal formula."[395]

To understand what it means, it's important to know that *regula*, or "rule," is a term from Roman law. These were the official summaries of the law, explaining them succinctly: "'a rule is that which briefly expounds a matter.' The legal rules are concise formulations drawn from the law which is in force: 'the law is not derived from rules (*regulae*) but a rule is derived from the existing law.' Therefore the rule itself does not create law."[396] In other words, the role of the Rule of Faith wasn't to replace the preaching of the apostles, or to add to it, but to summarize (and interpret) it. As Baylor's D.H. Williams explains, the Rule of Faith (called by some of the early Greek-speaking Christians the *Canon of Truth*) refers to "a brief description of what Christians believed about God and his story of salvation. The Rule of Faith was what the Church was preaching and teaching even before the various Gospels and epistles then circulating became canonized into one 'New Testament.' Indeed, the way the New Testament was formed is part of the legacy that emerged from this early tradition."[397] In other words, one of the ways that the early Christians could spot a false Gospel was that it didn't agree with the Rule of Faith that they already had.

The Rule also tells the faithful how to interpret Scripture: it shows how the pieces fit together. That image comes from St. Irenaeus, who describes heretics' misuse of Scripture by comparing it to taking a mosaic and rearranging the tiles:

Their manner of acting is just as if one, when a beautiful image of a king has been constructed by some skillful artist out of precious jewels, should then take this likeness of the man all to pieces, should rearrange the gems, and so fit them together as to make them into the form of a dog or of a fox, and even that but poorly executed; and should then maintain and declare that this was the beautiful image of the king which the skillful artist constructed.[398]

The problem isn't with the tiles (the biblical data), but with how those tiles are being arranged. That's where the Rule of Faith comes in. It's the instruction manual, so to speak, explaining how the different parts of Scripture fit together to form one orthodox whole. As Irenaeus explains, the one "who retains unchangeable in his heart the Rule of the truth which he received by means of baptism" will not be deceived by this rearrangement of the scriptural mosaic: "though he will acknowledge the gems, he will certainly not receive the fox instead of the likeness of the king."[399]

This also means that when the early Christians wanted to battle heresy, they didn't necessarily start with what the New Testament says. In the early 200s, Tertullian actually warns against using Scripture to combat heresy, saying that "our appeal, therefore, must not be made to the Scriptures; nor must controversy be admitted on points in which victory will either be impossible, or uncertain, or not certain enough." You don't just hand copies of the Bible to both the faithful and the heretics and ask each side what they think the text means. Doing that, Tertullian argues, places heresy "on equal footing" with orthodoxy: the heretics can just as easily fit the pieces together to make a fox as you can to make a king. Instead, we should be asking "'with whom lies that very faith to which the Scriptures belong. From what and through whom, and when, and to whom, has been handed down that Rule, by which men become Christians?' For wherever it shall be manifest that the true Christian Rule and faith shall be, there will likewise be the true Scriptures and expositions thereof, and all the Christian traditions."[400] In other words, the Church, with its Rule of Faith, is the only sure interpreter of Scripture and apostolic Tradition.

Following his own advice, when Tertullian writes against Praxeas (who seems to have taught the anti-trinitarian heresy of *Monarchianism*), he appeals to the Rule of Faith, explaining:

> [That t]his Rule of Faith has come down to us from the beginning of the gospel, even before any of the older heretics, much more before Praxeas, a pretender of yesterday, will be apparent both from the lateness of date which marks all heresies, and also from the absolutely novel character of our new-fangled Praxeas. In this principle also we must henceforth find a presumption of equal force against all heresies whatsoever—that whatever is first is true, whereas that is spurious which is later in date.[401]

This is an important claim, because even though the Rule might be expressed in different formulas,[402] at least Tertullian believed that the Rule of Faith was something ancient, dating back to "the beginning of the gospel," such that he was willing to wager his whole argument on the claim "that whatever is first is true."

One of the primary uses of the Rule seems to have been at the moment of baptism. Irenaeus describes the Rule as the "three points of our seal"[403]: in the sealing of baptism, a convert confesses faith in the Father, the Son, and the Holy Spirit. Irenaeus explains that "the baptism of our regeneration proceeds through these three points" because it "bids us bear in mind that we have received baptism for the remission of sins, in the name of God the Father, and in the name of Jesus Christ, the Son of God, who was incarnate and died and rose again, and in the Holy Spirit of God. And that this baptism is the seal of eternal life, and is the new birth unto God, that we should no longer be the sons of mortal men, but of the eternal and perpetual God."[404] Anyone accepting the authority of the Rule of Faith, therefore, has grounds to accept the canonical Gospels (and also baptismal regeneration!) while rejecting anti-trinitarian teachings or "Gospels."

Test #3: Liturgical Use

The third test MacArthur describes the early Christians using is whether a book was "read and used in the churches."[405] This test is helpful for two reasons.

First, it reminds us of Scripture's rightful context. In the prior section, I mentioned one modern distortion in our approach to revelation: our preference for the written word over (and even to the exclusion of) the spoken word. Another modern distortion is that we think of books as private rather than public. As Mary Mills explains in her commentary on Ecclesiastes, "in the modern world much reading is a private matter in which, through the possession of literacy skills, one individual engages with a text in a direct and personal manner."[406] The combined effect of those two distortions is that we conflate *Scripture* and *revelation* and then think of Scripture as something primarily "personal" rather than communal.

But that's not how the early Christians, or the Jews before them, thought of Scripture. The Law, and the Old Testament more broadly, was read in a liturgical context. God ordered a full reading of the Law to be proclaimed in its entirety every seven years, assembling "the people, men, women, and little ones, and the sojourner within your towns, that they may hear and learn to fear the Lord your God" (Deut. 31:12). Contrasting the Mosaic Law with the laws of other nations, the first-century Jewish historian Josephus explains that "every week men should desert their other occupations and assemble to listen to the Law and to obtain a thorough and accurate knowledge of it, a practice which all other legislators seem to have neglected."[407] We get a glimpse of this in Luke 4:16–21:

> And [Jesus] came to Nazareth, where he had been brought up; and he went to the synagogue, as his custom was, on the Sabbath day. And he stood up to read; and there was given to him the book of the prophet Isaiah. He opened the book and found the place where it was written, "The Spirit of the Lord is upon me, because he has anointed me to preach good news to the poor. He has sent me to proclaim release to the captives and recovering of sight to the blind, to set at liberty those who are oppressed, to proclaim the acceptable year of the Lord." And he closed the book, and gave it back to the attendant, and sat down; and the eyes of all in the synagogue were fixed on him. And he began to say to them, "Today this scripture has been fulfilled in your hearing."

Notice the little details. Jesus doesn't crack open his pocket Bible, because such a thing doesn't exist yet. Instead, he is handed a book, which he hands back at the end. And the book he's handed isn't a full Bible (or even a full Old Testament) because, again, such a thing doesn't exist yet. The Jewish Scriptures were kept on scrolls, with long books broken into more manageable parts (as we see with the books of Samuel, Kings, and Chronicles).[408] When it says Jesus opened Isaiah, the verb there is *anaptussó*, "unrolled." He's opening a scroll and must then find his place. Early Christians pioneered the shift from scrolls to codices (an early form of books),[409] but the expectation is still that Scripture is to be read communally and liturgically. The book of Revelation opens with blessings upon him "who reads aloud the words of the prophecy," as well as upon "those who hear" (1:3).

In other words, Scripture anticipates being read (and listened to) *publicly*, rather than being read privately in, say, the living room or den. Why? Partly the reasons are practical, surely. For one thing, ancient texts have "little or no division between words, sentences, or paragraphs, and little or no punctuation. Therefore, the reader was obliged to constitute the sense of a text by vocalizing it, and in this manner, the reader converted the written into the oral."[410] Additionally, prior to the printing press, books were incredibly expensive, since it took as much as two years to hand-copy a single Bible.[411] It also took years for ordinary people to amass the fortune needed to purchase one of these books. Eric Greitens points out that "today, almost any working person in any developed country can purchase almost any book for the equivalent of two or three hours of labor. Those two hours' worth of wages are precious, but books are much cheaper than they used to be. In medieval Byzantium, for example, an average laborer would have had to work for two or three *years* to buy a single book."[412]

Thus, the norm seems to have been that those who owned (and could read) books would read them aloud for those who didn't (or couldn't). We get a hint of this in an amusing anecdote St. Augustine shares about his mentor, St. Ambrose. Augustine says Ambrose spent what little free time he had either "refreshing his body with necessary sustenance, or his mind with reading."[413] But Augustine finds it fascinating that Ambrose read *silently*:

> But while reading, his eyes glanced over the pages, and his heart searched out the sense, but his voice and tongue were silent. Ofttimes, when we had come (for no one was

forbidden to enter, nor was it his custom that the arrival of those who came should be announced to him), we saw him thus reading to himself, and never otherwise; and, having long sat in silence (for who durst interrupt one so intent?), we were fain to depart, inferring that in the little time he secured for the recruiting of his mind, free from the clamor of other men's business, he was unwilling to be taken off. And perchance he was fearful lest, if the author he studied should express aught vaguely, some doubtful and attentive hearer should ask him to expound it, or to discuss some of the more abstruse questions, as that, his time being thus occupied, he could not turn over as many volumes as he wished; although the preservation of his voice, which was very easily weakened, might be the truer reason for his reading to himself. But whatever was his motive in so doing, doubtless in such a man was a good one.[414]

It's revealing that Ambrose's habit of silent, private reading was so unusual that Augustine wracks his brain to think of explanations for it. The norm for reading was that it was done publicly; communally; and, in the case of Scripture, liturgically and ecclesially. But of course, this wasn't simply an economic question: the Christian message is *personal*, but not *private*. Incorporation into Christ entails being part of "the Church, which is his body, the fulness of him who fills all in all" (Eph. 1:22–23).

There was a seismic shift in Christian thinking on this score after Johannes Gutenberg invented the printing press in 1439. The first major work that Gutenberg printed was the Latin Vulgate version of the Bible, and he printed around 180 copies.[415] That's a small number by today's standards but would have taken a scribe *centuries* to do by hand.

This increased supply caused the price of books to plummet eighty-five percent,[416] meaning that it was suddenly feasible for middle-class Christians to own their own Bibles.

It's hard to overstate the way that this single invention, the printing press, shifted the way people think about reading generally and about the Bible specifically. One consequence was that it made it much easier to think of the Bible as something that exists apart from the Church. Without denying the various other causes of the Reformation, the economic historian Jared Rubin has shown a "very strong connection between towns that adopted the printing press and those that accepted the Reformation."[417] Of the 100 largest cities in Europe in 1500, sixty of them had printing presses. Towns and cities with printing presses were twenty-nine to fifty-two percent more likely to become Protestants than those without.[xlviii]

The Protestant telling of this story is often that the printing press meant that "ordinary people could finally read the Bible for themselves," but it may be more accurate to say that "ordinary people could finally read the Bible *alone*"—that is, apart from the Church or other Christians. A half-millennium later, the attitude of many Western Christians can be encapsulated in the 1972 George Jones and Tammy Wynette duet "Me and Jesus": "Me and Jesus, we got our own things going / We don't need anybody to tell us what it's all about."[418] Indeed, that song should probably be a solo, given its message of radical individualism. As Cardinal Timothy Dolan laments, "We want a king without a kingdom; we want a shepherd without the other sheep; we want a father, with us as the only child;

---

xlviii "Towns with a [printing] press by 1500 were 52.1 percentage points more likely to accept the Reformation by 1530, 41.9 percentage points more likely to accept the Reformation by 1560, and 29.0 percentage points more likely to accept the Reformation by 1600." Rubin, p. 271.

we want a general without an army; we want to believe without belonging."[419] But as I hope is becoming clear in this chapter, such an attitude is logically inconsistent, as the early Christians well understood.

There's another reason why the test of liturgical use matters. When reading the writings of these early Christians, it's easy to discard them as "just one man's opinion," and it's not always clear if a book is being cited because the author views it as Scripture or just because it's a good quotation. St. Paul quotes the pagan poets Menander (Acts 17:28) and Epimenides (Titus 1:12), but no one thinks that makes those books canonical. But when we're looking at the corporate worship of whole churches, those problems are solved: the liturgical readings reveal the beliefs of the broader Church (at least locally), and they're reading not just good books, but ones they consider canonical.[xlix] We can see this clearly from the *Muratorian Fragment*'s treatment of the *Shepherd of Hermas*, which it considers orthodox but written too late to be of apostolic origin, concluding that "therefore it ought indeed to be read; but it cannot be read publicly to the people in church either among the prophets,[l] whose number is complete, or among the apostles, for it is after [their] time."[420]

So how do we know which books these early Christians used in the liturgy? As Valeriy Alikin of St. Petersburg

---

xlix Although, as we've seen, they wouldn't use the word *canonical* for this, since that term still refers to the Rule of Faith and baptismal formulas at this point in history.

l Both the *Muratorian Fragment* and Justin Martyr describe the readings as coming from either the apostles or "the prophets," leaving open the question of whether the Torah (the first five books, also known as the Law) was read at Mass in the early Church. See Alikin, pp. 156–57 (noting that the first clear references to Christians using the books of the Law in their liturgy come from the early third century). But "the prophets" could be used here as a shorthand for what we now call the Old Testament. For instance, Paul speaks of "the utterances of the prophets which are read every Sabbath" in the synagogue (Acts 13:27), but Paul's own address is delivered in the synagogue "after the reading of the law and the prophets" (v. 15).

Christian University explains, "Christians began to read apostolic epistles in their gatherings at the latest from the middle of the first century onwards."[421] At the end of his first letter to the Thessalonians, Paul instructs, "I adjure you by the Lord that this letter be read to all the brethren" (5:27). And after the Council of Jerusalem in Acts 15, the leaders of the Church send Paul and St. Barnabas to Antioch with a letter addressed to "the brethren who are of the Gentiles in Antioch and Syria and Cilicia" (v. 23). Alikin points out that this address signals that the letter was to be a "circular" (meaning that the church in Antioch would copy it and pass it along to the next local church), read liturgically in each of the local churches.[422] We get a more explicit example of this in Colossians 4:16: "when this letter has been read among you, have it read also in the church of the Laodiceans; and see that you read also the letter from Laodicea."

Do these books include the four Gospels? According to St. Justin Martyr, they do. Justin explains that "on the day called Sunday, all who live in cities or in the country gather together to one place, and the memoirs of the apostles or the writings of the prophets are read."[423] As we've already seen, "memoirs of the apostles" is the name Justin gives for the Gospels. He doesn't name them, but we can piece together which books he considered the "memoirs" (and thus, which Gospels were being used in his day) from some of his other references. For instance, he writes that "when a star rose in heaven at the time of his birth, as is recorded in the memoirs of his apostles, the Magi from Arabia, recognizing the sign by this, came and worshipped him."[424] That's a clear reference to Matthew 2, the only book to record those details. We've also already seen an apparent reference to the Gospel of Mark (calling it the memoir of Peter), in which Justin mentions that Christ gave the nickname *Boanerges* to James and John (Mark 3:17).[425]

Describing Christ in the garden of Gethsemane, he says that "in the memoirs which I say were drawn up by his apostles and those who followed them, [it is recorded] that his sweat fell down like drops of blood while he was praying, and saying, 'If it be possible, let this cup pass,'"[426] which includes a detail (Christ sweating blood) found only in the Gospel of Luke (22:44). And Justin calls Christ "the only-begotten of the Father of all things, being begotten in a peculiar manner Word and Power by him, and having afterward become man through the Virgin, as we have learned from the memoirs."[427] The reference to Christ as the Word (*Logos*) seems to be coming straight from John 1. Additionally, in his discussion on baptism, you may recall that Justin quotes John 3:3 to explain how we are born again in baptism. So even before we have clear evidence as to the names of the four Gospels, we have evidence that they were (a) recognized as of apostolic origin and (b) used in the Church's liturgy.

Even though Justin quotes from only the four Gospels, he doesn't explicitly deny that there are any others. The *Muratorian Fragment*, a decade later, *does* number the four Gospels.[li] But perhaps the clearest witness that these four are the *only* four comes from our friend Irenaeus, who says that "it is not possible that the Gospels can be either more or fewer in number than they are."[428] Irenaeus makes this argument from theological fittingness: there are four major covenants (Adam, Noah, Moses, Christ), and Revelation 7 speaks of "four angels standing at the four corners of the earth, holding back the four winds of the earth" (v. 1), along with four "living creatures" (v. 11): one like a lion, one like an ox, one like a man, and one like an eagle. Irenaeus reads this not as a

---

li   The fragment that we possess says that the names of the third and fourth Gospels are Luke and John, but it's clear from context that the author has just named two other Gospels.

prophecy of the end times or a literal description of heaven, but as a declaration about how God has "given us the gospel under four aspects,"[429] with each creature representing a specific evangelist.[lii]

Test #4: The Apostolic Fathers

The final test that MacArthur describes is whether a book was "recognized and used by the next generations after the early Church, especially by the Apostolic Fathers."[430] This is similar to the prior test, but the focus is on what the leading *theologians* of the early Church believe, rather than the general *liturgical practice*. As Michael W. Holmes explains, "the term 'Apostolic Fathers' is traditionally used to designate the collection of the earliest extant Christian writings outside the New Testament. These documents are a primary resource for the study of early Christianity, especially the post-apostolic period (ca. A.D. 70–150)."[431] In other words, it's a term for many of the people we've been looking at throughout this book. Since we've already seen what they said and why and when, we know that by the middle to the end of the second century, they're clearly using the four Gospels and no others.

---

lii Later theologians agreed, attempting to match which of the four "living creatures" represented which of the four Gospels. Jerome and Pope Gregory the Great argue that the four living creatures correspond to the four introductions to the Gospels. Following this reading, Matthew is the man, since he opens with Christ's genealogy (1:1). Mark is the lion because God compares the declarations of the prophets to a roaring lion (Amos 3:7–8) and Mark opens with St. John the Baptist, "the voice of one crying in the wilderness" (1:3). Luke is the ox, one of the two animals sacrificed in inaugurating the Levitical priesthood, because Luke opens with Zechariah the priest in the Temple (1:8–9). And John is the eagle because he doesn't begin on earth at all, but "flying like an eagle toward heaven" (Prov. 23:5). See Angela Russel Christman, *"What Did Ezekiel See?": Christian Exegesis of Ezekiel's Vision of the Chariot from Irenaeus to Gregory the Great* (Leiden: Brill, 2005), pp. 17–23.

How Might a Protestant Respond?

As you may have already noticed, the whole case for the four Gospels ends up turning on a single question: *Can we trust* that the beliefs and practices of the Church in the latter part of the second century faithfully reflect the beliefs and practices of the Church at the time of the apostles? Not coincidentally, that's also a question that arises when we talk about baptismal regeneration, the Eucharist, or the episcopacy.[liii] Saying we *can* trust the early Christians gives us good grounds for accepting the Gospels, but it also means they are trustworthy on baptism, the Eucharist, and the Church. Saying we *can't* trust the early Christians means avoiding those Catholic conclusions, but at the expense of undermining the Gospels.

One approach is to bite the bullet and say we don't know that the early Church was right about the four Gospels. Bethel's Mark L. Strauss argues that "uncertain authorship, of course, does not render questionable the authority or inspiration of the text. The authors of many Old and New Testament books are unknown."[432] But recall that the early Christians considered apostolicity a requirement for the Gospels to be included in the New Testament. Concluding that they erred in this determination *does* "render questionable the authority or inspiration of the text" (even if a believer can ultimately find some other grounds upon which to accept the Gospels).

The apologist William Lane Craig argues that it doesn't matter if the early Church misidentified the four evangelists because "when you think about it, the names of the Gospels'

---

liii   If there's a difference, it's simply that it would be easier to prove baptismal regeneration, episcopacy, and the Eucharist from the Christians pre-150 than it would be to prove the number and names of the Gospels.

authors are quite immaterial. At most, what matters is that the author, whether named Luke or Joshua or Herkimer or what have you, was in a position to deliver historically reliable information about the historical Jesus."[433] This is consistent with Craig's general approach to avoid "the misunderstanding, all too common among Evangelicals, that a historical case for Jesus' radical self-understanding and resurrection depends upon showing that the Gospels are generally reliable historical documents. The overriding lesson of two centuries of biblical criticism is that such an assumption is false."[434] Instead, Craig is content to argue that "even documents which are generally unreliable may contain valuable historical nuggets."[435] That minimalist approach makes sense in terms of proving the "historical case for Jesus' radical self-understanding and resurrection," but it does seem that Christians want (and need) more than that to have a sure understanding of orthodox doctrine.

A second approach is to argue that the early Christians used the wrong tests in determining the biblical books but still got it right (at least for the New Testament). Michael Kruger, one of the Reformed theologians I mentioned earlier, opposes any sort of "external" test of canonicity, since he views it as undermining Scripture. Instead, he claims:

> The canon, as God's word, is not just true, but the criterion of truth. It is an *ultimate* authority. So, how do we offer an account of how we know that an ultimate authority is, in fact, the ultimate authority? If we try to validate an ultimate authority by appealing to some other authority, then we have just shown that it is not really the ultimate authority. Thus, for ultimate authorities to be ultimate authorities, they have to be the standard for their own authentication.[436]

The argument here is logically unsound. St. John says that "Jesus did many other signs in the presence of the disciples, which are not written in this book; but these are written that you may believe that Jesus is the Christ, the Son of God, and that believing you may have life in his name" (John 20:30–31). John is hoping we will believe in Christ on the basis of his Gospel. Following Kruger's logic, does that mean that John is saying Christ "is not really the ultimate authority," but that his own Gospel is higher?

Regardless of the logical flaws, Kruger's commitment to the idea that the Bible must be the "ultimate authority" leads him to the position that "what is needed, then, is a canonical model that does not ground the New Testament canon in an external authority, but seeks to ground the canon in the only place it could be grounded, its own authority."[437] Kruger admits that his model suffers from "a certain degree of circularity,"[438] but he claims that this is unavoidable. But that's not the only problem: he also admits that "Scripture does not *directly* tell us which books belong in the New Testament canon."[439]

Kruger's solution is to propose "three attributes of canonicity: (1) divine qualities (canonical books bear the 'marks' of divinity), (2) corporate reception (canonical books are recognized by the Church as a whole), and (3) apostolic origins (canonical books are the result of the redemptive-historical activity of the apostles)."[440] Kruger hasn't fixed the problem he cites: he's still reliant upon the external standards of "corporate reception" and "apostolic origins." (Remember, it's on the basis of the early Church's testimony that we know that these books are genuinely apostolic.) What he's added is a third standard, "divine quality," which is vague, subjective, and question-begging.

To be clear, I believe that the books of Scripture do bear "divine qualities." What I deny is that individual Christians have such exquisite spiritual faculties that they can reliably discern these qualities, given that the early Christians sometimes disagreed over which books belonged in the Bible. This additional criterion is also unnecessary, since Kruger says that "any book with apostolic origins is a book constituted by the Holy Spirit and therefore will possess divine qualities."[441] To the extent that Kruger's model works, then, it's because it's just cleverly repackaging the means by which the early Christians actually determined which books belong in the canon of Scripture.

A third approach is to say we should just trust that God worked it out. The Reformed theologian Robert L. Reymond is skeptical of canonical tests, saying that "scholarship has not been able to establish a set of criteria for canonicity which does not at the same time threaten to undermine the New Testament canon as it has come down to us."[442] Like Kruger, Reymond rejects any tests reliant upon an authority external to Scripture (even if they work in producing the correct canon) because of his theological priors. But since he seems to be rejecting any rational basis upon which to accept the New Testament, he asks himself, "How can the Church be certain, without a direct statement from God on the matter, that it was only these particular books that he intended should be canonical? How can one be certain that the New Testament does not include a book that should not have been included or that it fails to include a book that should have been included? How can one be certain that the New Testament canon is even closed?"[443] Reymond answers the question this way:

> To such questions no answers can be given that will fully satisfy the mind that desires to think autonomously, that is, independently from Scripture. For regardless of

whether or not the Christian scholar thinks he possesses the one right criterion or the one right list of criteria for a given book's canonicity, at some point—and if at no other point, at least at the point of the established number, namely, twenty-seven New Testament books, not twenty-six or twenty-eight—the Christian must accept by faith that the Church, under the providential guidance of God's Spirit, got the number and the "list" right since God did not provide the Church with a specific list of New Testament books.[444]

There's a certain absurdity in criticizing people for thinking "independently from Scripture" for trying to figure out which books belong in Scripture. Reymond's theological priors seem to tear the Bible apart, by leaving it uncertain which books do and don't belong. Yet he responds to the (hypothetical) critics pointing this out by essentially calling their faith into question. It's also confusing to appeal to "the providential guidance of God's Spirit" working through the early Church while arguing that the early Christians shouldn't have used the tests they did—and that those tests don't actually work.

It's perfectly reasonable to say God preserves orthodoxy by working through the Church in a way that we can't neatly reduce to simple tests. But that would seem to be an argument in favor of the proposition that the early Church (including its universally held views on baptism, the Eucharist, and the structure of the Church) is reliable and trustworthy. At the very least, it would seem to entail that the Church got the canon of Scripture right.

Yet, strangely, Reymond doesn't think this. In arguing that we have exactly the right New Testament canon, he says that "the Third Council of Carthage demanded that nothing be read in the church under the title of divine Scripture except the 'canonical' books, and then it affirmed precisely the current collection of twenty-seven New Testament books as the New Testament canon. And because of the near-universal Christian conviction which has prevailed ever since then that the Lord of the Church had given these specific books and only these books to his people as the New Testament canon, the Church for the last 1,600 years has restricted the New Testament canon to the twenty-seven commonly received New Testament books."[445] But Reymond thinks the Third Council of Carthage actually got the biblical canon *wrong*, by including seven Old Testament books that he (quoting the *Westminster Confession*) considers as "not being of divine inspiration" and "no part of the canon of the Scripture," and therefore, they "are of no authority in the Church of God, nor to be any otherwise approved, or made use of, than other human writings."[446] So why doesn't Reymond's argument hold equally well against his own position, since from "the point of the established number . . . the Christian must accept by faith that the Church, under the providential guidance of God's Spirit, got the number and the 'list' right"?

The final approach is simply to pick and choose, without worrying about intellectual consistency. For instance, on the authorship of the Gospel of John, D.A. Carson writes that "even if Irenaeus, toward the end of the second century, is amongst the strongest, totally unambiguous witnesses, his personal connection with Polycarp, who knew John, means the distance in terms of personal memories is not very great."[447] But he doesn't take that same stance when it comes to other doctrines, like the Eucharist. In fact, later in the same book, he gets to the question of how to interpret

John 6 and admits that St. Ignatius "adopts a sacramentarian stance" on the Eucharist (calling it "the medicine of immorality, and the antidote which prevents us from dying, but a cleansing remedy driving away evil, [which causes] that we should live in God through Jesus Christ"), to which Carson replies:

> If John was not a sacramentarian, how could so near a contemporary and (presumably) a disciple use such language? But the argument is not convincing. Ignatius betrays a number of shifts that take us beyond anything the New Testament says. For instance, he introduces us to monarchical bishops who oversee several churches, though there is no evidence of such an office in the New Testament. He insists that where the bishop is, there is the church, though the New Testament writers would be unhappy with such a statement. In this and several other areas, Ignatius can be no sure guide to what John thought. Anyone who has followed theological developments in the twentieth century, let alone the sixteenth or the first, does not need convincing that major changes can be introduced in the space of twenty years, even by disciples of a revered leader.[448]

So Irenaeus can be trusted in 180 because he's still close to the time of the apostles, and John→ Polycarp→ Irenaeus is not a very great distance. But we can't trust Ignatius on how to understand John, because 107 is too late, and John→ Ignatius is meaningless, since "disciples of a revered leader" might introduce new doctrines. To put the matter another way, if Carson is right that major doctrinal errors ("shifts") occurred by the first decade of the 100s, of the sort that "the New Testament writers would be unhappy with," on what basis do we trust these erroneous Christians' theological *descendants* at the close of the second century? After all, remember that Irenaeus agrees with Ignatius about the Eucharist and even quotes him approvingly.[liv]

---

liv "As a certain man of ours [St. Ignatius] said, when he was condemned to the wild beasts because of his testimony with respect to God: 'I am the wheat of Christ, and am ground by the teeth of the wild beasts, that I may be found the pure bread of God.'" Irenaeus, *Against Heresies*, book 5, ch. 28, ANF 1:557. Ignatius's imagery here is eucharistic, but my point in citing it is simply to show St. Irenaeus's awareness of, and esteem for, Ignatius.

But Can We Trust the Early Christians?

SO FAR, we've looked at what the earliest Christians believed about theology, worship, the nature and structure of the Church, and the Gospels. In particular, we saw from numerous Christians living and writing before the year 200 that they believed the following:

- We are born again in the saving waters of baptism, in which we receive the gift of the Holy Spirit and become part of the Church.

- The Eucharist is the true flesh and blood of Jesus Christ, and their liturgies were structured around offering God the eucharistic sacrifice.

- Each true church had a bishop at its head.

- There were four inspired Gospels: Matthew, Mark, Luke, and John.

But we've seen more than this. In each of the above cases, these early Christians report that they're teaching what the apostles taught them. That means we cannot simply say, "Maybe they changed their minds about the best way to structure the Church," or "Maybe they decided to write a fourth Gospel so there would be an even number." They didn't view these as matters up for debate. Instead, they were beliefs and practices to be received and lived out. If the early Christians can be trusted, then we modern Christians should also share their theology, their worship, their Church, and their Gospels. In short, all Christians should be Catholics.

But that's a big *if*. How do we know that we *can* trust them? In this final chapter, I hope to answer three questions toward that end.

First, how do we know that the Christians we've looked at in this book speak for more than just themselves?

Second, how do we know that the early Christians knew what they were talking about? After all, these Christians weren't perfect. William Perkins, the "father of Puritanism," posed the question this way: even if "the ancient Fathers of the primitive Church avouch in their writings that they are apostolic traditions . . . how shall I know and be certain in conscience that the Fathers, subject to error, in saying so, have not erred?"[449]

Third, are we using this early Christian witness arbitrarily? Jean Daillé, a seventeenth-century Huguenot (French Calvinist) preacher, argued that "neither the Church of Rome nor the Protestants acknowledge the Fathers for their judges in points of religion; both of them rejecting such of their opinions and practices as are not suited to their taste."[450] So are Catholics guilty of picking and choosing what they believe from the early Christians—or are they taking a principled stance?

Always, Everywhere, and by All

One reason it's important to listen to the early Christians is that, left to their own devices, people don't interpret the

Bible the same way. As St. Vincent of Lérins put it back in 434,[lv] "Novatian expounds Scripture after his fashion, Photinus after another, Sabellius, after another," etc.[451] Vincent is listing early heretics: Novatian claimed that baptized Christians who fall into grave sin cannot be saved, Photinus denied the Incarnation, and Sabellius denied the Trinity, yet each of them (and several other heretics whom Vincent names) thought that the Bible supported their ideas.

What they were missing was not the true *text* of Scripture, but the *meaning*. So how do we ensure that we don't stray from the true meaning of Scripture?

To make sure that this doesn't happen to us, Vincent stresses that "great care is to be taken that we hold that which has been believed everywhere, always, and by all."[452] He thus offers three tools: *universality* ("the one true faith which the whole Church throughout the world professes"), *antiquity* (not departing from "those senses which it is manifest that our holy elders and fathers generally held"), and *consent* (holding to the views in antiquity "held by all, or at any rate, almost all, the priests and doctors together").[453] These three tools work together against heresy, as he explains:

> What, then, shall a Catholic Christian do, if some small part of the Church cut itself off from the communion of the universal faith? What, indeed, but prefer the soundness of the whole body to the pestiferous and corrupt member? Then shall he take care to adhere to antiquity, which is now utterly incapable of seduction by any fraud of novelty. What if in antiquity itself error be detected, of two

---

lv   Vincent is writing too late to be within the scope of the early Christians we've looked at (most of whom are writing pre-200), but he's a good early resource for telling us how to interpret those earlier Christians.

or three men, or possibly of one city, or even of some one province? Then shall he, by all means, take heed to prefer whatever has been decreed universally by the ancient universal Church, to the rashness and ignorance of a few.[454]

Many Protestant authors misstate Vincent's rule.[lvi] The Reformed theologian Keith Mathison, for instance, says that the Catholic Church claims "to accept as true tradition that which has been taught always, everywhere, and by all. The problem with this claim is the historical fact that the doctrines and practices peculiar to Rome have not been taught always, everywhere, and by all."[455] But Vincent's argument is not that we can believe *only* things that the early Christians were unanimous on. He even says explicitly that a case may arise "in which nothing of the sort can be found."[456] (For instance, the early Christians were not unanimous about which books belonged in the New Testament.) Instead, Vincent is arguing that where a consensus *does* exist, we should treat it as authoritative, since to stray from it is to stray from historic Christianity—a clear sign that one is drifting into heresy.[lvii]

The advantage to Vincent's rule is twofold. First, it gives some guardrails in our own interpretation of Scripture. If I read the New Testament and think it means something contrary to what everyone else thinks, I can be sure that I'm wrong. Second, it gives us principles in our approach to the

---

lvi   This is nothing new: St. John Henry Newman complained about the "unfair interpretation of Vincentius" by Anglican authors back in the nineteenth century. John Henry Newman, *An Essay on the Development of Christian Doctrine*, 7th ed. (London: Longmans, Green, and Co., 1890), p. 19.

lvii This is a lower standard than the one Mathison falsely claims for Vincent, but it's a standard that Protestantism still cannot meet. Whether it's regenerative baptism or the sacrifice of the Mass or the necessity of bishops or countless other issues not explored in this book, we find "all, or at any rate, almost all" of the early Christians believing in practicing in a particular way, only for Protestants to come along more than a 1,000 years later and claim that everyone misunderstood Jesus and the apostles.

writings of the early Christians. I can't just pick and choose the teachings that happen to agree with me. Instead, I should be looking for the consensus of the broader Church. But how do we know where that consensus exists? To answer that, we need to unpack the difference between theologians and eyewitnesses and to see the role of the "dogs that didn't bark."

Theologians and Eyewitnesses

The early Christians we've looked at in this book are often doing the same three things: offering their own theological opinions, reporting what their church (and the broader Church) believes, and highlighting which teachings the apostles had expressly given them. For the sake of clarity, we can call them *theologians* when they're sharing their own opinions and *eyewitnesses* when they're testifying to the consensus of the early Church or to what they have received from the apostles.[lviii]

Take the Calvinist idea of *double predestination*, for example. The Westminster Confession of Faith (1647) puts the belief this way: "By the decree of God, for the manifestation of his glory, some men and angels are predestinated unto everlasting life; and others foreordained to everlasting death."[457] In this view, faith doesn't save. Instead, saved people get the gift of faith. Reformed thinkers going all the way back to John Calvin will cite St. Augustine of Hippo (354–430) in support of this doctrine,[458] and modern Calvinists will claim that this view of predestination reflects "the position of the Church from its early years to more recent history."[459]

---

lviii This distinction is found in Scripture. Writing to the Corinthians, Paul distinguishes between those teachings he "received from the Lord" (1 Cor. 11:23, 15:3) and those that are his own personal view, not from the Lord (7:12).

The truth is that Augustine has a well-documented shift in his thinking about predestination in the mid-390s, amid his battles against the Pelagian heresy.[460] Although Augustine was never a Calvinist,[461] his later works on predestination *do* sound more "Calvinistic." The change in thought is first seen in a lengthy letter he wrote in response to questions from his friend St. Simplician, the bishop of Milan. Simplician asks him to explain Romans 9:10–29, to which Augustine responds,

> You ask that the whole passage be discussed, and indeed, it is rather obscure. But, to be sure, I know your regard for me and am certain that you would not bid me expound that passage unless you had prayed the Lord to give me the ability to do so. With confidence in his help I approach the task.[462]

In other words, Augustine is *not* claiming to be passing on a clear teaching that was handed on to him or giving voice to the widespread belief of the Church. Instead, he's making an educated (and prayerful) guess, one that he would later retract in part.[463] He's acting as a theologian, not as an eyewitness.

In fact, Augustine's later views *aren't* what earlier Christians believed about predestination.[464] Shawn Wright, of Southern Baptist Theological Seminary, went looking for "'Calvinists' Before Calvin" but had to conclude that prior to Augustine, "the earliest Christian writers after the close of the New Testament canon did not stress God's predestination of his elect."[465] This leads him to ask, "Why did some great thinkers in the history of the Church (people like Justin Martyr, Irenaeus, Tertullian, and Athanasius), who thought deeply and wrote thoughtfully, not address a doctrine that seems so apparent throughout both the Old and the New Testaments?"[466]

But it's not just that they didn't "address" Calvinist beliefs about total human depravity and double predestination; it's that they actively *denied* them. The idea that you are predetermined to be good or evil, apart from anything you say or do, was popular in the first few centuries after Christ—just not among Christians. Instead, it was popular among different pagan groups, including "astrologers, Gnostics, and Stoics."[467] St. Justin Martyr responds to the idea in the mid-100s by explaining it's not what Christians believe, since

> we have learned from the prophets and we hold it as true that punishments and chastisements and good rewards are distributed according to the merit of each man's actions. Were this not the case, and were all things to happen according to the decree of fate, there would be nothing at all in our power. If fate decrees that this man is to be good and that one wicked, then neither is the former to be praised nor the latter to be blamed.[468]

That doesn't mean that the early Christians ignored (or rejected) the biblical idea of predestination. They rejected only the pagan (and later Calvinist) interpretation of that idea. As Craig Keener explains, "most early Church Fathers predicated predestination on foreknowledge in the sense that God's 'choice depends on our foreseen response to his invitation.'"[469] In other words, they believed in a type of predestination that didn't involve God ignoring our faith and works (or lack thereof).

Nor was Justin alone in understanding Christian teaching in this way. Wright quotes the Dutch Calvinist theologian Herman Bavinck, who says that the view of the early Christians was that, "though humans had been more or less corrupted by sin, they remained free and were able to accept the proffered grace of God. The Church's teaching did not include a doctrine of absolute predestination and irresistible grace."[470] Here, the early Christians don't appear to be theologizing or giving their personal opinions; rather, they appear to be speaking as eyewitnesses to what was already (in the 100s) the widespread belief of the Church, something they "learned from the prophets." Augustine is arguably a superior *theologian* to Justin Martyr and the other earlier writers. But Justin and the others are in a better position as *eyewitnesses*, since they know which teachings could and couldn't be traced to the apostles.

So how can Calvinists defend as central a doctrine unknown to (and even rejected by) the earliest Christians? Wright suggests that perhaps the early Christians "were just wrong in their interpretation of the biblical text and the conclusions they drew from it."[471] After all, "they erred in other doctrines (at least this confessional Baptist thinks they did), such as in their swift move toward episcopal authority in their churches, some of the magical views they associated with the Lord's Supper, their turn toward infant baptism, and some of their overly allegorical biblical interpretation."[472] There's a certain logic to Wright's dismissive attitude toward the early Christians: if you're going to ignore or reject what the earliest Christians believed about so many other basic Christian doctrines, what's one more? But this attitude reveals how far Protestantism has drifted from the faith of the early Christians.

The Dogs That Didn't Bark

Another way we can tell that the Church (and not just a handful of spokesmen) was Catholic is because of the dogs that didn't bark. That expression derives from a Sherlock

Holmes detective story called "Silver Blaze." Investigating the theft of a racehorse, Holmes points out "the curious incident of the dog in the night-time." When the Scotland Yard detective protests that "the dog did nothing in the night-time," Holmes responds, "That was the curious incident."[473]

At the end of the story, he reveals what he meant: "a dog was kept in the stables, and yet, though someone had been in and had fetched out a horse, he had not barked enough to arouse the two lads in the loft. Obviously the midnight visitor was someone whom the dog knew well."[474] In other words, there are times where the lack of a response is telling.

Imagine that Protestantism is true and that the apostles taught some form of (what we now call) Protestantism to their followers: that baptism and the Eucharist are just symbols, that being "born again" is a matter of a personal commitment to Christ rather than anything to do with baptism, that churches should be governed by elders and not a single bishop, and so on. In that world, we would see two things. First, we would see the early Christians saying things that can't be harmonized with Catholicism. After all, listen to a Protestant preacher discuss baptism or the Eucharist, and likely it won't be long before he says (or does)[lix] something with which Catholics can't agree. Yet, when we read the writings of the early Christians, there's a lack of anything

---

lix   To give an example in the opposite direction, it's clear that the early Christians brought the Eucharist to the sick and homebound. Justin Martyr says the deacons commune those present for the liturgy, "and to those who are absent they carry away a portion." Justin Martyr, *First Apology* 65, ANF 1:185. This is also borne out in the lives of saints like Tarcisius, who was martyred while bringing Communion to the sick. Yet Lutherans have traditionally argued that this was "a bad habit of some in the early Church." Salomon Deyling, quoted in (and translated by) Roland F. Ziegler, "Should Lutherans Reserve the Consecrated Elements for the Communion of the Sick?," *Concordian Theological Quarterly*, vol. 67, no. 2 (April 2003), p. 132. But where are examples of widespread liturgical practices contrary to Catholicism?

distinctly Protestant in these areas.[lx] That dog doesn't bark.

And there's a second dog we should find barking. As we've seen in this book, prominent early Christians were saying explicitly Catholic things right away, at the beginning of the history of the Church. If this had been a departure from what the apostles had so recently taught, surely there would have been an outcry.

Imagine if the Protestant televangelist Pat Robertson went before Regent University (where he serves as CEO) and declared that from now on, they were going to replace Protestant services with the Catholic Mass so they could offer the true sacrifice of Christ's flesh and blood to the Father. Oh, and by the way, don't forget to submit to your bishop because without the bishop, there is no church. Would the students simply nod along? Or might these Protestants . . . *protest*? Yet there is no protest in the early Church— apparently because there were no Protestants.

Some Protestant theologians have noticed the strangely silent dogs of the early Church and tried to explain them away. The nineteenth-century Scottish theologian William Cunningham argues that it's "by no means certain that important changes of doctrine may not have taken place in what is called the early Church, without our having any very specific evidence regarding them."[475] Put plainly, he is suggesting that almost immediately, the Church fell into heresy, but we don't have evidence of this because it happened "privily"—that is, secretly.[lxi]

---

lx   To be sure, there are times where an author says something generic enough that both Catholics and Protestants can agree with it. What's missing is anything obviously Protestant.

lxi If the "creeping heresy" theories we explored in chapter one explain this away because the change happened too slowly, Cunningham's theory seems to be that it happened so quickly that we didn't notice it.

How does Cunningham defend such a theory? First, he says that "the history of the Church abundantly confirms what the Scripture gives us reason to expect, viz., that errors and heresies may creep in *privily*—the enemy sowing the tares while men are sleeping." That's a reference to Christ's parable of the weeds among the wheat. But in that parable, the weeds didn't replace the wheat. The enemy introduces weeds, but the wheat still "came up and bore grain" (Matt. 13:26). Nor are the good silent once they see the weeds: "the servants of the householder came and said to him, 'Sir, did you not sow good seed in your field? How then has it weeds?'" (v. 27). If anything, the parable proves the opposite: that good Christians wouldn't allow the devil to overcome the Church with heresy without speaking out!

Cunningham's second argument is historical: "the history of the Church fully proves, moreover, that very considerable changes may be effected in the prevalent opinions of a church or nation, and of course of many churches or nations, in a comparatively short period of time; and without, perhaps, our being able to trace them to any very definite or palpable cause."[476] Cunningham offers no evidence of either "churches or nations" that rapidly changed without leaving a trail of historical evidence. To be sure, there are plenty of times in which a church or nation radically changes,[lxii] but where are the times where a radical change happened both quickly and quietly?

---

lxii The Puritans founded Congregationalist churches that became Unitarian, denying the Trinity, within the span of about a century. That's a dramatic change, but it didn't happen quietly—rather, "it was one of the most bitter and significant controversies in American religious history," and we can trace four successive stages of the controversy. David Raymond, "Echoes of a Distant Thunder?: The Unitarian Controversy in Maine,1734–1833," *Maine History*, vol. 46, no. 1 (2011), p. 5. Likewise, there were rapid and radical cultural shifts in the U.S. (and many Western countries) during the Sexual Revolution in the mid-twentieth century, but these hardly went unnoticed.

In any case, the question isn't whether we can trace the changes in the Church to some "very definite or palpable cause"; it's whether we can prove that any change occurred. The problem isn't that Protestants don't know exactly *why* the early Christians jettisoned their twofold Church structure for a threefold structure with bishops. It's that they can't point to any clear evidence that this ever happened in the first place.

What Cunningham shows us is that there's a serious evidentiary problem for Protestantism: Where were the early Christians saying distinctly Protestant things? And where were the early Christians protesting the distinctly Catholic things that Ignatius, Justin, Irenaeus, and the rest were saying? The most logical way of reading this evidence is that the early Christian churches were Catholic, which is why they greeted the writings of people like Ignatius warmly instead of "correcting" them for being too Catholic as Protestants would have done.

Are We Superior to the Early Christians?

But if the early Church was the Catholic Church, why can't we say that Christians just lost their way early on? That's the argument many Mormon and Protestant theologians make. In Mormon theology, this idea is expressed in terms of a *Great Apostasy* that followed the death of the apostles:

Following the death of Jesus Christ, wicked people persecuted and killed many Church members. Other Church members drifted from the principles taught by Jesus Christ and his apostles. The apostles were killed, and priesthood authority—including the keys to direct and receive revelation for the Church—was taken from the earth. Because the Church was no longer led by priesthood authority, error crept into Church teachings. Good people and much truth remained, but the gospel as established by Jesus Christ was lost. This period is called the Great Apostasy.[477]

But in 1820, "Father in Heaven again chose a prophet to restore the gospel and the priesthood to the earth. That prophet's name was Joseph Smith."[478]

One problem with this story is that it's really two stories that don't agree with one another. The first story is of the early Church, 2,000 years ago. As Scripture says, Jesus built the Church "upon the foundation of the apostles and prophets, Christ Jesus himself being the cornerstone, in whom the whole structure is joined together and grows into a holy temple in the Lord" (Eph. 2:20–21). But according to Mormons, the followers of Jesus quickly lost the structure of the Church that he intended, and each generation drifted farther from the fullness of the gospel. The first story, in other words, is a tragedy.

But then there's a second story, a story beginning in 1820, in which God (through Joseph Smith) restores "the complete gospel."[479] If the second story were like the first story, you'd then hear about how Joseph Smith's teachings were quickly corrupted by his followers, and the priesthood was lost again. But the second story isn't a tragedy: it's about how the gospel and the Church were restored, and then stayed restored from one generation to the next.

It's not clear how these two stories can be reconciled. Is Joseph Smith superior to Jesus? Were his followers superior to the apostles? Were Mormons in the nineteenth century holier than the early Christian martyrs? If none of those things are true, then why would a Church directly started by Jesus quickly fail, but a church restarted by Smith endure forever?

My point here isn't exclusively about Mormonism. Many Protestants, including theologians and Church historians, settle for a version of Church history that sounds more like Mormonism than Christianity. The seventeenth-century Protestant preacher Jean Daillé, whom we met earlier, wrote an entire book on how to approach the "Church Fathers" in deciding religious controversies. In it, he argues:

> Now according to this hypothesis, which, as I conceive, is equally common to all Protestants, the doctrine of the Church must necessarily have suffered some alteration in the second age of Christianity, by admitting the mixture of some new matter into its faith and discipline: and so likewise in the third age some other corruption must necessarily have crept in: and so in the fourth, fifth, and the rest that follow; the Christian religion continually losing something of its original purity and simplicity, and on the other side still contracting all along some new impurities, till at length it came to the highest degree of corruption.[480]

In other words, the standard Protestant narrative (as expressed by Daillé)[481] is basically the same as the first of the two Mormon stories: Jesus built the Church, but it fell apart almost immediately. What's more, this theological erosion "must necessarily" have occurred, because the second generation of Christians simply could not be counted on to faithfully preserve what their parents taught them, even though their parents were taught directly by the apostles. This story is a tragedy, and its logical conclusion is a complete loss of faith in Christianity. For if the second generation of Christians couldn't figure out the gospel, and the third generation was worse, and Daillé is writing some 1,600 years later, what hope could he (or we) possibly have of knowing what Christ really taught?

But Daillé has a second story, beginning with the Reformation, in which Protestants "have now at last, by the guidance of the Scriptures," restored the Church "to the self-same state wherein it was at the beginning; and have, as it were, fixed again upon its true and proper hinge."[482] For some reason, it's not the case that the second generation of Protestants "must necessarily" have fallen farther from the truth than the original Reformers in the same way that the second generation of Christians allegedly fell from the truth of Christ.

Daillé explains that this is because, unlike early Christianity, Protestant "doctrine is the very same that was in the time of the apostles, as being taken immediately out of their books."[483] By this reasoning, all that the Christians of the second century needed to avoid the "progress of corruption" was to ignore what they had learned about the apostles from their elders (those who had learned from the apostles in person) and rely only upon the information that could be found in books.

Of course, Protestantism isn't really "taken immediately out of" the Bible, which is why serious Protestants read biblical commentaries and works of spirituality and theology and try to educate themselves beyond their own best guesses about what the biblical texts mean.[lxiii] No one, including the Reformers, ever arrived at a full-fledged Protestant theology simply by picking up a Bible to read by himself. If you could arrive at a complete and orthodox faith that way, how did it

---

lxiii Daillé's description of Protestant theology reads like wishful thinking. In what other areas of life does expertise come only from reading the book and not listening to experts in the field? Imagine a constitutional lawyer who decided to skip law school because he could read the Constitution on his own, or a Shakespeare scholar who refused to read any prior scholarship.

take Christians 1,500 years to realize this? Moreover, if what Daillé calls the "pure and simple doctrine of the apostles"[484] was immediately obvious from the biblical texts, how did anyone (let alone *everyone*) fall into doctrinal error in the first place? Why didn't the first generation of Christians simply say, "Everything you need to know is in the text, so don't worry about Tradition"?

Daillé's description of Scripture contrasts starkly with the Bible's description of Scripture. In Acts 8, St. Philip (one of the first deacons) is inspired by the Holy Spirit to approach a man reading the book of Isaiah and ask, "Do you understand what you are reading?" The man replies, "How can I, unless someone guides me?" and he invites Philip to sit with him in his chariot (vv. 26–31). By Daillé's reasoning, the man should instead have objected that getting Christianity from Philip (who got it from the apostles, who got it from Christ)[lxiv] was a clear example of "the progress of corruption in religion," and that he would instead just get his beliefs "immediately" from the book (in this case, Isaiah). But the man in Acts 8 saw what Daillé failed to see: how can we hope to arrive at an orthodox interpretation of Scripture unless someone guides us?

In the end, we come back to the same types of questions we come to with Mormonism. Was Martin Luther superior to Jesus? Were the Reformers superior to the apostles? Are modern Protestants holier than the early Christian martyrs? And if none of those things is true, then why would a church directly started by Jesus quickly fail and a church restarted by the Reformers endure forever?

---

lxiv When the Samaritans converted at Philip's preaching, the Church sent St. Peter and St. John to administer what we now call the sacrament of confirmation (Acts 8:14–17). This suggests that the "Philip" in question is the deacon (6:5) and not the apostle (1:13), since the latter could have administered the sacrament himself.

Daillé is not alone in imagining that modern Protestants understand Christianity better than the early Christians did. John Piper argues that "we are in a better position today to know Jesus Christ than anyone who lived from A.D. 100 to 300. They had only parts of the New Testament rather than the collected whole."[485] Piper singles out A.D. 100 as "a precarious and embattled time" since the apostle John died that year, meaning that "the churches had neither the collected New Testament nor a living apostle."

By Piper's reasoning, we are better able to understand John's Gospel now, reading it (usually in translation) more than 1,900 years later, than were the first recipients of the Gospel, who knew and walked with the man, whom he personally taught for years, and who had the ability to ask him questions when they were confused about the meaning of something he said or wrote. This is a bit like insisting that we know more about Paris than Parisians because we've read a travel guide. When we read the book of Acts, we're reading *about* the early Church, whereas the Christians of 100 lived it.

Piper argues that "the Church did not rescue the New Testament from neglect and abuse. The New Testament rescued the early Church from instability and error."[486] Although it's true that these Christians didn't "rescue the New Testament from neglect and abuse," that's only because they weren't neglecting or abusing the New Testament in the first place. As W. Bradley Shelton (himself a Southern Baptist theologian) explains of St. Irenaeus:

Perhaps most important is [Irenaeus's] treatment of Scripture, which was not yet in canonical form throughout Christian communities. Irenaeus successfully appeals to a notion of catholicity, that most churches everywhere in the late second century see a certain collection of writings to be Scripture. He helps to prove that churches were not in disarray, uncertain of authoritative texts of the Faith, but generally united in agreeing on most books and especially not agreeing on an entirely different and threatening genre of books: Gnostic writings.[487]

In other words, neither the "neglect and abuse" of the New Testament nor the "instability and error" of second-century Christianity is borne out by the historical evidence. Even though the precise contours of the New Testament weren't settled yet, the core of it (including the Gospels) was well established, and these early Christians were conversant in Scripture and sound theology. After all, as we saw in the previous chapter, we know which books are Gospels (the same is true for the rest of the New Testament) because we trust the orthodoxy and reliability of these early Christians.[lxv]

Standing on the Shoulders of Giants

Fortunately, some Protestants perceive the dangers of treating the early Christians this way. They grasp that not only did these first generations of Christians prove their fidelity, even to the point of the shedding of blood, but they laid the theological foundations upon which all mainstream Christianity is built. We have an orthodox sense of the mystery of the Trinity (three persons in one essence) and of the natures of Jesus (a single divine person with two natures, fully God and fully man) because they put the pieces together. It's true

---

lxv In Piper's version of history, "the New Testament" comes along and saves an erring Church. But if the Church was in error, how can we trust the Church that the books really are apostolic?

that we may sometimes see things that they didn't, but only because we're perched upon their shoulders.

These Protestants understand that those who reject or ignore the theology of the early Church are doomed to (at best) continually reinvent the wheel or (at worst) resurrect old heresies. Joel R. Beeke, president of Puritan Reformed Theological Seminary, puts it this way:

> When we survey Church history, we discover giants of the Faith, such as Aurelius Augustine (354–430), Martin Luther (1483–1546), John Calvin (1509–1564), John Owen (1616–1683), and Jonathan Edwards (1703–1758). Amid those giants the Puritans also rise as giants of exegetical ability, intellectual achievement, and profound piety. Upon this mountain our Reformed "city" is built. We are where we are because of our history, though we are dwarves on the shoulders of giants.[488]

Beeke's heart is in the right place in trying to call Protestants to recognize something deeper than the ephemeral present and to rediscover a theology rooted in more than one's own personal reading of the Bible. But even he is prone to speaking as if the Church began with Luther in the sixteenth century rather than with Christ in the first. And the figures he draws upon from the last 500 years are exclusively Protestants who rejected the Church of the first fifteen centuries. His "city" is ultimately built on a foundation of sand, not rock. Even in his well-intentioned call to "rediscover giants of the Faith," Beeke illustrates a problem highlighted by Northern Baptist Theological Seminary's Scot McKnight:

> Most Evangelicals know almost nothing about the early Fathers, and what they do know (they think) supports what

they already believe, so why bother studying them? When it comes to realities, however, few have read even a page of the Fathers. However, very few Evangelicals are drawn to either the Fathers or the medieval theologians to strengthen their faith and interpretation. The *only* theologian from this era most of them bother reading[lxvi] is St. Augustine (whom they hesitantly call "saint" out of courtesy).[489]

It's hard to stand on the shoulders of giants if you ignore (or worse, try to topple) the even bigger giants on whose shoulders *they're* standing.

Dupes, Deceivers, or . . . Devout Catholics

In *Mere Christianity*, C.S. Lewis famously poses a *trilemma*, sometimes called the *Liar, Lunatic, or Lord* argument, which works like this: Jesus presents himself as the Messiah, as the Son of God, and even as God. Given this, the three ways we can make sense of him are to conclude that he was *delusional* (believing he was God when he wasn't), *deceptive* (knowing he wasn't God but duping his followers into believing he was), or *divine*. The argument is straightforward enough, but Lewis thought it important "to prevent anyone saying the really foolish thing that people often say about him: 'I'm ready to accept Jesus as a great moral teacher, but I don't accept his claim to be God.'"[490] After all, "a man who was merely a man and said the sort of things Jesus said would not be a great moral teacher." He concludes that we must not "come with any patronizing nonsense about his being a great human teacher.

---

lxvi To be clear, I'm *not* suggesting that Augustine is the only theologian from the first three quarters of the Church's history whom Beeke has bothered reading. It seems more likely that Augustine is the only early Christian he could count on his Reformed readers both recognizing and accepting.

He has not left that open to us. He did not intend to."[491]

I'd like to close this book by proposing another trilemma of sorts. We have seen that the early Christians were Catholics. Although we didn't look at every aspect of their belief and practice, I hope you've seen enough to realize that they believed what Catholics believe (for instance, on the saving nature of baptism), that they worshiped as Catholics worship (with the holy sacrifice of the Mass), that their churches were Catholic churches (complete with bishops), and that their Gospels were the same four Gospels that Catholics use today.

There are three ways to respond to all of this. First, we could conclude that the early Christians were *duped*. Someone somehow tricked them into thinking false things about Christianity. As we saw in chapter one, it's difficult to see how anyone can settle for this theory because the timeline is just too short. I might fool someone about ancient history, but I'd have a harder time fooling people about the teachings of the apostles when the apostles or the students of those apostles lived among them.

Second, we could conclude that they were themselves *deceivers*, knowingly peddling a false version of Christianity and lying by claiming that they had received this from the apostles when they knew they hadn't. It's hard, though, to square this cynical view of the early Christians with the faithfully selfless lives we know they led.[lxvii]

---

lxvii Pliny, the governor of Pontus/Bithynia in the early second century, wrote to the Emperor Trajan about his experiences with the early Christians. Although Pliny viewed Christianity as generally harmless (saying they were guilty of "nothing else but depraved, excessive superstition"), that didn't stop him from killing those who refused to renounce the Faith. In his words, "In the case of those who were denounced to me as Christians, I have observed the following procedure: I interrogated these as to whether they were Christians; those who confessed I interrogated a second and a third time, threatening them with punishment; those who persisted I ordered executed. For I had no doubt that, whatever the nature of their creed, stubbornness and inflexible obstinacy surely deserve to be punished." Pliny, *Letters*, book 10, in *Roman Civilization: Selected Readings*, vol. 2, 3rd ed., eds. Naphtali Lewis and Meyer Reinhold (New York: Columbia University Press, 1990), pp. 551–552.

It's worth recognizing, too, that if we opt for either of these first two approaches, we can hardly have confidence in the Bible. For how can we trust a bunch of dupes or liars when they tell us they're accurately preserving the writings of the apostles? It does no good to say, "Maybe the Holy Spirit preserved the biblical texts" while expressly denying that he guided the preservation of their *meaning*. The promise Jesus made at the Last Supper is that the Holy Spirit would guide the Church into "all the truth" (John 16:13), not that he would abandon the Church while protecting the book.

Moreover, our trust in the Holy Spirit is based in no small part upon what we read in the same Scripture whose reliability is now in question. And so, concluding that the early Christians are untrustworthy is even *worse* for Protestantism than assuming they're trustworthy.

That leaves us with a third option: that the early Christians, for all of their individual faults, are faithful disciples. They listened attentively to what the apostles taught, they lived by those teachings, and they defended those teachings, no matter the price. And what it looks like to live out what the apostles taught is simply the Catholic Church.

ABOUT THE AUTHOR

KANSAS CITY NATIVE Joe Heschmeyer is a staff apologist for Catholic Answers. A popular author, speaker, blogger, and podcaster, he joined the apostolate in March 2021 after three years as an instructor at Holy Family School of Faith in Overland Park, Kansas.

While at School of Faith, Joe focused primarily on formation for the Kansas City Archdiocese's elementary and high school teachers. He also spent a year helping to manage the Catholic Spiritual Mentorship program.

Prior to his work at School of Faith, he discerned the priesthood from 2012–17 for the Archdiocese of Kansas City. During that time, he earned both a bachelor's degree in philosophy from Kenrick-Glennon Seminary in St. Louis and a baccalaureate degree in sacred theology (S.T.B.) from Rome's Pontifical University of Saint Thomas Aquinas (Angelicum).

A regular contributor to *Catholic Answers Live*, *Catholic Answers Focus*, and *Catholic Answers Magazine* (print and online) even before joining the apostolate, Joe has blogged at his own "Shameless Popery" website and co-hosted a weekly show called "The Catholic Podcast."

To date, he has authored three books, including *Pope Peter* for Catholic Answers Press.

A former practicing attorney in Washington, D.C., Joe received his Juris Doctor degree from Georgetown University in 2010 after earning a bachelor's degree in history from Topeka's Washburn University.

Joe and his wife, Anna, along with their children Stella and James reside in the Kansas City area. In his free time, Joe enjoys reading, listening to podcasts, and tormenting his loved ones with terrible puns.

ENDNOTES

1   Charles Reign Scoville, *Evangelistic Sermons Delivered During the Great Meetings at Pitts-burg and Des Moines* (Des Moines: Christian Union Publishing Company, 1902), p. 24.

2   Id., p. 26.

3   James Aitken Wylie, *The History of Protestantism*, vol. 1 (Lond: Cassell, Petter, Galpin, & Co., 1883), p. 3.

4   Ibid.

5   Mormonism's legitimacy requires a *Great Apostasy*—that is, that both the gospel and orthodox Christianity disappeared from the earth shortly after the death of the apostles, necessitating the "restoration" brought about through Joseph Smith in the nineteenth century. *The Restoration of the Gospel of Jesus Christ* (Salt Lake City: Intellectual Reserve, 2008), p. 8. We take a closer look at this idea in the final chapter of the book.

6   The teaching of the Quran is that the original revelations to the Jews and Christians were inspired but that these revelations were corrupted (which explains why the Quran can speak of Jews and Christians as "people of the Book," even though their scriptures do not constitute part of the Islamic canon). As the Institute of Islamic Knowledge explains, "Islam requires the Muslims to believe in all the prior scriptures including Taurat (To-rah) and Injeel (Gospel / Bible) that they were the true revelations from Allah. Because of not preserving in original languages in written form and translating them in various languages from oral narrations through centuries, human words were mingled with di-vine words, therefore, they lost their pure forms." *What is Islam? Who are the Muslims?* (Houston: The Institute of Islamic Knowledge, 2008), p. 8; see Quran 5:46–48.

7   For instance, Bart Ehrman argues that there was a "major leap" in the twenty years fol-lowing the death of Jesus Christ, "from seeing Jesus as his own disciples did during his ministry, as a Jewish man with an apocalyptic message of coming destruction, to seeing him as something far greater, a preexisting divine being who became human only tem-porarily before being made the Lord of the universe. It was not long after that that Jesus was declared to be the very Word of God made flesh, who was with God at creation and through whom God made all things." Bart Ehrman, *How Jesus Became God: The Exaltation of a Jewish Preacher from Galilee* (New York: HarperOne, 2014), p. 371. But as Larry Hurtado points out, neither the New Testament nor later Christian writings depict Jesus as "a preexisting divine being who became human only temporarily," since "Jesus' assumption of humanity was emphatically portrayed as irrevocable" both in the New Testament and later. Larry Hurtado, "How Jesus became 'God,' per Ehrman," Larry Hurtado's Blog, May 29, 2014, available at larryhurtado.wordpress.com.

8   For instance, Charles Taze Russell, the founder of Jehovah's Witnesses, "taught that after the death of the first-generation apostles, Christianity became corrupt, and ab-sorbed ideas from pagan philosophies, and in particular from Greek thought." George D. Chryssides, "Jehovah's Witnesses: Anticipating Armageddon," in *Handbook of Glob-al Contemporary Christianity*, ed. Stephen Hunt (Leiden: Brill, 2016), p. 425.

9   For almost any historical document from this period, you can find scholarly debates about authorship and dating. I've largely avoided getting into the weeds of those dis-putes, but this document is particularly hard to date, since it is internally anonymous, and we don't find it quoted by other early authors. Generally, scholars place it some-where between A.D. 120 and 310, although you can find more extreme views in both

directions. See Clayton N. Jefford, *The Epistle to Diognetus (with the Fragment of Quadratus)* (Oxford: Oxford University Press, 2013), pp. 15–29.

10   Letter to Diognetus 5, Office of Readings for Wednesday, Easter Week V, pp. 840–42. For an alternate translation, see ANF 1:26–27.

11   Charles Haddon Spurgeon, "The Former and the Latter Rain," July 11, 1869, available at spurgeon.org.

12   Michael J. Kruger, "The Early Christians Were Odd, Too," The Gospel Coalition, November 18, 2017.

13   Ibid.

14   Ibid.

15   Markus Bockmuehl, *The Remembered Peter: In Ancient Reception and Modern Debate* (Tubingen: Mohr Siebeck, 2010), p. 120.

16   Ibid (emphasis in original).

17   Patrick Anderson, "Holy Paper Chase!," *Washington Post*, April 7, 2003.

18   Jehovah's Witnesses make a similar claim about Constantine. A 1998 article in the official Jehovah's Witness magazine *The Watchtower* claims that at the Council of Nicaea, "after two months of furious religious debate, this pagan politician [Constantine] intervened and decided in favor of those who said that Jesus was God." "Constantine the Great—A Champion of Christianity?" *The Watchtower*, March 15, 1998, pp. 26–30.

19   Dan Brown, *The Da Vinci Code* (New York: Anchor Books, 2009), p. 306.

20   Thomas Jefferson to John Adams, August 15, 1820, quoted in Bruce Baden, *Ye will Say I am no Christian* (Amherst: Prometheus Books, 2006), p. 211.

21   Irenaeus, *Against Heresies*, Book 1, preface, ANF 1:315.

22   Jerome, *The Dialogue Against the Luciferians* 28, NPNF 2/6:334.

23   Cf. Stacia McKeever, "A Staff or Not?" in *Demolishing Supposed Bible Contradictions*, vol. 1, ed. Ken Ham (Green Forest, AR: Master Books, 2010), pp. 104–05 (claiming that "the issue can be cleared up studying the Greek words used for provide or take in the original manuscript," before conceding that Luke and Mark use the same verb).

24   I trace this in greater depth in Joe Heschmeyer, "The Bible . . . and Other Traditions," *Catholic Answers Magazine Online*, March 13, 2018.

25   Matthew Barrett, "The Sufficiency of Scripture," The Gospel Coalition, 2020, available at thegospelcoalition.org.

26   Tim Challies, "The Five Tests of False Doctrine," February 6, 2017, available at challies.com.

27   Ibid.

28   Ibid.

29   In introducing his test, Challies presents several popular heretical teachings, from prosperity gospel preachers to Mormon doctrine. But the last teaching he includes is the Catholic teaching on justification: "Roman Catholicism says we are justified by faith, but not by faith alone." Ironically, the Catholic teaching can pass each of Challies's five tests. Scripture says we are "justified by faith apart from works of law" (Rom. 3:28), but not by faith *alone*. As St. James taught, "you see that a man is justified by works and not by faith alone" (James 2:24). Martin Luther, encountering that part of Scripture, concluded that James was "flatly against St. Paul and the all the rest of Scripture in ascribing justification to works." Martin Luther, *Word and Sacrament I*, p. 395, quoted in Martin Foord, "The 'Epistle of Straw': Reflections on Luther and the Epistle of James," *Themelios*, vol. 45, no. 2 (August 2020), p. 294. Luther's disgust with the epistle of James was sufficient that he would later say, "I almost feel like throwing Jimmy [the book of James] into the stove." Luther, *Career of the*

Reformer IV, ed. Helmut T. Lehmann and Lewis W. Spitz, *Luther's Works* 34 (St. Louis: Concordia, 1960), p. 317, quoted in Foord, p. 294. In other words, Luther (the originator of the Protestant teaching that justification is by "faith alone") was emphatic that this teaching *was not* "consistent with the whole" of what modern Protestants accept as Scripture. By Challies's own fivefold test, then, it's the Protestant doctrine of justification by faith *alone* (not the Catholic doctrine of justification by faith) that fails the test of doctrinal orthodoxy.

30   Quoted in Terry Johnson, "Just Me and My Bible?," *Tabletalk Magazine*, March 1, 2015.

31   "Lasting evolutionary change takes about one million years," *Oregon State University*, August 22, 2011, available online at today.oregonstate.edu.

32   "There has been [a] considerable amount of debate on this dating, although this range of years [A.D. 155–160] seems generally acceptable to most scholars." Jackson Lashier, *Irenaeus on the Trinity* (Leiden: Brill, 2014), p. 21, fn. 11. That the account of his martyrdom was written within the year is based in part on the internal evidence of the text itself, which dates Polycarp's death on both the ancient Macedonian ("the second day of the month Xanthicus") and ancient Roman ("the seventh day before the Kalends of May") calendars, and which is written in anticipation of the upcoming "birth-day" (that is, the first anniversary) of the martyr's death. See *The Martyrdom of Polycarp* 18 & 21, ANF 1:43. Cf. Candida Moss, "On the Dating of Polycarp: Rethinking the Place of the *Martyrdom of Polycarp* in the History of Christianity," *Early Christianity* vol. 1, no. 4 (2010), pp. 544–45; *id.*, p. 557, fn. 39. (Moss concedes that the majority view of scholars is that the text is an eyewitness account dating to within a year of Polycarp's death—a view that she rejects—but argues that "a distinction should be drawn between scholars who view *MPol* as an authentic record of events and scholars who offer the more nuanced view that the text is a 'theologized' authentic eyewitness event.")

33   *Martyrdom of Polycarp* 9, ANF 1:41.

34   *Martyrdom of Polycarp* preface & 16, ANF 1:39, 42.

35   Irenaeus, *Against Heresies*, book 3, 3, ANF 1:416.

36   James Ussher, *The Whole Works of the Most Rev. James Ussher, D.D.*, vol. 7 (first published 1641), p. 50.

37   *Martyrdom of Polycarp* 15, ANF 1:42.

38   See Alexander Roberts and James Donaldson, "Introductory Notice," ANF 1:312 (explaining that "the general date assigned to his birth is somewhere between A.D. 120 and A.D. 140"). A fuller examination is provided by Eric Osborn: "There is wide disagreement on the date of his birth, with estimates from those of Dodwell (AD 98), Grabe (108), Tillémont and Lightfoot (120), Ropes (126), Harvey, (130), to those of Dupin, Massuet and Kling (140), Böhringer, Ziegler and others (147). The most probable date lies between 130 and 140. The early estimates ignore the late development of his writing. The early estimates probably make him too young for episcopacy in 177, when he succeeded the ninety-year-old Pothinus. Irenaeus' claim (5.30.3) that the Apocalypse was written towards the end of the reign of Domitian († 96) and near to the time of his own generation makes a year of birth much after 130 improbable, since a generation was commonly reckoned as thirty or forty years." Eric Osborn, *Irenaeus of Lyons* (Cambridge: Cambridge University Press, 2001), p. 2.

39   The city is known in English both as *Lyon* (based on modern French) and *Lyons* (from medieval French), and style guides offer contradictory advice. Cf. Bill Granger, "What's in a Name? Well, Excuuuuse Us, Nueva York, but we Shakawgoans Know," *Chicago Tribune*, June 14, 1987 (noting that the *New York Times* calls it *Lyons*, whereas the *Chicago Tribune* and the *Wall Street Journal* prefer *Lyon*). I've opted for *Lyons* simply

because the saint is typically referred to as *Irenaeus of Lyons*, particularly in older texts. Strict accuracy would demand "Irenaeus of Lugdunum," since that's what the city was called in Irenaeus's day.

40 Jared Secord, "The Cultural Geography of a Greek Christian: Irenaeus from Smyrna to Lyons," in *Irenaeus: Life, Scripture, Legacy*, eds. Paul Foster and Sara Parvis (Minneapolis: Fortress Press, 2012), pp. 25, 30.

41 Irenaeus, *Against Heresies*, book 3, 3, ANF 1:416.

42 Eusebius, *Church History*, book 5, ch. 5, NPNF 2/1:220.

43 Irenaeus, quoted in Eusebius, *Church History*, book 5, ch. 20, NPNF 2/1:238–39.

44 *Martyrdom of Polycarp*, 22, ANF 1:43.

45 W. Brian Shelton, "Irenaeus," in *Shapers of Christian Orthodoxy: Engaging with Early and Medieval Theologians*, ed. Bradley G. Green (Downers Grove: IVP Academic, 2010), p. 20.

46 Anthony Briggman, "Irenaeus," *Oxford Classical Dictionary*, eds. Simon Hornblower and Antony Spawforth. Shelton adds: "In his Isaiah commentary, Jerome makes a passing but interesting comment about 'Irenaeus, bishop of Lyons and martyr', but scholars suspect it to be a redaction, given the silence of Jerome in his biographical entry of Irenaeus in *Lives of Illustrious Men* and the lack of any other patristic mention." Shelton, p. 20.

47 Thomas B. Slater, "Dating the Apocalypse to John," *Biblica*, vol. 84, no. 2 (2003), p. 253.

48 In fact, the question of the age of John (and the other disciples) is one to which too little scholarly attention has been paid. For one of the few articles on the subject, see Otis and Frank Cary, "How Old Were Christ's Disciples?," *The Biblical World*, vol. 50, no. 1 (July 1917) (arguing that the oldest of the Twelve were likely "nearer twenty than twenty-five," and that John may have been younger than sixteen). There are serious methodological shortcomings in the approach that Cary and Cary take, but it does point to the fact that the Twelve may have been younger than artistic depictions suggest. Beyond this journal article, my research was unable to find much careful examination of the question beyond a pair of doctoral dissertations.

49 Richard Carrier, "Did Polycarp Meet John the Apostle?," Richard Carrier Blogs, October 31, 2019, available at richardcarrier.info.

50 Richard Carrier, *On the Historicity of Jesus* (Sheffield: Sheffield Phoenix Press, 2014), p. 151.

51 J.D. Montagu, "Length of life in the ancient world: a controlled study," *Journal of the Royal Society of Medicine*, vol. 87 (January 1994), pp. 25–26.

52 Karen Cokayne, *Experiencing Old Age in Ancient Rome* (London: Routledge, 2003), p. 100. For Livia's death, see Walter Scheidel, "Emperors, Aristocrats, and the Grim Reaper: Towards a Demographic Profile of the Roman Élite," *The Classical Quarterly*, vol. 49, no. 1 (1999), p. 257, fn. 6. Of course, the apostle John wasn't an emperor. But neither was he a soldier or slave, which points to the difficulty in Carrier's one-size-fits-all mathematical model.

53 Tim G. Parkin, *Demography and Roman Society* (Baltimore: Johns Hopkins University Press, 1992), p. 109. Those three are the senator Gaius Manlius Valens (A.D. 6–96), the consul Lucius Volusius Saturninus (38 B.C.–A.D. 56), and the consul Lucius Julius Ursus Servianus (A.D. 45–136).

54 Osborn, p. 2. See also Eusebius, *Church History*, book 5, 5, NPNF 2/1:220. This Pothinus was another disciple of Polycarp, who sent him to Gaul (France) to establish the church in Lyons. See Roberts and Donaldson, "Introductory Note to Irenæus *Against Heresies*," ANF 1:309.

55 Irenaeus, *Against Heresies*, book 3, 3, ANF 1:416.

56 Andrew Wright, *Christianity and Critical Realism: Ambiguity, Truth and Theological Lit-*

eracy, p. 93.

57 Irenaeus, quoted in Eusebius, *Church History*, book 5, ch. 20, NPNF 2/1:238.

58 Ibid.

59 Bockmuehl, p. 120.

60 Barna Group Press Release, "Is Evangelism Going Out of Style?," Barna Group, December 17, 2013. Barna Group was founded by George Barna, the co-author of the book *Pagan Christianity?*, which I respond to in chapter three on the Eucharist.

61 These are the two major views on baptism, but they are not the only ones. *Understanding Four Views on Baptism*, eds. John H. Armstrong and Paul E. Engle (Grand Rapids: Zondervan, 2007), compares and contrasts these two views with two other views: the Reformed view of baptism as a "sacrament of the covenant" and the Christian Church/Churches of Christ's view of "believer's baptism as the biblical occasion of salvation." There are in fact a *variety* of Reformed/Calvinist positions on baptism, and many Calvinists today reject Calvin's own position on baptism. See John W. Riggs, *Baptism in the Reformed Tradition* (Louisville: Westminster John Knox Press, 2002), p. 90 ("Where Calvin was careful to insist that baptism actually did something at the time of administration—offer God's promise of grace attached to an outward sign—Reformed orthodoxy backed away from such sacramental language by insisting that baptism outwardly sealed what God internally did otherwise," creating a distinction between "outward baptism" and "inward baptism"). Major thinkers within the Reformed tradition, like Karl Barth in the twentieth century, evince this lack of a single clear "Reformed" position on baptism: over the course of writing *Church Dogmatics*, his *magnum opus*, Barth went from thinking (and speaking) of baptism as a sacrament to rejecting its sacramentality. See Karl Barth, *The Teaching of the Church Regarding Baptism* (Eugene: Wipf and Stock Publishers, 2006); Tracey Mark Stout, *A Fellowship of Baptism: Karl Barth's Ecclesiology in Light of His Understanding of Baptism*, (Eugene: Pickwick Publications, 2010), pp. 68–86; W. Travis McMaken, *The Sign of the Gospel: Toward an Evangelical Doctrine of Infant Baptism After Karl Barth* (Minneapolis: Fortress Press, 2013).

62 Wayne Jackson, "A History of the Baptism Apostasy," *Christian Courier*, n.d., available at christiancourier.com.

63 Aruna Koneru contrasts the sentence "the accident was never investigated" ("who failed to investigate? No one is to blame") with "the police never investigated the accident." Aruna Koneru, *Professional Communication* (New Delhi: Tata McGraw-Hill Publishing Co. Ltd., 2008), p. 163.

64 Castelein is part of the "Churches of Christ" and denies that baptism is a sacrament. His view is similar to (but not the same as) the Baptist view. See John D. Castelein, "Christian Churches / Churches of Christ View: Believers' Baptism as the Biblical Occasion of Salvation," in *Understanding Four Views on Baptism*, eds. John H. Armstrong and Paul E. Engle (Grand Rapids: Zondervan, 2007), p. 143; Thomas J. Nettles, "A Baptist Response," *Understanding Four Views on Baptism*, p. 145 ("Dr. Castelein and I have much in common in our views of baptism" but disagree over "Castelein's view of baptism as the occasion of salvation").

65 Castelein, p. 130.

66 Cyprian, Letter 75, ANF 5:400–01.

67 Everett Ferguson, *Baptism in the Early Church: History, Theology, and Liturgy in the First Five Centuries* (Grand Rapids: Wm. B. Eerdmans Publishing Company, 2009), p. 854.

68 I am personally indebted to the tremendous research done by Bryan Cross in "The Church Fathers on Baptismal Regeneration," Called to Communion, June 15, 2020, available at calledtocommunion.com.

69 Jonathan Pennington, "Why Did Jesus Need to Be Baptized?," The Gospel Coalition, May 8, 2019. I leave the reader to make sense of a Christology in which the fully divine Christ dedicates himself to following God at age thirty.

70 See Stephen D. Ricks, "Miqvaot: Ritual Immersion Baths in Second Temple (Intertestamental) Jewish History," *Brigham Young University Studies*, vol. 36, no. 3 (1996–97), pp. 277–86.

71 Maurice Lamm, *Becoming a Jew* (Middle Village: Jonathan David Publishers, Inc., 1991), p. 156.

72 Talmud Vavli, The William Davidson Talmud, Yevamot 47b, available at sefaria.org.

73 Lamm, p. 158.

74 Ignatius, Epistle to the Ephesians 18, ANF 1:57.

75 William R. Schoedel, *A Commentary on the Letters of Ignatius of Antioch*, ed. Helmut Koester (Philadelphia: Fortress Press, 1985), p. 85.

76 Ibid.

77 Jonathan A. Draper, "The Apostolic Fathers: The Didache," *The Expository Times*, vol. 117, no. 5 (2006), p. 178. ("Few scholars now date the text later than the end of the first century CE or the first few decades of the second," and "a number of recent studies have even argued for a very early date in the mid first century.")

78 *Didache* 7, in *The Apostolic Fathers*, vol. 1, trans. Kirsopp Lake (London: William Heinemann, 1914), pp. 320–21.

79 E.g., Bruce Edwards, Jr., "Immersion, Pouring and Sprinkling: A History," *Truth Magazine*, vol. 19, no. 27 (May 15, 1975), pp. 422–24 (claiming that "on an eventful day circa 253 A.D., a man named Novatian lay in illness, apparently upon his deathbed. Believing in the necessity of immersion for salvation, but unable to leave his bed, he was permitted by a local 'bishop' to substitute the pouring of water all about him in its place. This episode, reported by the famous church historian, Eusebius [Church History VI. xliii. 14, 17], constituted the first known historical substitution of another action in the place of immersion."). Eusebius is describing Novatus, the leader of the Cathar heresy, and says nothing one way or another about him "believing in the necessity of immersion for salvation." Novatus's emergency baptism was defective for other reasons, as Eusebius's account explains: "when he was healed of his sickness he did not receive the other things which it is necessary to have according to the canon of the Church, even the being sealed by the bishop. And as he did not receive this, how could he receive the Holy Spirit?" Eusebius, Church History 6, NPNF 2/1:288–89. In any case, the permission for affusion given in the first-century *Didache* debunks the idea that Novatus was anything like the first person to be baptized this way.

80 Tyler Scarlett, "Baptism: For Believers Only, by Immersion Only," Forest Baptist Church, available at forestbaptistchurch.org. Scarlett's views are consistent with *The Baptist Faith and Message (2000)*, the official statement of beliefs of the Southern Baptist Convention, which describes baptism as "the immersion of a believer in water in the name of the Father, the Son, and the Holy Spirit." Article 7 of *Baptist Faith & Message 2000*, available at bfm.sbc.net. But they are *not* consistent with the *Didache* or other early Christian testimonies.

81 "The Epistle of Barnabas can be dated any time between the mid-90s CE and the 130s CE." James Carleton-Paget, "The Epistle of Barnabas and the Writings that later formed the New Testament," in *The Reception of the New Testament in the Apostolic Fathers*, eds. Andrew F. Gregory and Christopher M. Tuckett (Oxford: Oxford University Press, 2005), p. 229.

82 "The writer of this epistle is supposed to have been an Alexandrian Jew of the times of Trajan [98 to 117] and Hadrian [117–138]. He was a layman; but possibly he bore the name of 'Barnabas,' and so has been confounded with his holy and apostolic name-sire. It is more probable that the epistle, being anonymous, was attributed to St. Barnabas, by those who supposed that apostle to be the author of the epistle to the Hebrews, and who discovered similarities in the plan and purpose of the two works." A. Cleveland Coxe, "Introductory Note to the Epistle of Barnabas," ANF 1:133.

83 The Epistle of Barnabas 9, ANF 1:144.

84 Ibid.

85 Ibid.

86 On the dating of the fragment, see Everett Ferguson, "Canon Muratori: Date and Provenance," *Studia Patristica*, vol. 17, ed. Elizabeth A. Livingstone (Oxford: Pergamon Press, 1982), pp. 677–83; Eckhard J. Schnabel, "The Muratorian Fragment: The State of Research," *Journal of the Evangelical Theological Society*, vol. 57, no. 2 (2012), pp. 231–64.

87 Muratorian Fragment 73–80, quoted in Schnabel, p. 238. See also Bruce Metzger, *The Canon of the New Testament* (Oxford: Clarendon Press, 1987), pp. 193–94.

88 *Shepherd of Hermas*, book 3, simil. 9, ch. 16, ANF 2:49.

89 John V. Fesko, *Word, Water, and Spirit: A Reformed Perspective on Baptism* (Grand Rapids: Reformation Heritage Books, 2010).

90 *Shepherd of Hermas*, book 2, comm. 4th, ch. 3, ANF 2:22.

91 Tertullian, *On Repentance* 4, ANF 3:659.

92 Daniel H. Williams, *Retrieving the Tradition and Renewing Evangelicalism* (Grand Rapids: Wm. B. Eerdmans Publishing Company, p. 116. He continues: "In keeping with the successionist model, 'Baptists' can be found, if not in name, in every age since the apostolic era. Moreover, the number of dissenting groups that are identified as proto-Baptists was enlarged as the paradigm became a fixture in historical interpretation. Modern theorists identify groups from every epoch—Montanists, the so-called 'Novations,' Donatists, St. Patrick, the Bogomils, the Albigenses, the Lollards, the Waldensians, and, of course, the Anabaptists—as doctrinal precursors." Williams, pp. 117–18. To be clear, Williams is describing this theory, not endorsing it: he in fact rejects it as false and as making historical claims while "exhibiting little knowledge of the primary works themselves." Williams, p. 119.

93 Joe Heschmeyer, *Pope Peter* (El Cajon: Catholic Answers, 2020), pp. 218–19.

94 See Roger Scott, "Narrating the Reign of Constantine in Byzantine Chronicles," in *Byzantine Culture in Translation*, eds. Amelia Brown and Bronwen Neil (Leiden: Brill, 2019), pp. 9, 11.

95 Justin Martyr, *First Apology* 61, ANF 1:83. Jerome is describing the baptism of an adult convert. He's silent on the question of when those raised in the faith were baptized (i.e., his views on infant baptism).

96 Ibid.

97 Ibid.

98 See John Farrelly, *The Trinity: Rediscovering the Central Christian Mystery* (Lanham: Rowman & Littlefield Publishers, 2005), p. 75.

99 Theophilus, To Autolycus, book 2, ch. 16, ANF 2:101.

100 Irenaeus, *Against Heresies*, book 3, ch. 17, ANF 1:444.

101 Irenaeus, Fragment 34 from the Lost Writings of Irenaeus, ANF 1:574.

102 Irenaeus, *Against Heresies*, book 2, ch. 22, ANF 1:391.

103 "It is hard to see what Irenaeus can mean if infant baptism is not in mind." Anthony N.S. Lane, "Did the Apostolic Church Baptise Babies? A Seismological Approach," *Tyndale*

Bulletin, vol. 55, no. 1 (2004), p. 126. Lane's conclusions are worth the read: "If the problem with infant baptism is *inconclusive* evidence that it happened in the first 150 years of the church, the problem with the alternative theory is *total lack* of evidence. . . . The meagre evidence from the first two centuries is consistent with the practice of infant baptism but does not demand it. The evidence from the third and fourth centuries un-ambiguously reveals a diversity in practice where the initiation of Christian children is concerned. There is a total lack of evidence in the first four centuries of any objection *in principle* to either the baptism or the non-baptism of babies. Given this evidence, what is most likely to have occurred in the apostolic church? That the practice of infant baptism was unknown seems to me to be the least likely hypothesis. That it was practised seems very likely. That it was *universally* practised is much less likely given the freedom that later Christians felt not to baptise their children." Layne, pp. 128, 130.

104 Irenaeus, *Against Heresies*, book 1, ch. 21, ANF 1:345.

105 Timothy Kaufman, "That He Might Purify the Water, Part 1," White Horse Blog, August 17, 2014, available at whitehorseblog.com.

106 Ibid.

107 Ibid.

108 Timothy Kaufman, "That He Might Purify the Water, Part 3," White Horse Blog, August 31, 2014, available at whitehorseblog.com.

109 Tertullian, *On Baptism* 16, ANF 3:677.

110 Ibid.

111 See Clement of Alexandria, *Stromata*, book 2, ch. 18, ANF 2:368.

112 Kauffman, "That He Might Purify the Water, Part 3."

113 Tertullian, *On Baptism* 3, ANF 3:670.

114 Tertullian, *On Baptism* 5, ANF 3:670–71.

115 "T.A. McMahon & Ron Merryman (Part 1)," *The Berean Call*, November 2, 2013, transcript available at thebereancall.org.

116 Thomas R. Schreiner, "Baptism in the Epistles," in *Believer's Baptism*, eds. Thomas R. Schreiner and Shawn D. Wright (Nashville: B&H Academic, 2006), pp. 92–93.

117 Gregg R. Allison and Andreas J. Köstenberger, *The Holy Spirit*, eds. David S. Dockery, Nathan A. Finn, and Christopher W. Morgan (Nashville: B&H Academic, 2020), p. 369.

118 Eugene R. Schlesinger, "Sacrament," *The Lexham Bible Dictionary*, eds. John D. Barry, et al (Bellingham: Lexham Press, 2016), as found in the Verbum study software program.

119 I explore this in greater detail in Joe Heschmeyer, "Stripping Sacraments Down to Ordinances," *Catholic Answers Magazine Online*, May 18, 2021.

120 John MacArthur, The MacArthur New Testament Commentary: Acts 1–12 (Chicago: Moody Publishers, 1994), p. 74.

121 James White, "A Brief Rebuttal of Baptismal Regeneration," Alpha & Omega Ministries, May 8, 1998, available at aomin.org. To hold to White's position, you would have to believe that the entire early Church rejects the biblical teaching on sin. And yet somehow, if you follow Allison's and Köstenberger's argument, it's precisely their concern over the impact of original sin that leads them into baptismal regeneration in the first place.

122 R.C. Sproul, *Essential Truths of the Christian Faith* (Carol Stream: Tyndale House Publishing, 1992), p. 235.

123 Dennis W. Jowers, "A Reformed Perspective on the Doctrine of Baptismal Regeneration," *WRS Journal*, vol. 14, no. 23.

124 Ibid.

125 MacArthur, p. 74.

126 Augustine, Tractate 5 on the Gospel of John 18, *NPNF* 1/7:38.

127 *Fortress Commentary on the Bible: The New Testament*, eds. Margaret Aymer, Cynthia Briggs Kittredge, and David A. Sánchez (Minneapolis: Fortress Press, 2014), p. 339.

128 Bruce M. Metzger, *Manuscripts of the Greek Bible* (New York: Oxford University Press, 1991), p. 96. ("There is no reason why scribes should have omitted the confession if it had originally stood in the text. On the other hand, its insertion into the text seems to have been due to the feeling that Philip could not have baptized the Ethiopian without securing a confession of faith, which needed to be expressed in the narrative.") But see Irenaeus, *Against Heresies*, ANF 1:433.

129 Irenaeus, *Against Heresies*, book 3, ch. 12, ANF 1:436.

130 "God does not command impossible things, does he?" John Chrysostom, *Hom. Act.* 23.3, quoted in Benjamin A. Edsall, *The Reception of Paul and Early Christian Initiation* (Cambridge: Cambridge University Press, 2019), p. 175, fn. 28.

131 Dennis W. Jowers, "A Reformed Perspective on the Doctrine of Baptismal Regeneration," *WRS Journal*, vol. 14, no. 23.

132 Irenaeus, *Against Heresies*, book 1, ch. 21, ANF 1:345.

133 Eugene F. Rice, Jr. (with Anthony Grafton), *The Foundations of Early Modern Europe, 1460–1559*, 2nd ed. (New York: W.W. Norton & Co., 1971), p. 152.

134 Michael Reeves, *The Unquenchable Flame: Discovering the Heart of the Reformation* (Nashville: B & H Academic, 2010), p. 17.

135 Reeves, p. 18.

136 Benedict XVI, *Sacramentum Caritatis* 77, February 22, 2007; John Paul II, Paul VI, *Lumen Gentium* 11, November 21, 1964.

137 John Paul II, *Ecclesia de Eucharistia* 1, April 17, 2003.

138 Scott Hendrix, "Rerooting the Faith: The Reformation as Re-Christianization," *Church History*, vol. 69, no. 3 (September 2000), p. 561.

139 Frank Viola and George Barna, *Pagan Christianity: Exploring the Roots of Our Church Practices* (Carol Stream: Tyndale House, 2008), p. 51; fn. 10. Viola and Barna cite the (lapsed Catholic) historian Will Durant for support, although Durant actually argues that the weekly Christian liturgy "had taken the form of the Christian Mass" by "the close of the second century." Will Durant, *Caesar and Christ* (vol. 3 of *The Story of Civilization*), (New York: Simon and Schuster, 1944), p. 599.

140 Typically, *transubstantiation* is usually used (by both Catholic and non-Catholic authors) to describe the change of the bread and wine into the body and blood of Christ, and *Real Presence* is to describe that reality post-change. See, e.g., "The Real Presence of Jesus Christ in the Sacrament of the Eucharist: Basic Questions and Answers," United States Conference of Catholic Bishops (USCCB), 2001; cf. Matt Slick, "Transubstantiation and the Real Presence," The Christian Apologetics & Research Ministry (CARM), December 3, 2008. However, there are some who believe that Christ is really present in the Eucharist, but not through transubstantiation. See Paul VI, *Mysterium Fidei* 11, September 3, 1965 (rejecting explanations like *transignification* or *transfinalization* that fail to express clearly "the marvelous conversion of the whole substance of the bread into the body and the whole substance of the wine into the blood of Christ"). For instance, Martin Luther's view was that "the Sacrament of the Altar" consists of "the true body and blood of the Lord Christ, *in and with* the bread and wine through Christ's word." Martin Luther, *Luther's Large Catechism*, trans. Friedemann Hebart (Adelaide: Lutheran Publishing House, 1983), p. 188 (emphasis added). This is the same, or a similar, view to the *consubstantiation* view for which John Wyclif was condemned as a heretic in the fourteenth century.

See Anthony Kenny, *Wyclif*, pp. 80–81 (explaining the distinction between *Real Presence* and *transubstantiation*). There are serious metaphysical problems with consubstantiation (is Christ fully God and fully man *and* fully bread?), but they lie beyond the scope of this book. My point here is simply that the earliest Christians believed in the Real Presence, a point with which Lutheran and Anglican readers will probably happily agree.

141 J.N.D. Kelly, *Early Christian Doctrines*, 4th edition (London: Adam & Charles Black, 1968), p. 452. Kelly says this in his chapter on the Christians living from Nicaea to Chalcedon (325–451), but he traces this history of eucharistic realism to a yet earlier period.

142 The question of which heretics Ignatius was writing against is one on which there is some scholarly disagreement. See Andreas J. Köstenberger and Michael J. Kruger, *The Heresy of Orthodoxy* (Wheaton: Crossway, 2010), p. 43 (arguing that Ignatius's opponents were Docetists); John P. Meier, "Part One: Antioch" in John P. Meier and Raymond Brown, *Antioch and Rome* (New York: Paulist Press, 1982), p. 78 (Gnostics or Docetists); but see Michael D. Goulder, "Ignatius' 'Docetists,'" *Vigiliae Christianae*, vol. 53, no. 1 (February 1999), pp. 16–30 (arguing that they were instead Ebionites).

143 Ignatius, Epistle to the Smyrnaeans 5, ANF 1:88.

144 Luke Wayne, "Ignatius of Antioch and Transubstantiation," CARM, November 28, 2018.

145 Ignatius, Smyrnaeans 6, ANF 1:88–89.

146 Ignatius, Smyrnaeans 7, ANF 1:89.

147 Justin Martyr, *First Apology* 67, ANF 1:186.

148 Ibid.

149 Ibid.

150 *First Apology* 65, ANF 1:185.

151 The word Justin uses for the presider literally means "president" or "ruler." See T.G. Jalland, "Justin Martyr and the President of the Eucharist," *Studia Patristica, Texte und Untersuchungen*, vol. 80 (Berlin: Akademie-Verlag, 1962), pp. 83–85.

152 It is translated in this way in, for instance, *The Christianity Reader*, trans. Leslie William Barnard, eds. Mary Gerhart & Fabian E. Udoh (Chicago: University of Chicago Press, 2007), p. 350; James T. O'Connor, *The Hidden Manna: A Theology of the Eucharist*, 2nd ed. (San Francisco: Ignatius Press, 2005), p. 19. The Greek word Justin uses is *eucharistēthentos*.

153 *First Apology* 66, ANF 1:185.

154 Ibid.

155 Luke Wayne, "Justin Martyr and Transubstantiation," CARM, February 19, 2017.

156 For instance, Tim Staples, "What Catholics Believe about John 6," *Catholic Answers Magazine Online*, November 1, 2010; Charles Pope, "Eating the Eucharist is not cannibalism—here's why," *Our Sunday Visitor*, April 21, 2020; Michael Foley, "The Eucharist & Cannibalism," *The Catholic Thing*, August 6, 2011.

157 To use CARM itself as an example: As of this writing, a search for "cannibalism" on CARM's website produces multiple articles falsely accusing Catholics of cannibalism, at least two articles mentioning how this charge was falsely levied against the early Church, and none on why Protestant theology isn't cannibalistic. And why not? Probably because Protestant eucharistic theology is so obviously different from what the early Christians and modern Catholics believe that it couldn't be mistaken as such.

158 Gregory of Nyssa, *The Great Catechism* 37, NPNF 2/5:503–04.

159 Cardinal Ratzinger beautifully captures this theology when he says: "It is truly the one, identical Lord, whom we receive in the Eucharist, or better, the Lord who receives us and assumes us into himself. St. Augustine expressed this in a short passage which he

perceived as a sort of vision: 'eat the bread of the strong; you will not transform me into yourself, but I will transform you into me.' In other words, when we consume bodily nourishment, it is assimilated by the body, becoming itself a part of ourselves. But this bread is of another type. It is greater and higher than we are. It is not we who assimilate it, but it assimilates us to itself, so that we become in a certain way 'conformed to Christ,' as Paul says, members of his body, one in him." Cardinal Ratzinger, "Lecture by H.E. Cardinal Ratzinger at the Bishops' Conference of the Region of Campania in Benevento (Italy) on the Topic: 'Eucharist, Communion And Solidarity,'" June 2, 2002, available online at vatican.va.

160 James R. Payton, Jr., *Irenaeus on the Christian Faith* (Eugene: Pickwick Publications, 2011), p. ix.

161 Irenaeus, *Against Heresies*, book 5, 2, ANF 1:528.

162 Aristotle, *The Prior Analytics*, book 1, 5, in *The Organon*, trans. Octavius Freire Owen (Altenmünster: Jazzybee Verlag, 2015), p. 50.

163 To give a real-life example of how shifting mindsets can impact the rhetorical effectiveness of a *reductio ad absurdum*, when the Supreme Court ruled against Texas's anti-sodomy laws in 2003, Justice Kennedy was careful to explain that the Court *wasn't* redefining marriage to include same-sex couples, since the case did "not involve whether the government must give formal recognition to any relationship that homosexual persons seek to enter." *Lawrence v. Texas*, 539 U.S. 558, 563 (2003). But as Justice Scalia pointed out in his dissent, this was true "only if one entertains the belief that principle and logic have nothing to do with the decisions of this Court." *Lawrence*, 539 U.S. at 605 (Scalia, J., dissenting). Once the Supreme Court decided that there was no "rational basis" to distinguish between homosexual and heterosexual relationships, it was only a matter of time until it said the same for marriage. Scalia's *reductio ad absurdum* amounted to "if you accept this, logically, you have no argument against 'gay marriage.'" At the time, this argument worked, because Americans were overwhelmingly against the idea of "gay marriage": as the *New York Times* noted at the time, even "a majority of people traditionally viewed as supportive of gay rights, including Democrats, women and people who live on the East Coast," supported a constitutional amendment against it. Katharine Q. Seelye and Janet Elder, "Strong Support is Found for Ban on Gay Marriage," *New York Times*, December 21, 2003. Sure enough, twelve years later, Justice Kennedy wrote the majority opinion for the Supreme Court finding a constitutional right to "gay marriage," even citing his earlier opinion in *Lawrence* for support. Scalia's *reductio ad absurdum* had come true. But in those intervening years, attitudes on marriage had changed such that the same people who thought Scalia was a scare-monger for claiming that the *Lawrence* decision logically led to "gay marriage" were now *agreeing* with his reasoning but accepting the "absurd" conclusion. The logic of the argument remained the same, but the rhetorical effectiveness was lost as the culture shifted. Something similar has happened with Ignatius's and Irenaeus's *reductio ad absurdum*. In the early Church, "if you accept this, you'd logically have to reject the Real Presence" was enough to show the absurdity of a particular idea. But for many Christians today, that's no longer the case.

164 *Against Heresies*, 5, 2, ANF 1:528.

165 Id., 5, 3, ANF 1:528.

166 Ibid.

167 *Against Heresies*, 4, 18, ANF 1:486.

168 The A.D. 180 dating is approximate, but we know from *Against Heresies*, 3, 3 that he wrote during the reign of Pope Eleutherius (174–189). Denis Minns, *Irenaeus: An Intro-*

duction (London: T&T Clark, 2010), p. 2.

169 The first theologian to use the word *Trinity* to describe the Godhead (at least in any work that we still possess) was St. Theophilus of Antioch, in *Ad Autolycus*, which William A. Jurgens dates to c. 181. William A. Jurgens, *The Faith of the Early Fathers*, vol. 1 (Collegeville: Liturgical Press, 1970), p. 73. Riemer Roukema suggests "from around 180." Riemer Roukema, *Jesus, Gnosis, and Dogma* (London: T&T Clark, 2010), p. 170.

170 *Against Heresies*, 4, 18, ANF 1:486.

171 Hubmaier, *Eighteen Articles*, quoted in Danijel Časni, "Balthasar Hubmaier and His Eighteen Articles," *KAIROS - Evangelical Journal of Theology*, vol. 12, no. 1 (2018), p. 57.

172 Quoted in Keith D. Lewis, "'*Unica Oblatio Christi*': Eucharistic Sacrifice and the first Zürich Disputation," *Renaissance and Reformation*, New Series, vol. 17, no. 3 (Summer 1993), p. 20.

173 Gregg Allison, "The Mass They Made," Desiring God, March 17, 2018.

174 John MacArthur, "Explaining the Heresy of the Catholic Mass, Part 1," April 30, 2006.

175 Martin Luther, *On the Babylonish Captivity of the Church*, in *First Principles of the Reformation* ("*Babylonish Captivity*"), ed. Henry Wace and C.A. Buchheim (London: John Murray, 1883), p. 161.

176 John Calvin, *Institutes of the Christian Religion*, book 4, ch. 18, trans. Henry Beveridge (Grand Rapids: Wm. B. Eerdmans Publishing Co., 1989), p. 607.

177 Luther, *Babylonish Captivity*, p. 176. Luther referred to these prayers as "that abominable concoction drawn from everyone's sewer and cesspool." Martin Luther, *An Order of Mass and Communion for the Church at Wittenberg (1523)*, in *Martin Luther's Basic Theological Writings*, 3rd ed., eds. William R. Russell and Timothy F. Lull (Minneapolis: Fortress Press, 2012), p. 312.

178 Calvin, p. 607.

179 Lewis, p. 22.

180 Luther, *Babylonish Captivity*, p. 177.

181 *Ibid.* Luther offers a second argument, that we could reinterpret the innumerable references to the eucharistic sacrifice as *actually* being references to the "sacrifice" of bringing food and drink to share with the poor, but even he doesn't seem to think this is a strong argument: he explicitly offers it in order "that we may keep the Fathers too."

182 Quoted in Lewis, p. 20.

183 *Didache* 14, in *The Apostolic Fathers*, vol. 1, trans. Kirsopp Lake (London: William Heinemann, 1914), p. 331.

184 Justin Martyr, *Dialogue with Trypho* 117, ANF 1:257–58.

185 Irenaeus, *Fragment 37*, ANF 1:574.

186 Even John Wesley, the founder of Methodism, appears to fall into this error in *A Letter to a Roman Catholic* when he writes: "I say not a word to you about your opinions or outward manner of worship. But I say, all worship is an abomination to the Lord, unless you worship him in spirit and in truth, with your heart as well as your lips, with your spirit and with your understanding also. Be your form of worship what it will, but in everything give him thanks, else it is all but lost labor. Use whatever outward observances you please; but put your whole trust in him, but honor his holy name and his word, and serve him truly all the days of your life." John Wesley, *A Letter to a Roman Catholic*, in *The Works of the Rev. John Wesley, A.M.*, vol. 10, 5th ed. (London: John Mason, 1860), p. 83. But Jesus' response is about worshipping "in spirit and truth," not about using "whatever outward observances you please."

187 Candice Lucey, "What Does 'Worship in Spirit and Truth' Really Mean?" *Crosswalk*, April 20, 2020.

188 See Tovah Lazaroff, "In Pictures: Samaritans perform sacrificial Passover ritual," *Jerusalem Post*, April 22, 2016.

189 Irenaeus, *Fragment 37*, ANF 1:574.

190 Clement, *1 Clement* 44, ANF 1:17, fn. 5; Ignatius, Epistle to the Philadelphians 4, ANF 1:81. An excellent succinct exploration of Clement's eucharistic theology can be found in Homersham Cox, *The First Century of Christianity* (London: Longmans, Green, and Co., 1886), pp. 236–37.

191 "We can also credit Cyprian with the notion that when the priest offered the Eucharist, he was actually offering up the death of Christ on behalf of the congregation. To Cyprian's mind, the body and blood of Christ are once again sacrificed through the Eucharist. Consequently, it is in Cyprian that we find the seeds of the medieval Catholic Mass." Viola and Barna, p. 116.

192 *This Holy Mystery: A United Methodist Understanding of Holy Communion*, adopted by the 2004 General Conference of The United Methodist Church, p. 17.

193 For instance, Mark W. Stamm, *Let Every Soul Be Jesus' Guest: A Theology of the Open Table* (Nashville: Abingdon Press, 2006).

194 For instance, David M. Knight, "Should Protestants receive Communion at Mass?," *La Croix International*, July 23, 2020.

195 CNA Staff, "Catholics and Protestants in Germany announce intercommunion move despite Vatican objections," *Catholic News Agency*, March 16, 2021.

196 Bobby Jamieson, *Going Public: Why Baptism Is Required for Church Membership* (Nashville: B&H Academic, 2015), p. 8 (arguing that from a Baptist perspective, "a huge number of Christians simply haven't been baptized because sprinkling an infant is not what Jesus and the apostles meant by 'baptism'").

197 Article 8 of *Baptist Faith & Message 2000*, available at bfm.sbc.net.

198 Carol Pipes, "Lord's Supper: LifeWay surveys churches' practices, frequency," *Baptist Press*, September 17, 2012. *Lifeway* surveyed 1,066 SBC pastors, asking, "Who may participate in the Lord's Supper at your church?" The results, in descending order: "anyone who has put faith in Christ" (52%); "anyone baptized as a believer" (35%); "anyone who wants" (5%); "only members of the local church" (4%); "have no specifications" (4%).

199 John Bunyan, *Differences in Judgment About Water Baptism,* in *The Works of that Eminent Servant of Christ John Bunyan*, vol. 3 (New Haven: Nathan Whiting, 1833), pp. 333, 330.

200 Bunyan, p. 335.

201 Mark W. Stamm, *Let Every Soul Be Jesus' Guest: A Theology of the Open Table* (Nashville: Abingdon Press, 2006).

202 If the Eucharist is the earthly preparation for the wedding feast of the Lamb (Rev. 19:6–8), then it's worth listening to Jesus' parable of the wedding feast in Matthew 22. There, the king says, "The wedding is ready, but those invited were not worthy. Go therefore to the thoroughfares, and invite to the marriage feast as many as you find" (Matt. 22:8–9), a none-too-subtle reference to the incorporation of the Gentiles into the Church. If the parable ended there, it might sound like Stamm's argument. But it doesn't: instead, it ends with the king confronting a guest who attended the feast without first putting on a wedding garment, ultimately casting him into "the outer darkness" (vv. 11–13).

203 *Didache* 9, in *The Apostolic Fathers*, vol. 1, p. 323.

204 Ignatius, Epistle to the Philadelphians 3, ANF 1:80.

205 *First Apology* 66, ANF 1:185.

206 "Protestants reject the idea of transubstantiation but maintain divergent understandings of the precise significance of the [Lord's] Supper." Jonathan Griffiths, "The Lord's Supper," The Gospel Coalition, 2020, available at thegospelcoalition.org.

207 R.C. Sproul, *Knowing Scripture*, 2nd ed. (Downers Grove: IVP Books, 2009), p. 17 (emphasis in original).

208 Martin Luther, *The Bondage of the Will*, trans. Henry Cole (London: T. Bensley, 1823), p. 17.

209 Alister E. McGrath, *Reformation Thought: An Introduction*, 4th ed. (Malden: Wiley-Blackwell, 2012), p. 82.

210 See "The Lord's Supper in the Present," *Tabletalk Magazine*, October 2016.

211 *Understanding Four Views on the Lord's Supper*, ed. John H. Armstrong (Grand Rapids: Zondervan, 2007). His book highlights and contrasts four major views—Baptist, Reformed, Lutheran, and Catholic—but even the contributing authors note that these are not the only views on offer.

212 Armstrong, "Do This in Remembrance of Me," in *Understanding Four Views on the Lord's Supper*, p. 13.

213 A helpful resource for those wanting more primary-source evidence is Fr. James Thomas O'Connor's *The Hidden Manna: A Theology of the Eucharist*, 2nd ed. (San Francisco: Ignatius Press, 2005).

214 Wayne is extreme even by CARM's standards. His colleague Matt Slick admits that "there were Church Fathers who held to a similar view of the Roman Catholic transubstantiation—though not articulated in the same way," even though he claims that they didn't *unanimously* hold the Catholic position. Matt Slick, "Did the Early Church Fathers all agree with the Catholic view of the Eucharist?," CARM, February 19, 2020. But Wayne goes farther, insisting that "the Church Fathers closest to the time of the New Testament are actually *all* on our side." Luke Wayne, "Clement of Alexandria and Transubstantiation," CARM, December 3, 2018 (emphasis added).

215 Luke Wayne, "Did Justin Martyr Teach the Eucharist as a Propitiatory Sacrifice?," CARM, February 9, 2018.

216 Wayne, "Ignatius of Antioch and Transubstantiation."

217 Wayne, "Did Justin Martyr Teach the Eucharist as a Propitiatory Sacrifice?"

218 Also, Ignatius and Justin were venerated from the earliest days as martyrs, saints, and models of Christian discipleship. For instance, Polycarp offers to the Philippians the witness given by "the blessed Ignatius, and Zosimus, and Rufus, but also in others among yourselves, and in Paul himself, and the rest of the apostles." Polycarp, Epistle to the Philippians 9, ANF 1:35. If Ignatius is a heretic promoting idolatry and cannibalism, what should we make of the Smyrnaeans, or Polycarp, or any of the innumerable others who venerate and emulate Ignatius?

219 Bradford Littlejohn, *Davenant Digests: What Divides Protestants and Catholics on the Eucharist?*, January 2019, p. 3.

220 Littlejohn, p. 13.

221 *Heidelberg Catechism* 80, quoted in Wim H.Th. Moehn, "A Lasting Controversy on Mass and Supper? Meaning and Actuality of HC 80," in *The Spirituality of the Heidelberg Catechism*, ed. Arnold Huijgen (Göttingen: Vandenhoeck & Ruprecht, 2015), p. 149. Although many Protestant denominations have moved away from the sweeping condemnations of the *Heidelberg Catechism*, you can still find Protestants defending this view. See, e.g, Kevin DeYoung, "Is the Mass Idolatrous?," The Gospel Coalition, August 18, 2009.

222 Timothy George, "Baptist Real Presence?," *Pray Tell*, January 25, 2019.

223 Congregation for Divine Worship and the Discipline of the Sacraments, *Redemptionis*

Sacramentum 129, March 25, 2004.

224 *First Apology* 65, ANF 1:185. Regarding the translation, see endnote 152, *supra*.

225 O. Wesley Allen, Jr., *Protestant Worship* (Nashville: Abingdon Press, 2019), p. 178.

226 Kelly, p. 440.

227 See David Noel Power, *The Eucharistic Mystery: Revitalizing the Tradition* (New York: Crossroad, 1992), p. 146; Brett Salkeld, *Transubstantiation: Theology, History, and Christian Unity* (Grand Rapids: Baker Academic, 2019), pp. 58–59.

228 Kelly, p. 440.

229 Nathan Busenitz, "Did the Early Church Teach Transubstantiation?" *The Master's Seminary Blog*, April 21, 2016.

230 Ibid.

231 William R. Crockett, *Eucharist: Symbol of Transformation* (Collegeville: Liturgical Press, 1990), p. 80.

232 Power, p. 146.

233 Robert B. Eno, *The Rise of the Papacy* (Eugene: Wipf and Stock, 2008), p. 29.

234 Kenneth J. Collins and Jerry L. Walls, *Roman but Not Catholic: What Remains at Stake 500 Years after the Reformation* (Grand Rapids: Baker Academic, 2017), p. 242.

235 Philip Dixon Hardy, *The New Testament [The New Covenant] of Our Lord and Saviour Jesus Christ* (London: Elliot Stock, 1874), p. 119.

236 We would do well to heed Alistair Stewart-Sykes's caution against "the illegitimate assumption that, because Paul discusses charisma and not office when listing functions within the congregation, he intends thereby to denigrate official ministries, or even to deny their existence." Alistair Stewart-Sykes, "Prophecy and Patronage: The Relationship between Charismatic Functionaries and Household Officers in Early Christianity," in *Trajectories Through The New Testament and the Apostolic Fathers*, eds. Andrew F. Gregory and Christopher M. Tuckett (Oxford: Oxford University Press, 2005), p. 168.

237 Earl S. Johnson, Jr., *The Presbyterian Deacon* (Louisville: Geneva Press, 2014), p. 5.

238 The Twelve are described as "apostles" even during the ministry of Jesus (Mark 6:30; Luke 6:13), but their roles necessarily change after Jesus ascends into heaven and is no longer physically present to settle controversies. Likewise, the New Testament describes local church leadership, but the way such leadership operates necessarily changes with the death of the apostles. Eamon Duffy writes, "To 'preside' seems to me in this context a verb apt to describe a stable local ministry, presumably including some form of eucharistic presidency, but less useful in characterising the remote-control though certainly strong and overriding authority of an absent apostle. Some such day to day 'presidency' must surely have coexisted in the earliest church alongside apostolic authority, but while the apostles lived, they can hardly have been considered to be the same sort of thing." Eamon Duffy, "Was There a Bishop of Rome in the First Century?," *New Blackfriars*, vol. 80, no. 940 (June 1999), p. 303.

239 Article 6 of *Baptist Faith & Message 2000*, available at bfm.sbc.net.

240 Office of the Stated Clerk of the General Assembly of the Presbyterian Church in America, *The Book of Church Order of the Presbyterian Church in America* (BCO), (Lawrenceville: Committee on Discipleship Ministries, 2021), §7-2.

241 BCO §8-1.

242 *The Book of Discipline of the United Methodist Church* (Nashville: The United Methodist Publishing House, 2016), paras. 402–03.

243 See Article 36 of the Thirty-Nine Articles.

244 "Appendix to the Articles of Smalcald" (1537), *The Christian Book of Concord* (New-

market: Solomon D. Henkel and Brs.), pp. 318–19. See also Article 14 of Philip Mel-
anchthon's *Apology of the Augsburg Confession*.

245 John Calvin, *Calvin: Theological Treaties*, trans. J.K.S. Reid (Philadelphia: Westminster,
1954), p. 58. Calvin seems to have been influenced in this by the German Reformer
Martin Bucer. Amy Nelson Burnett, "Church Discipline and Moral Reformation in
the Thought of Martin Bucer," *The Sixteenth Century Journal*, vol. 22, no. 3 (Autumn
1991), p. 448 ("It is generally recognized that Calvin developed his four offices of the
ministry—pastors, teachers, elders and deacons—under Bucer's influence during his
stay in Strasbourg between 1538 and 1542," although "Bucer was not quite so clear in
his discussion of church office").

246 Even this somewhat oversimplifies matters, as you will find contradictory models of the
Church being affirmed within the same denomination or communion. In "Mission and
Ministry in Covenant," the Faith and Order bodies of the Church of England and Methodist Church noted that "different theologies of the episcopate exist among Anglicans
and in other churches that are in communion with the Church of England, notably the
Nordic and Baltic Lutheran members of the Porvoo Communion of Churches, where
teaching that there is one order of ministry only, not three, would be common, and
where there were significant changes to the form of the episcopacy at and after the Reformation." "Mission and Ministry in Covenant: Report from The Faith and Order bodies
of the Church of England and the Methodist Church," §30, pp. 11–12.

247 "Yet it is striking that of the five New Testament occurrences of *episkopos* in the sense of
an office holder, three are in the singular (with only Philippians 1.1 and Acts 20.28 in the
plural)," while "of the forty-seven references to *presbuteroi* meaning office holders, only
one is in the singular [1 Timothy 5.19]—and this itself is indefinite and echoes a reference
in the plural only two verses previously." David Albert Jones, "Was there a Bishop of
Rome in the First Century?," *New Blackfriars*, vol. 80, no. 937 (March 1999), p. 131.

248 "Acts 12:17 has often been understood as marking the 'passing of the baton' from Peter
to James, after which Peter became a traveling missionary to the Jews living in the
Diaspora (i.e., outside of Palestine). Current scholars who support this view include the
conservatives Richard Bauckham, Ralph P. Martin, and Luke Timothy Johnson—and
also, interestingly, the extremely liberal Gerd Lüdemann. A maverick voice arguing
for a different interpretation is, again, John Painter." Jeffrey J. Butz, *The Brother of Jesus
and the Lost Teachings of Christianity* (Rochester: Inner Traditions, 2005), pp. 58–59; cf.
John Painter, *Just James: The Brother of Jesus in History and Tradition*, 2nd ed. (Columbia:
University of South Carolina Press, 2004), p. 44 (arguing that "the notion that Peter
was the leader runs contrary to tradition concerning the Jerusalem church. That tradition names James as the first leader ('bishop'). The nomenclature is anachronistic, but
the leadership of James is supported by the way in which James is portrayed in Acts 15
and 21 as well as in Paul's letter to the Galatians"). Although I think Painter's "maverick" view is incorrect, it's significant that both sides of the debate treat the church in
Jerusalem as having a leader, and that the early Christians were clear that James was the
first "bishop."

249 A.T. Robertson, *Studies in the Epistle of James* (New York: George H. Doran Co. 1915), p. 43.

250 Witness Lee, *Life-Study of Galatians* (Anaheim: Living Stream Ministries, 1990), p. 56.

251 D.A. Carson, *For the Love of God*, vol. 1 (Wheaton: Crossway, 2006), p. 28.

252 Jerome, *Lives of Illustrious Men* 2, NPNF 2/03:361.

253 Hegesippus, quoted in Jerome, *Lives of Illustrious Men* 2, NPNF 2/03:361.

254 Colin J. Hemer, *Letters to the Seven Churches of Asia in Their Local Setting* (Sheffield: Shef-

field Academic Press, 1989), p. 32.

255 Id., p. 33.

256 L.L. Morris, "Church Government," in *Evangelical Dictionary of Theology*, 2nd ed., ed. Walter A. Elwell (Grand Rapids: Baker Academic, 2001), p. 256.

257 David J. Stagaman, *Authority in the Church* (Collegeville: Liturgical Press, 1999), p. 73.

258 Margaret R. Miles, *The Word Made Flesh: A History of Christian Thought* (Malden: Blackwell Publishing, 2005), p. 50

259 Michael J. Kruger, *Christianity at the Crossroads: How the Second Century Shaped the Future of the Church* (Downers Grove: IVP Academic, 2018), p. 7.

260 Clement, 1 Clement 1, ANF 1:5.

261 1 Clement 42, ANF 1:16.

262 1 Clement 40–41, ANF 1:16.

263 Constitutions of the Holy Apostles 8, ANF 7:482. The Oxford manuscript has "grant that this thy servant whom thou hast chosen to the holy office of thy bishop, may discharge the duty of a high priest to thee." Ibid.

264 *Episcopal Ministry: The Report of the Archbishops' Group on the Episcopate* (London: Church House Publishing, 1990), pp. 31–32. Henry Chadwick (one of the members of the group, and the likely author of this portion of the report) makes the same claim, verbatim, in "Episcopacy in the New Testament and Early Church," in *Henry Chadwick: Selected Writings*, ed. William G. Rusch (Grand Rapids: Wm. B. Eerdmans Publishing Co., 2017), p. 15.

265 *The Marketplace Ministry Handbook*, eds. R. Paul Stevens and Robert Banks (Vancouver: Regent College Publishing, 2005), p. 36.

266 John Calvin, *Institutes of the Christian Religion*, book 1, ch. 13, trans. Henry Beveridge (Edinburgh: Calvin Translation Society, 1845), p. 186.

267 Jaroslav Pelikan, *Development of Christian Doctrine: Some Historical Prolegomena* (New Haven: Yale University Press, 1969), p. 58. As background: There were three different sets of letters (called *recensions*) that were ascribed to Ignatius: a short Syriac collection of three letters ("short recension"), a set of seven Greek letters ("middle recension"), and a set of thirteen Greek letters ("long recension"). The Lutheran scholar Theodor Zahn and Anglican Bishop Joseph B. Lightfoot convincingly demonstrated the authenticity of the middle recension (most likely, the short recension is a translation or summary into Syriac, while the long recension is compromised by later forgeries). As Pelikan notes, this was despite their own theological biases as Protestants: "The highly developed hierarchical conceptions of the bishop of Antioch were not at all congenial to Zahn, nor even to Bishop Lightfoot. . . . Both Zahn and Lightfoot developed their literary, textual, and historical analysis with such careful attention to methodology and sound scholarship that there is now virtually unanimous acceptance of the seven epistles in their middle recension. The dispute was not settled by *a priori* theories about doctrinal development on either side, but by philological history and honest historical research into the facts of the development." Pelikan, pp. 58–59.

268 Paul N. Anderson, "The Community that Raymond Brown Left Behind: Reflections on the Johannine Dialectical Situation," in *Communities in Dispute: Current Scholarship on the Johannine Epistles*, eds. R. Alan Culpepper and Paul N. Anderson (Atlanta: Society of Biblical Literature Press, 2014), p. 91.

269 Ignatius, Magnesians 2, ANF 1:59.

270 Ignatius, Magnesians 3, ANF 1:60.

271 Ignatius, Magnesians 6, ANF 1:61.

272 Cyril Hovorun, *Scaffolds of the Church: Towards Poststructural Ecclesiology* (Cambridge:

James Clarke & Co., 2018), p. 152.

273 Ignatius, Ephesians 4, ANF 1:50–51.

274 Ignatius, Ephesians 6, ANF 1:51.

275 Ignatius, Ephesians 1, ANF 1:49.

276 F.F. Bruce, *The Pauline Circle* (Eugene: Wipf & Stock, 2006), p. 72.

277 Douglas Moo is right that "the name was common enough that this identification is by no means clear." Douglas J. Moo, *The Letters to the Colossians and to Philemon* (Grand Rapids: Wm. B. Eerdmans Publishing Co., 2008), p. 374.

278 Ignatius, Trallians 7, ANF 1:68–69.

279 Ignatius, Trallians 3, ANF 1:67.

280 Eamon Duffy, *Saints and Sinners: A History of the Popes*, 4th ed. (New Haven: Yale University Press, 2014), p. 2.

281 David W. Kling, *The Bible in History: How the Texts Have Shaped the Times* (Oxford: Oxford University Press, 2004), p. 60.

282 Ignatius, Philadelphians 4, ANF 1:81.

283 Alistair Stewart-Sykes, "Prophecy and Patronage: The Relationship between Charismatic Functionaries and Household Officers in Early Christianity," in *Trajectories Through the New Testament and the Apostolic Fathers*, eds. Andrew F. Gregory and Christopher M. Tuckett (Oxford: Oxford University Press, 2005), p. 173.

284 Ignatius, Magnesians 15, ANF 1:65.

285 Ignatius, Smyrneans 8, ANF 1:89.

286 Id., ANF 1:90.

287 Ignatius, Polycarp 1, ANF 1:93.

288 Ignatius, Polycarp 6, ANF 1:95.

289 Raymond E. Brown, "Part Two: Rome," in Raymond E. Brown and John P. Meier, *Antioch and Rome: New Testament Cradles of Catholic Christianity* (New York: Paulist Press, 2004), p. 163, fn. 347.

290 Brown, p. 163.

291 Duffy, *Saints and Sinners*, p. 10.

292 James A. Kleist, *The Epistles of St. Clement of Rome and St. Ignatius of Antioch* (Westminster: The Newman Bookshop, 1946), p. 4.

293 Michael J. Svigel, *The Center and the Source: Second Century Incarnational Christology and Early Catholic Christianity* (Piscataway: Gorgias Press, 2016), p. 111.

294 Ignatius, Romans 2, ANF 1:74.

295 Ignatius, Romans 9, ANF 1:77.

296 Brown, p. 202.

297 Ignatius, Trallians 3, ANF 1:67.

298 Hegesippus, Concerning His Journey to Rome, and the Jewish Sects, ANF 8:764.

299 Ibid.

300 As Irenaeus laments, if you argue against them from Scripture, "they turn round and accuse these same Scriptures, as if they were not correct, nor of authority, and [assert] that they are ambiguous," but if you "refer them to that Tradition which originates from the apostles, [and] which is preserved by means of the succession of presbyters in the Churches, they object to Tradition, saying that they themselves are wiser not merely than the presbyters, but even than the apostles, because they have discovered the unadulterated truth." Irenaeus, *Against Heresies*, book 3, ch. 2, ANF 1:415.

301 Id., ch. 3, ANF 1:415.

302 Ashish Badiye, Neeti Kapoor, and Ritesh G. Menezes, "Chain of Custody," *StatPearls*,

February 24, 2021, available at ncbi.nlm.nih.gov.

303 Irenaeus, quoted in Eusebius, *Church History*, book 5, ch. 20, NPNF 2/1:238.

304 Irenaeus, *Against Heresies*, book 3, ch. 3, ANF 1:415.

305 Id., ANF 1:416.

306 Ibid.

307 "It is generally admitted that Peter and Paul died in Rome (A.D. 64–67) as martyrs in the persecution of Christians under Nero. Indeed, it is plausible that Peter died by crucifixion in the Circus of Nero south of Vatican Hill (in which vicinity he was buried) and Paul died by beheading on the Ostian Way, as commemorated by subsequent churches and shrines." Brown, p. 97.

308 For the dating of Tertullian's writing, see Bernard P. Prusak, *The Church Unfinished: Ecclesiology Through the Centuries* (Paulist Press, 2004), p. 125. Significantly, this is one of Tertullian's earlier writings. (He would later become a Montanist heretic.)

309 Tertullian, *Prescription Against Heretics* 30, ANF 3:257.

310 Tertullian, *Prescription Against Heretics* 32, ANF 3:258.

311 Ibid.

312 Ibid.

313 John Chrysostom, Homily 1 on Philippians, NPNF 1/13:184.

314 Jerry L. Walls, "'If Christ be not Raised'; If Peter was not the First Pope: Parallel Cases of Indispensable Doctrinal Foundations," *Journal of Biblical and Theological Studies*, vol. 4, no. 2 (2019), p. 251. I present, and respond to, Walls's argument more thoroughly in Joe Heschmeyer, "How Strong is the 'STRONGEST Argument Against Catholicism'?," Word on Fire, October 5, 2020, available at wordonfire.org.

315 Duffy, *Saints and Sinners*, p. 2.

316 Ibid.

317 Markus N.A. Bockmuehl, *The Remembered Peter: In Ancient Reception and Modern Debate*, p. 118. Bockmuehl refers here to F.J. Foakes-Jackson's famous remark that "it must strike every student that, whereas the unanimous voice of the Church from the first acknowledges and reverences St. Peter as the founder of the Roman Church, when we search for a strictly historic proof of even his having ever visited Rome, we have to acknowledge that it is wanting." F.J. Foakes-Jackson, *Peter: Prince of Apostles* (New York: George H. Doran Company, 1927), p. vii. But as Bockmuehl points out, Foakes-Jackson adds an important (and largely forgotten) caveat: "Yet to the candid historian it seems far more perverse to deny that St. Peter was actually at Rome than to affirm that he was the founder of its church." Foakes-Jackson, p. vii; Bockmuehl, *The Remembered Peter*, p. 118, fn. 12.

318 As Bockmuehl says, "the identification of Babylon with Rome (rather than a place in Mesopotamia or a small Roman garrison near modern-day Cairo) is widely agreed upon today and was certainly understood this way in antiquity." Markus N.A. Bockmuehl, *Simon Peter in Scripture and Memory: The New Testament Apostle in the Early Church* (Grand Rapids: Baker Academic, 2012), p. 31.

319 Clement, 1 Clement 5, ANF 1:6.

320 Ignatius, Romans 4, ANF 1:75.

321 Duffy writes that it "is possible that the excavation unconverted the site of Peter's execution, rather than his burial," but that "whether it is Peter's grave or his cenotaph, however, the mere existence of the shrine is overwhelming evidence of a very early Roman belief that Peter had died in or near the Vatican Circus." Duffy, *Saints and Sinners*, p. 8. Bockmuehl points out that "the absence of rival sites is striking and attests, if not necessarily to historicity, then certainly to an early and universal consensus."

Bockmuehl, *Simon Peter in Scripture and Memory*, p. 149.

322 Michael D. Goulder, "Did Peter Ever Go to Rome?," *Scottish Journal of Theology*, vol. 57, no. 4 (November 2004), p. 377.

323 Id., pp. 394–95.

324 Fred Lapham, *Peter: The Myth, the Man, and the Writings* (New York: T. & T. Clark, 2013), p. 248.

325 Bockmuehl, *Simon Peter in Scripture and Memory*, p. 32.

326 Paula Fredriksen, *From Jesus to Christ*, 2nd ed. (New Haven: Yale University Press, 2000), pp. xiii–xiv. Fredriksen is not exaggerating: in foonote 1 on page xiii, she cites the irreconcilable "Jesuses" presented by Stevan L. Davies, Gerald F. Downing, Burton Mack, John Dominic Crossan, Marcus Borg, Richard Horsely, and N.T. Wright.

327 Duffy, *Saints and Sinners*, p. 10.

328 Duffy, "Was There a Bishop of Rome in the First Century?," p. 304.

329 Ignatius, Magnesians 2, ANF 1:59.

330 Laurie Guy, *Introducing Early Christianity* (Downers Grove: InterVarsity Press, 2004), p. 92.

331 Eamon Duffy, *Saints and Sinners: A History of the Popes* (New Haven: Yale University Press, 1997), p. 7.

332 Johannes Brosseder, "Teaching Office: Roman Catholic," in *Encyclopedia of Christianity*, vol. 5 (Grand Rapids: Wm. B. Eerdmans Publishing Co., 2008), p. 316.

333 Karen Jo Torjesen, "Clergy and Laity," in *The Oxford Handbook of Early Christian Studies*, eds. Susan Ashbrook Harvey and David C. Hunter (Oxford: Oxford University Press, 2008), p. 398.

334 Cyril Hovorun, *Scaffolds of the Church: Towards Poststructural Ecclesiology* (Cambridge: James Clarke & Co., 2018), p. 152.

335 John P. Meier, "Part One: Antioch," in Raymond E. Brown and John P. Meier, *Antioch and Rome: New Testament Cradles of Catholic Christianity* (New York: Paulist Press, 2004), p. 75.

336 Peter Lampe, *Christians at Rome in the First Two Centuries: From Paul to Valentinus*, trans. Michael Steinhauser (London: Continuum, 2003), p. 402.

337 *Shepherd of Hermas*, book 1, vis. 2, ch. 4, ANF 2:12.

338 Ibid.

339 Ibid.

340 Lampe, p. 403.

341 Lampe, p. 404.

342 Meier, p. 76.

343 Michael C. McGuckian, "The Apostolic Succession: A Reply to Francis A. Sullivan," *New Blackfriars*, vol. 86, no. 1001 (January 2005), p. 88.

344 John MacArthur, *Essential Christian Doctrine: A Handbook on Biblical Truth* (Wheaton: Crossway, 2021), p. 80.

345 First Vatican Council, *Dei Filius* 7, in Decrees of the Ecumenical Councils, vol. 2, ed. Norman P. Tanner (London: Sheed & Ward, 1990), p. 806.

346 John MacArthur, *Why Believe the Bible?*, 3rd ed. (Grand Rapids: Baker Publishing Group, 2015), pp. 77–78.

347 Lee Martin McDonald, *The Biblical Canon* (Grand Rapids: Baker Academic, 2007), p. 405. He adds that "two other features of ancient Scripture, namely, its adaptability and inspiration, also figure in the process."

348 Ibid.

349 Robert H. Gundry, *A Survey of the New Testament*, 4th ed. (Grand Rapids: Zondervan,

2003), p. 81.

350 Augustine's *Confessions* is perhaps the most influential Christian book outside the Bible. It's orthodox, morally edifying, and beloved, yet it isn't part of the New Testament, since it was written in the late fourth century.

351 Michael J. Kruger, *Canon Revisited: Establishing the Origins and Authority of the New Testament Books* (Wheaton: Crossway, 2012), p. 182, fn. 102.

352 Id., p. 182.

353 The Gospel of Mark was written by Peter's scribe (see 1 Pet. 5:13), and Luke was the traveling companion of Paul (see Col. 4:14; 2 Tim. 4:11).

354 Bart D. Ehrman, *Lost Christianities: The Battles for Scriptures and the Faiths We Never Knew* (Oxford: Oxford University Press, 2003), p. 235.

355 "None of the Gospels came with an 'about the author' section. The closest we get to a claim of authorship is at the very end of the book of John, where the author implies that the book was written by 'the disciple whom Jesus loved.'" Zondervan Academic, "Who Wrote the Gospels, and How Do We Know for Sure?," ZA Blog, September 20, 2017, available at zondervanacademic.com. Ehrman says something similar: "In John's case the text *is* authorized: the author claims to be basing his account on the traditions passed on by 'the disciple Jesus loved.' The author's own identity doesn't matter—only that of his source does." Bart Ehrman, "Why Are the Gospels Anonymous?," The Bart Ehrman Blog, November 28, 2014, available at ehrmanblog.org.

356 F.F. Bruce, *The Gospel of John* (Grand Rapids: Wm. B. Eerdmans Publishing, 1994), p. 1.

357 Ehrman, "Why Are the Gospels Anonymous?"

358 *Didache* 15, in *The Apostolic Fathers*, vol. 1, trans. Kirsopp Lake (London: William Heinemann, 1914), p. 331.

359 Irenaeus, quoted in Eusebius, *Church History*, book 3, ch. 39, NPNF 2/1:170.

360 Papias, quoted in Eusebius, *Church History*, book 3, ch. 39, NPNF 2/1:171.

361 Papias, in *Church History*, NPNF 2/1:173.

362 Papias, in *Church History*, NPNF 2/1:172–73.

363 Justin Martyr, *Dialogue with Trypho*, ch. 106, ANF 1:252.

364 These three interpretations are explored in Timothy P. Henderson, *The Gospel of Peter and Early Apologetics* (Tübingen: Mohr Siebeck, 2011), pp. 10–11.

365 See Ernst Haenchen, *John: Chapters 1–6*, trans. Robert W. Funk, eds. Robert W. Funk and Ulrich Busse (Philadelphia: Fortress Press, 1984), p. 17; Andrew F. Gregory, *The Reception of Luke and Acts in the Period Before Irenaeus* (Tübingen: Mohr Siebeck, 2003), pp. 43–44.

366 See Everett Ferguson, "The Problem of Eusebius," *Christian History*, no. 72 (2001).

367 On the dating of the fragment, see Everett Ferguson, "Canon Muratori: Date and Provenance," *Studia Patristica*, vol. 17, ed. Elizabeth A. Livingstone (Oxford: Pergamon Press, 1982), pp. 677–83; Eckhard J. Schnabel, "The Muratorian Fragment: The State of Research," *Journal of the Evangelical Theological Society*, vol. 57, no. 2 (2012), pp. 231–64.

368 *Muratorian Fragment* 73–77, quoted in Schnabel, p. 238.

369 *Muratorian Fragment* 1–15, quoted in Schnabel, pp. 236–37.

370 Irenaeus, *Against Heresies*, book 3, ch. 1, ANF 1:414.

371 Theophilus, *To Autolycus*, book 2, ch. 22, ANF 2:103.

372 D.A. Carson, *The Gospel According to John* (Leicester: Apollos, 1991), p. 68

373 See Timothy Paul Jones, *Misquoting Truth* (Downers Grove: IVP Books, 2007), p. 100.

374 David Alan Black, *Why Four Gospels?*, 2nd ed. (Gonzalez: Energion Publications, 2010), p. 36.

375 Id., pp. 36–37.

376 Paula Fredriksen, *From Jesus to Christ*, 2nd ed. (New Haven: Yale University Press, 2000), p. xvi.

377 Ibid. For a list of (and thorough rebuttal to) scholars arguing for Gentile authorship of the Gospel of Matthew, see W.D. Davies and Dale C. Allison, Jr., *A Critical and Exegetical Commentary on the Gospel According to Saint Matthew*, vol. 1 (New York: T&T Clark Ltd., 2010), pp. 9–58.

378 Paula Fredriksen, *From Jesus to Christ*, 2nd ed. (New Haven: Yale University Press, 2000), p. xvi.

379 For a (now somewhat dated) state of critical research on this question, see Michael W. Holmes, "From 'Original Text' to 'Initial Text': The Traditional Goal of New Testament Textual Criticism in Contemporary Discussion," in *The Text of the New Testament in Contemporary Research*, 2nd ed., eds. Bart D. Ehrman and Michael W. Holmes (Leiden: Brill, 2013), pp. 665–667 (Helmut Koester, William L. Petersen, and David C. Parker arguing that we know little about the original biblical texts, whereas Barbara Aland, Kim Haines-Eitzen, K.S. Min, Tommy Wasserman, Holger Strutwolf, Martin Heide, and Martin Holmes argue that the biblical texts around A.D. 200 are "reasonably close" to their original forms).

380 William L. Peterson, "The Genesis of the Gospel," in *New Testament Textual Criticism and Exegesis*, ed. A. Denaux (Leuven: University Press, 2002), p. 62.

381 Petersen actually claims that this is true not only for the four Gospels, but for all of the New Testament documents.

382 "In the first half of the second century—that is, in the age of the Apostolic Fathers—and even later, into the time of Tatian and Clement of Alexandria (near the end of the second century), there was neither a fixed canon nor a fixed text for any of the New Testament documents. Rather, 'clusters' of sayings/episodes/parts of (what later became our canonical) Gospels and epistles circulated, initially (for the Gospels, at least) probably without a title, and then, later, with a title. But the *contents* of the 'cluster' bearing the title 'Mark' or 'Romans' was still very much in flux and subject to change. Additions were being made, as were deletions; the sequence of the text was still being modified." William L. Petersen, "Textual Traditions Examined: What the Text of the Apostolic Fathers tells us about the Text of the New Testament in the Second Century," in *The Reception of the New Testament in the Apostolic Fathers*, eds. Andrew F. Gregory and Christopher M. Tuckett (Oxford: Oxford University Press, 2005), p. 40.

383 Michael W. Holmes, "What Text is Being Edited? The Editing of the New Testament," in *Editing the Bible: Assessing the Task Past and Present*, eds. John S. Kloppenborg and Judith H. Newman (Atlanta: Society of Biblical Literature, 2012), p. 117.

384 Howard M. Jackson, "Ancient Self-Referential Conventions and their Implications for the Authorship and Integrity of the Gospel of John," *The Journal of Theological Studies*, New Series, vol. 50, no. 1 (April 1999), p. 1. More recently, Hugo Méndez points out that "a small but vocal set of critics has taken aim at the lack of any external evidence for the existence of a Johannine community and the uncertain methods used to reconstruct its history." Hugo Méndez, "Did the Johannine Community Exist?," *Journal for the Study of the New Testament*, vol. 42, no. 3 (2020), p. 351.

385 "Unless one is to resort to the hypothesis of pure accidental survival, one must hold to the improbable thesis that all the posited redactions (i.e., published editions) of John prior to the sole-surviving final one were circulated so exclusively within the hermetically-sealed-off confines of a closed Johannine community or group of communities that the earlier editions could be so successfully superseded by later ones as to leave no

trace of their existence." Jackson, p. 2. To give a modern example: One of the texts I used in preparing this chapter was Craig Blomberg's "The Historical Reliability of the New Testament," a chapter he wrote for the second edition of William Lane Craig's book *Reasonable Faith*, even though Craig removed Blomberg's chapter from the most recent edition of the book. Why? Because the older version of the book didn't just disappear. So where did these rejected versions of the canonical Gospels go?

386 Martin Luther, *Prefaces to the New Testament*, trans. Charles M. Jacobs and E. Theodore Bachmann (Wildside Press, 2010), p. 48.

387 MacArthur, *Why Believe the Bible?*, p. 78.

388 Tim Lewis, "Were the Apostles' [sic] Inspired? Or Was It Something They Wrote?," Proclaim & Defend, February 25, 2020, available at proclaimanddefend.org.

389 Karen Swallow Prior, "Screens Are Changing the Way We Read Scripture," *Christianity Today*, November 1, 2018.

390 John Piper, "Why We Believe the Bible: Session 2," *Desiring God*, February 15, 2008, available at desiringgod.org.

391 Papias, in *Church History*, NPNF 2/1:171.

392 Everett Ferguson, "Defining the Faith," *Christian History*, no. 96, 2007.

393 Theodor Zahn, "Regula Fidei ('Rule of Faith')," in *The New Schaff-Herzog Encyclopedia of Religious Knowledge*, vol. 9, eds. Samuel Macauley Jackson and George William Gilmore (New York: Funk and Wagnalls Co., 1911), p. 445. For instance, in the late second century, as Pope Victor and other bishops are beginning to demand that all Christians observe Easter on the same Sunday, Bishop Polycrates of Ephesus responds by listing saintly Christians who had gone before them who "observed the fourteenth day of the passover according to the Gospel, deviating in no respect, but following the rule of faith." Polycrates, quoted in Eusebius, *Church History*, book 5, ch. 24, NPNF 2/1:242.

394 Ibid.

395 Zahn, pp. 445–46.

396 Adolf Berger, *Encyclopedic Dictionary of Roman Law*, vol. 43, part 2 (Philadelphia: American Philosophical Society, 1991), p. 672 (internal citations omitted).

397 D.H. Williams, "The Earliest Mere Christianity," *Christianity Today*, 2007.

398 Irenaeus, *Against Heresies*, book 1, ch. 8, ANF 1:326.

399 Id., ch. 9, ANF 1:330.

400 Tertullian, *On Prescription Against Heretics*, ch. 18–19, ANF 3:251–52.

401 Tertullian, *Against Praxeas*, ch. 2, ANF 3:598.

402 Williams catalogues several early Rules in *Tradition, Scripture, and Interpretation: A Sourcebook of the Ancient Church*, ed. D.H. Williams (Grand Rapids: Baker Academic, 2006), pp. 67–79.

403 Irenaeus, *The Demonstration of the Apostolic Preaching*, trans. J. Armitage Robinson (London: Society for Promoting Christian Knowledge, 1920).

404 Id., pp. 75–76, 72.

405 MacArthur, *Why Believe the Bible?*, p. 74.

406 Mary E. Mills, *Reading Ecclesiastes: A Literary and Cultural Exegesis* (London: Routledge, 2017), p. 16.

407 Josephus, *Contra Apionem*, book 2, quoted in Herold Weiss, *A Day of Gladness: The Sabbath Among Jews and Christians in Antiquity* (Columbia: University of South Carolina, 2003), p. 68.

408 John Bergsma and Brant Pitre, *A Catholic Introduction to the Bible* (San Francisco: Ignatius Press, 2018), p. 385.

409 "At some point someone had the very clever idea of stringing a few tablets together in a bundle. Eventually the bundled tablets were replaced with leaves of parchment and thus, probably, was born the codex. But nobody realized what a good idea it was until a very interesting group of people with some very radical ideas adopted it for their own purposes. Nowadays those people are known as Christians, and they used the codex as a way of distributing the Bible. One reason the early Christians liked the codex was that it helped differentiate them from the Jews, who kept (and still keep) their sacred text in the form of a scroll. But some very alert early Christian must also have recognized that the codex was a powerful form of information technology—compact, highly portable and easily concealable. It was also cheap—you could write on both sides of the pages, which saved paper—and it could hold more words than a scroll. The Bible was a long book. . . . Over the next few centuries the codex rendered the scroll all but obsolete." Lev Grossman, "Mechanical Muse: From Scroll to Screen," *New York Times*, September 2, 2011.

410 Valeriy A. Alikin, *The Earliest History of the Christian Gathering: Origin, Development and Content of the Christian Gathering in the First to Third Centuries* (Leiden: Brill, 2010), p. 148.

411 Margaret Leslie Davis, *The Lost Gutenberg* (New York: Tarcher Perigee, 2019), p. 19.

412 Eric Greitens, *Resilience* (Boston: Houghton Mifflin Harcourt, 2015), pp. 120–21. See Joanne Filippone Overty, "The Cost of Doing Scribal Business: Prices of Manuscript Books in England, 1300–1483," *Book History*, vol. 11 (2008), pp. 1–32.

413 Augustine, *Confessions*, book 6, ch. 3, NPNF 1/1:91.

414 Ibid.

415 Davis, p. 9.

416 Jared Rubin, "Printing and Protestants: An Empirical Test of the Role of Printing in the Reformation," *The Review of Economics and Statistics*, vol. 96, no. 2 (May 2014), p. 272.

417 Id., p. 271.

418 George Jones, "Me and Jesus," available at youtube.com.

419 Timothy Dolan and John L. Allen, Jr., *A People of Hope* (New York: Image, 2011), p. 186.

420 *Muratorian Fragment* 77–80, quoted in Schnabel, p. 238.

421 Alikin, p. 158.

422 There have been many theories about this "Laodicean Epistle" to which Paul apparently refers. Notice that Paul talks about the Laodiceans sending a letter on to the Thessalonians but doesn't specify that the letter was addressed to them originally. Charles H. Talbert mentions several (a letter written from Laodicea to Paul; a letter of Epaphras to Laodicea; Philemon; Ephesians; a lost letter; the apocryphal Epistle of Paul to Laodicea), of which the most likely theory is the oldest: that Paul is referring to the letter to the Ephesians, a copy of which was sent to Laodicea. Charles H. Talbert, *Ephesians and Colossians* (Grand Rapids: Baker Academic, 2007), p. 242; William Barclay, *The Letters to the Galatians and Ephesians* (Louisville: Westminster John Knox Press, 2002), pp. 80–82; F.F. Bruce, *The Epistles to the Colossians, to Philemon, and to the Ephesians* (Grand Rapids: Wm. B. Eerdmans Publishing Co., 1984), p. 184.

423 Justin Martyr, *First Apology*, ch. 67, ANF 1:186. The similarities between Justin's description of the weekly Christian gathering and Josephus's description of weekly Jewish gathering are revealing, even though Alikin claims that "there is no continuity between the readings in the synagogue and that in the church." Alikin, p. 158.

424 Justin Martyr, *Dialogue*, ch. 106, ANF 1:252.

425 Ibid.

426 Justin Martyr, *Dialogue*, ch. 103, ANF 1:251.

427 Id., ch. 105, ANF 1:252.

428 Irenaeus, *Against Heresies*, book 3, ch. 11, ANF 1:428.

429 Id., ANF 1:428–29.

430 MacArthur, *Why Believe the Bible?*, p. 78.

431 Michael W. Holmes, *The Apostolic Fathers in English* (Grand Rapids: Baker Academic, 2006), p. 17.

432 Mark L. Strauss, *Four Portraits, One Jesus* (Grand Rapids: Zondervan, 2007), p. 253.

433 William Lane Craig, "#Question of the Week 373: Gospel Authorship—Who Cares?," *Reasonable Faith*, June 8, 2014, available at reasonablefaith.org.

434 William Lane Craig, *Reasonable Faith* (Wheaton: Crossway Books, 2008), p. 11.

435 Ibid.

436 Kruger, p. 91.

437 Kruger, p. 89.

438 Kruger, p. 92.

439 Kruger, p. 94.

440 Ibid.

441 Kruger, p. 290.

442 Robert L. Reymond, *A New Systematic Theology of the Christian Faith* (Nashville: Thomas Nelson Publishers, 1998), p. 61.

443 Id., p. 66.

444 Id., p. 67.

445 Id., p. 64.

446 Id., p. 59, *ff*, quoting *Westminster Confession of Faith*, I/iii.

447 D.A. Carson, *The Gospel According to John* (Grand Rapids: Wm. B. Eerdmans Publishing Co., 1991), p. 68.

448 Id., pp. 277–78. Elsewhere, Carson laments that "although he made noted advancements concerning the doctrine of baptism," Martin Luther wasn't Protestant enough on baptism: "Luther failed to undo every rope that the medieval sacramental system had used to bind the Christian. By maintaining that baptism is the ordinarily necessary occasion of justification and by holding to an essentially *ex opere operato* understanding, Martin Luther unwittingly compromised his cherished doctrine of justification by faith alone. Stressing the objectivity of baptism as God's saving word and work . . . is not enough to vindicate Luther. For when baptism becomes the means of justification, responding to the gospel in faith is no longer sufficient. One must believe and be baptized." D.A. Carson, "*Sola Fide* Compromised? Martin Luther and the Doctrine of Baptism," *Themelios*, vol. 34, no. 2 (2009), p. 192. So we know that Carson does not view fidelity to the views of the early Christians as necessary.

449 William Perkins, *A Discourse of Conscience and The Whole Treatise of Cases of Conscience*, ed. Thomas F. Merrill (Nieuwkoop: B. De Graaf, 1966), p. 42.

450 Ibid.

451 Vincent of Lérins, *The Commonitory*, trans. John Jebb (Baltimore: Joseph Robinson, 1847), p. 5.

452 Ibid.

453 Id., p. 6.

454 Id., pp. 6–7.

455 Keith Mathison, *The Shape of Sola Scriptura* (Moscow, ID: Canon Press, 2001), p. 213.

456 Vincent, p. 7.

457 *Westminster Confession* 3.3., quoted in Shawn Wright, "'Calvinists' Before Calvin?,"

Desiring God, October 15, 2019, available at desiringGod.org. R.C. Sproul explains the Reformed view of predestination by saying that "God from all eternity decrees some to election and positively intervenes in their lives to work regeneration and faith by a monergistic work of grace. To the non-elect God withholds this monergistic work of grace, passing them by and leaving them to themselves." R.C. Sproul, "'Double' Predestination," *Ligonier*, March 17, 2012.

458 See John Calvin, *Institutes of the Christian Religion*, book 3, ch. 21, §4.

459 Michael Horton, *Putting Amazing Back into Grace: Embracing the Heart of the Gospel*, 2nd ed. (Grand Rapids: Baker Books, 2005), pp. 234, 237–240.

460 See, e.g., David Roach, "From Free Choice to God's Choice: Augustine's Exegesis of Romans 9," *Evangelical Quarterly*, vol. 80, no. 2 (April 2008), pp. 129–141; Josef Lössl, "Augustine on Predestination: Consequences for the Reception," *Augustiniana*, vol. 52, no. 2/4 (2002), pp. 241–272. Peter J. Thuesen offers a nice, short summary of the shift in Augustine's thinking: "it is sometimes forgotten that the greatest thinker of the early Western Church, Augustine of Hippo (354–430), also at first insisted that 'God only predestined those whom he knew would believe and follow the call.' Augustine drew this conclusion partly from Romans 8:29 ('For those whom he foreknew he also predestined to be conformed to the image of his Son'), upon which he remarked in an unfinished pair of commentaries in 394–395. Yet barely two years later, in his first literary work as bishop of Hippo Regius in North Africa, Augustine turned again to Romans in response to a friend's query and reached a radically different conclusion: God did not choose Jacob (or anyone else) in view of foreseen faith." Peter J. Thuesen, *Predestination: The American Career of a Contentious Doctrine* (Oxford: Oxford University Press, 2009), p. 19.

461 There are some significant differences between what Augustine and Calvin taught on predestination and free will, but this is not the space to engage in a nuanced exploration of the question. Suffice it to say that "Augustine, who came to emphasize predestination more than most Eastern fathers, continues to connect predestination and foreknowledge in some sense: 'There is, in the foreknowledge of God, a predetermined limit and number of saints who love God.'" Keener, p. 59.

462 Augustine, *To Simplician—on Various Questions*, book 1, q. 2, in *Augustine: Earlier Writings*, trans. John H.S. Burleigh (Philadelphia: Westminster Press, 1953), pp. 385–386.

463 Augustine, *The Retractions*, book 2, ch. 27, trans. M. Inez Bogan (Washington, D.C.: Catholic University of America Press, 1968), pp. 119–122.

464 My aim here is not to engage in any kind of nuanced discussion of Augustine's views of predestination, or how they differ from the views of the Protestant Reformers. It's rather to show two things: that Calvinism was clearly not what the early Christians believed, and that Calvinists misuse the testimony of the early Christians when they disregard the earliest witnesses and ignore the distinction between a theologian and an eyewitness.

465 Wright, "'Calvinists' Before Calvin?"

466 Ibid.

467 Thuesen, p. 19.

468 Justin Martyr, *First Apology* 43, ANF 1:177.

469 Craig S. Keener, *1 Peter: A Commentary* (Grand Rapids: Baker Academic, 2021), p. 59.

470 Herman Bavinck, *Reformed Dogmatics*, ed. John Bolt, trans. John Vriend, vol. 2, God and Creation (Grand Rapids: Baker, 2004), p. 348, quoted in Wright, "'Calvinists' Before Calvin?"

471 Wright, "'Calvinists' Before Calvin?"

472 Ibid.

473 Arthur Conan Doyle, *The Complete Sherlock Holmes* (New York: Race Point Publishing, 2013), p. 359.

474 Id., p. 363.

475 William Cunningham, *Historical Theology*, vol. 1, 2nd ed. (Edinburgh: T. & T. Clark, 1864), p. 177.

476 Ibid.

477 *The Restoration of the Gospel of Jesus Christ* (Salt Lake City: Intellectual Reserve, 2008), p. 8.

478 Id., p. 11.

479 Ibid.

480 Jean Daillé, *A Treatise on the Right Use of the Fathers in the Decision of Controversies Existing at this Day in Religion*, 2nd ed., trans. T. Smith, ed. G. Jekyll (London: Henry G. Bohn, 1843), pp. 294–295.

481 In support of this idea that this dismissive attitude toward the early Christians is characteristic of Protestantism, Daillé writes that "it is true, I confess, that some of their first authors, as Bucer, Peter Martyr, and J. Jewel of Salisbury, and in a manner all the later writers also, allege the testimonies of the Fathers; but (if you but mark it) it is only by way of confutation, and not of establishing anything: they do it only to overthrow the opinions of the Church of Rome, and not to strengthen their own." Id., p. 296. John Harrison, a nineteenth-century Anglican author, agrees with this assessment, arguing that the Reformers used the early Christians only to attack medieval teachings, since as "bad as was the teaching of the leading authorities of the Church of antiquity, it was far worse in the fourteenth and fifteenth century." John Harrison, *Who Are the Fathers?* (London: Longmans, Green, and Co., 1867), p. 13.

482 Daillé, p. 295.

483 Ibid.

484 Ibid.

485 John Piper, "Don't Equate Historically Early with Theologically Accurate," Desiring God, January 19, 2011, available at desiringGod.org.

486 Ibid.

487 W. Brian Shelton, "Irenaeus," in *Shapers of Christian Orthodoxy: Engaging with Early and Medieval Theologians*, ed. Bradley G. Green (Downers Grove: IVP Academic, 2010), p. 51.

488 Joel R. Beeke, "Reading the Puritans," *Southern Baptist Journal of Theology*, vol. 14, no. 4 (Winter 2010), p. 20.

489 Scot McKnight "From Wheaton to Rome: Why Evangelicals become Roman Catholic," *Journal of the Evangelical Theological Society*, vol. 45, no. 3 (September 2002), p. 463

490 C.S. Lewis, *Mere Christianity* (New York: HarperOne, 2001), p. 52.

491 Ibid.